VOICE
of the Turtle

VOICE
of the Turtle

American Indian
Literature
1900–1970

Edited and with an Introduction by

Paula Gunn
Allen

ONE WORLD

BALLANTINE BOOKS · NEW YORK

Grateful acknowledgment is made to the following
for permission to reprint previously published material:

HARPERCOLLINS PUBLISHERS, INC.:
Excerpts from *Pretty-shield, Medicine Woman of the Crows*
by Frank B. Linderman. Copyright 1932 by Frank B. Linderman. Reprinted
by permission of HarperCollins Publishers, Inc.

SIMON J. ORTIZ:
"Woman Singing"; permission granted by the author, Simon J. Ortiz.

SUNSET MAGAZINE:
"Singing Bird" by John Oskison. Reprinted courtesy of *Sunset* magazine.

THE UNIVERSITY OF ARIZONA PRESS:
"The Problem of Old Harjo" by John Oskison from *The Singing Spirit* by Peyer.

THE UNIVERSITY OF NEBRASKA PRESS:
Excerpt from *Black Elk Speaks* by John G. Neihardt.
Copyright 1932, 1959, 1972 by John G. Neihardt. Copyright © 1961
by the John G. Neihardt Trust. Reprinted by permission
of the University of Nebraska Press.

UNIVERSITY OF OKLAHOMA PRESS:
Excerpt from *Sundown* by John Joseph Mathews.
Copyright © 1987 by the University of Oklahoma Press. Reprinted
by permission of the University of Oklahoma Press.

YALE UNIVERSITY PRESS:
Excerpt from *Sun Chief*, edited by Simmons and Hine. Copyright © 1942
by Yale University Press. Copyright renewed © 1970 by Leo W. Simmons.

LIBRARY OF CONGRESS CATALOGING-IN-PUBLICATION DATA
Voice of the turtle: American Indian Literature 1900–1970 / edited and with an
introduction by Paula Gunn Allen.
    v.—cm.
    Includes bibliographical references (p.320).
    Contents: v. 1. 1900–1970
    ISBN 0-345-37526-2 (v. 1)
    1. Indians of North America—Fiction. 2. American fiction—Indian au-
thors. 3. American fiction—20th century. I. Allen, Paula Gunn.
PS508.I5V64 1994
813'.5080897—dc20   93-39438
                                                                   CIP

Text design by Holly Johnson

Manufactured in the United States of America

First Edition: July 1994

10 9 8 7 6 5 4 3 2

This anthology is dedicated to

Mourning Dove
D'Arcy McNickle
N. Scott Momaday

And to Turtle Island, out of which they write,
in which we live, and into which all disappear.

There are no boundaries here.

Contents

CONTENTS

Editor's Preface

Readers will quickly discover that some of the selections in this volume have been taken from larger works. Those who dislike reading "excerpts" in the belief that any work is "self-contained" might keep in mind that short stories are read by people familiar with the cultural assumptions, materials, and practices of the writer because they share them. Any given narrative arises out of a vast constellation of stories, formal and informal, personal or "high art," and it is this all-encompassing matrix that provides a given work its apparently "self-contained" meaning. In short, every story is an excerpt.

Rather than viewing narratives extracted from longer works as "excerpts," readers might approach each of them as a chapter in *Voice of the Turtle*, and, beyond that, as one of many interconnecting portions of the vast Native Narrative Tradition that encompasses and informs every aspect of Native life. As I have conceptualized the experience of reading *Voice of the Turtle*, it should be as much as possible like participating in storytelling sessions over several weeks.

Imagine that you, dear reader, are part of a gathering of a

number of people who like to share stories they've heard, stories that pertain to a theme or a group of themes that have arisen in conversation. They each contribute to the common story pot—it's a narrative Pot Luck, you see. You may not be familiar with all of the unspoken assumptions, background, and narrative threads employed, but you have an interpreter who provides some of the missing information.

The true joy of story sessions is taking the stories home to reflect on, to apply to your own experience, to learn and grow from, to share with someone else. It is in this spirit that *Voice of the Turtle* is offered, so that the stories can be experienced as living things, part and parcel of all that is, as refracted through a Native lens. It is, as well, the spirit in which Native writers fashion their works—not as individual pieces that have neither father nor mother, grandparent, aunt, or uncle, but as one of the multitude of petals gracing the great flower of Native life.

Paula Gunn Allen
Albuquerque, July 1993

For, lo, the winter is past, the rain is over and gone. The flowers appear on the earth; the time of the singing of birds is come, and the voice of the turtle is heard in our land.

—SONG OF SOLOMON 2:11–12

This is the account of how all was in suspense, all calm, in silence; all motionless, still, and the expanse of the sky was empty.

This is the first account, the first narrative. There was neither man, nor animal, birds, fishes, crabs, trees, stones, caves, ravines, grasses, nor forests; there was only the sky.

—*POPUL VUH*, PART I, CHAPTER 1

VOICE
of the Turtle

American Indian
Literature
1900–1970

Introduction

For myth is at the beginning of literature,
and also at its end.

—*JORGE LUIS BORGES*

A s the Western world approaches its second millennium
and as we look back over five hundred years of multicul-
tural encounters of the devastating kind, we who belong to the
Turtle Island branch of the encounter see the words of the
prophecies of the Maya and Aztec being realized. According to
those prophecies, there would be nine "descents" for Native
peoples; nine periods lasting in total about five hundred years,
western standard time, in which the situation for Native Indian
peoples would deteriorate to levels all but unthinkable. They
wrote that the People would reach the depths of poverty, degradation, humiliation, and devastation during that time. But then
the new time would come, and the First Nations of the Amer-
icas would lead a worldwide renaissance in thought, understanding, and values that would in turn bring about a new age of

peace, reason, and beauty. Then indeed "the last would be first," and "the meek would inherit the earth" as another prophecy from another part of the world foretold.

As we approach the year 2013, the Mayan date of the Great Transformation (or so some scholars have said), the prophecies of the major parties to the encounter between two worlds—the Native spiritist and the Christian spiritist—converge into a single moment. This process and its culmination have been chronicled in Native American personal narratives, folktales, and fiction, spanning the past one hundred years. *Voice of the Turtle: American Indian Literature, 1900–1970* is the first volume of a projected two-volume work. Together these two volumes will provide a kind of a map, a template of that complex, vast, and myriad chronicle.

The old stories come to us from the ancients. But during the nineteenth and twentieth centuries they found a new shape in personal narratives requested by (or more often recorded and intensely edited by) Anglo-Europeans who were curiosity seekers or who were engaged in research, publishing, or social reform. Many Anglo-European visitors, and not a few citizens of Native nations, have contributed to this vast collection of folktales and ceremonial literature, quite a bit of which has never been published.

By the late nineteenth century the transformation of Native traditional materials, historical and political data and perspective, into formal fiction had also begun. This process gained some momentum between 1900 and 1940, and then dwindled. The selections contained in this volume represent every major writer of that era, along with writers whose personal narratives and autobiographies formed the preponderance of Native writings in the twentieth century, particularly during the long silence that occurred between the mid-thirties and the late sixties.

A number of factors contributed to the sudden silencing

of Native voices in publishing circles, the most important of these being the Great Depression and World War Two. The very influential work of the American historian Frederick B. Turner played a large role in the redefinition of Native people as forever beyond the pale of "civilized" culture, as did a dramatic rise in xenophobia, cultural chauvinism, and white supremacist thought that culminated in the establishment of the Third Reich in Germany but was by no means confined to that unhappy nation.

In the bland and blinding white cocoon of the 1950s, with its Red Scare, Cold War, and suburban fixations, a reawakened consciousness stirred in the United States. As a result, the nation returned to its former self in the 1960s, as though recovering from profound shock. In the ferment of the sixties, via Hippies, Civil Rights, the Peace Movement, Kennedy's Manpower Act, Johnson's War on Poverty, and especially the GI Bill that educated thousands of Native vets from the Second World War and the Korean and Vietnam Wars, Native writers began to publish fiction once again. The signal events of those years were the publication of N. Scott Momaday's *House Made of Dawn* in 1968 and John Milton's anthology, *The American Indian Speaks* which was published in 1969—the year Momaday was awarded the Pulitzer Prize for fiction. In a sense, 1970 marked the end of literary and cultural dispossession. As the last quarter of the century has unfolded, the tiny trickle of fiction begun by Native writers during the first seventy years has become a broad and stately river.

There were few Native writers publishing fiction from 1900–1970, but almost all who did are represented in this volume. They, along with their most influential counterparts who were publishing autobiographies and folktales during this period form the core of Native writers, a Native canon, and their works have been reissued over the past decade. Of their works, I have selected stories that speak to the fundamental theme of transformation, for it is that theme, both in content and in structure, that informs Native life and thought.

Nonfiction works have also formed a major part of the narrative materials read by American readers. Because certain of these are seen as classics, and because they have markedly influenced the Native short story at least as thoroughly as have the more exotic folk and ceremonial traditions, including a reasonable sampling of these seemed necessary to a proper, full-bodied representation of Native literature. My intent is for non-Native readers to experience something of the wholeness of Native thought, which, though it varies community by community, contains common threads of historical and political events and perspectives.

From E. Pauline Johnson to Simon J. Ortiz the stories are an aggregate of U.S. history, national and international Native American history, spirituality, and personal narrative. Their structures, especially as the formative period of Native fiction drew to a close in 1970, came to resemble traditional Native Narrative more and more while the voice, tone, and style ever more closely replicated a communal voice: multiple, integral, and accretive.

The process recorded in these pages is not "evolutionary," a white materialist-determinist notion that has no vital part in the Native Narrative Tradition; it is, rather, an account of how the transitory and the enduring interact. That dynamic is sometimes tragic, sometimes comic; sometimes it seems to venture into the unknown world of the Anglo-Europeans, sometimes it returns to its original and forever home; but however much it changes, it always remains what it is. Going out and coming in, is that not the process of weaving? Baskets, rugs, kilts, sashes: In design and process they replicate that primal movement: in and out. White science styles it breathing—in, out; systolic, diastolic. Sacred traditions from all over the world tell seekers that the Universe is about Breath—it goes in; it goes out. But to say that is to speak of waves—the kind identified as sine and cosine by mathematicians and physicists, woven as edging patterns on Navajo rugs, danced intricately by Native dancers everywhere. Such a construct reminds us that breath goes on and on, and whether one inhales or exhales, one breathes; that inbreath is not superior to outbreath; that wherever you go, there you are.

Modern people think of change as progress, and that is the primary organizing principle—motivating force and raison d'être—of modern life. But Native people see change as the fundamental sacred process, as Transformation, as Ritual, as intrinsic to all of existence whenever and wherever, in whatever form or style it takes. Transformation: to change someone or something from one state or condition to another. Magic. What mages, wise ones, shamans do. Also what all peoples, human or otherwise, participate in. The wise are conscious of the process of Ritual Transformation in every facet of life.

Native American fiction in the twentieth century has two sides: the Oral Tradition of the Native Nations, and Western fiction and its antecedents. As does the Bible for the thought and literature of the West, ceremonial texts provide a major source of the symbols, allusions, and philosophical assumptions that inform our world and thus our work. It is a mistake to believe that ceremonial texts are "dated" and thus irrelevant to the work of modern writers. Which of these is inhalation, sine, and which exhalation, cosine, is impossible to say. They interact, as wings of a bird in flight interact. They give shape to our experience. They *signify*.

In order to make clear the process of interaction of which I speak, I have included a number of entries from the informal oral tradition and from personal narratives that depend on it. Their inclusion will provide readers with an experience analogous to that enjoyed by Native writers, as the latter draw from it explicitly and implicitly for narrative structures as well as events, symbols, and imagery, whether the story is identified as traditional narrative or contemporary fiction.

The narrative tradition of Native America can easily be thought of as a novel. It is characterized by certain structural features—diversity, event-centeredness, nonlinear development of story line, and transitional modes—that become less startling as one becomes more familiar with the tradition in its entirety. In content, the Native Narrative Tradition revolves around the theme of magical transformation, but within that rubric it employs a number of subthemes, of which the major ones are social change, cultural transition, and shifting modes of identity. While these subthemes may seem to result from the presence of Anglo-Europeans on Native soil, they have informed the tradition since time immemorial. White presence has, perhaps, caused writers to focus on narratives that highlight social change, cultural transition, and shifting identities, and it has also transformed structural possibilities in some fundamental ways.

The publication of John Rollin Ridge's melodramatic western *The Life and Adventures of Joaquin Murieta* in 1854 marked the beginning, a trickle at first, of publishing by Native American writers in the United States. His novel was followed by "thundering silence." Nothing else fictional was published by Native writers for more than forty years. In addition, little fiction made it into print during the first two-thirds of the 20th century, as can be seen from the selections contained in this volume. But in an odd twist of the Oral Tradition, Ridge's novel became folklore central to the Mexican-American community in California, a peculiarity of literature acknowledged by Borges as shown by the quote cited above.

During the period of engulfment by whites that stretched from the seventeenth to the late twentieth century and from the Southwest and Northeast to Washington State, Alaska, and Hawaii, Native writers addressed our situation, bringing it to the attention of the reading public, placing it in a context that aimed to give voice to traditional Native values and points of view. E. Pauline Johnson, a Mohawk writer from what had become the Canadian side of the Iroquois (actually their proper name is Haudenoshonee) Confederacy was known as "Poet Laureate" in Canada. Most of her work is concerned with the dilemma Native people of the early Reservation era faced. She also devotes considerable thought to the status of women, Native or white, in the brawling world of the American and Canadian frontiers in the late nineteenth century and makes the parallels in the treatment of Native Americans and of women plain.

"A Red Girl's Reasoning," Johnson's first published short story, is exemplary of her work. It clearly delineates the difference in worldview possessed by the different parties to Red/White encounters. Hers might seem an early feminist voice as she portrays women as self-sufficient, self-determining, strong, and capable people, but her position is one generally seen in the Native Narrative Tradition.

Charles A. Eastman (Ohiyesa) was a writer whose work crossed genre boundaries, a practice that would become commonplace among Native authors as the century wore on, revealing Native style more and more. A medical doctor, Dr. Eastman, in collaboration with his Anglo-American wife, Eliza, published several volumes of autobiographical, historical, and fictional works. Like a number of early American Indian writers, Eastman was a survivor of the devastating warfare between the Anglo-European invaders and the Native peoples. He was raised by his grandparents in the Minnesota woods until in adolescence he was retrieved by his father when the latter was finally released from prison for his part in the Minnesota Uprising of 1862, which saw a number of Santee resisters hanged by the United States.

Around the turn of the century several kinds of Native narratives began finding their way into print. Personal narratives, a little like what is usually thought of as fiction, are by far the greatest in number, followed by stories from the Oral Tradition. While this volume focuses primarily on what is usually called fiction, I have included some personal and traditional narratives. It is significant to the development of Native Narrative in this century that the three forms developed simultaneously. While they were largely separate, many writers did some of each, and many incorporate features from each in their work. Indians were never good at recognizing Anglo-European boundaries, whether geopolitical, aesthetic, or social.

Seneca writer Arthur C. Parker devoted his considerable writing abilities to recording Seneca stories from their oral tradition. Like many of his literary descendants, he worked as a journalist when he was young. Eventually, he turned to collecting and rendering the stories he had heard since his youth. Being of a creative turn of mind, Parker came up with a methodology that would be paralleled by Native authors for the rest of the century. His discussion of that methodology is worth quoting, as it aptly describes both the process involved in Native narrative writing and the effect I have envisioned for this anthology: ". . . the transcriber['s] object is to produce the same emotions in the mind of [readers] which is produced in the [native] mind, which entertains the story without destroying the native style or warping the facts of the narrative." (*Myths and Legends*, 12)

Unlike Parker, who was born and well educated on the New York side of the Haudenoshonee Confederacy of which the Seneca Nation is a part, Okanogan Montana, writer Mourning Dove (Humishuma; white name Cristal Quintasket Galler) was virtually uneducated and worked as a migrant farmworker. Like Parker, she was obsessed with the desire to write. She cherished the idea of publishing a novel, and eventually secured the aid of a folklorist, Lucullus Virgil McWhorter, to help her realize her ambition. She gathered the traditional "little stories" from her Okanogan relatives and friends, typing them after work while sitting on the ground outside her tent. In that fashion she also completed her novel, *Cogewea: The Half-Blood*.

A deeply feminist novel cast in the mode of the popular western of the day, *Cogewea* draws from protest and ceremonial themes to clarify the struggle for identity that characterizes Native writing in the United States in the twentieth century. Mourning Dove is awkwardly successful in this novel, employing a complex interweaving of modern and traditional themes. Her process, which integrates ceremonial and historical Native themes and structure within a Western conflict-crisis-resolution plot, was not duplicated again until N. Scott Momaday published his novel *House Made of Dawn* in 1968. D'Arcy McNickle did write one such work, titled *"En roulant ma boule, roulant . . . ,"* "Roll along my ball, roll on . . . ," but it remained unpublished until 1992 when it was published in *The Hawk Is Hungry*, a collection of McNickle's short stories edited by Birgit Hans.

Also out of Montana at about the same time as Mourning Dove was Pretty-shield. The memoirs of the Crow medicine woman, gathered by Frank B. Linderman, represent a trend in Native publishing and Native narrative that would characterize much of the middle portion of the century. As actual Native presence visibly waned, public and academic interest in Native traditions and testimony about our defeat grew.

While Linderman took advantage of the academic interest in the demise of Native life and thought, he was soon followed by scores of scholars and writers seeking publication. Unlike Parker, however, Linderman employed the ethnological process Franz Boas, known as the father of modern anthropology, preferred; Pretty-shield's voice was not passed on to us verbatim. Instead her voice is reproduced on Linderman's page as through an interpreter. She was a canny as well as wise woman though, and her ironic assessment of the reality of Linderman's interest in Crow traditions comes through, providing a sharply perceptive portrait of Native views of anthropology.

Estelle Armstrong, like the much better known Luther Standing Bear, attended Carlisle Indian School in Pennsylvania, and like him she writes out of that experience. Carlisle provided the model for government-run educational institutions for Indian children throughout the United States. Its founder, Colonel Richard Henry Pratt, believed along with most progressive Americans that cultural genocide was preferable to physical genocide, and he convinced Washington to fund educational establishments that could accomplish his purpose. One wonders why American policymakers perceived only genocidal alternatives. Perhaps they couldn't think of more than one possibility at a time, complexity being beyond them.

Clearly a product of the liberal vision of Indian people in the United States, Armstrong published her stories in *The Red Man*, the Carlisle Indian School student newspaper; that seems to be all that is known about her. Her career apparently ended upon graduation, and whether she returned home or where that home might have been is unrecorded. Her disappearance, like her stories-in-exile, provides a profound insight into what happened to Natives under Anglo-American rule, as does Luther Standing Bear's book, *My People, the Sioux*.

Standing Bear's chronicle of life at Carlisle constitutes one of the clearest pictures we have of life under the aegis of the boarding school system. Such establishments realized most of Pratt's goals: Children who survived were profoundly alienated from their people and often became the primary proponents of Anglo-Christian values in their home communities after graduation. However, survivors were fewer than victims, for boarding schools left far more dead of malnutrition, neglect, physical abuse, and epidemics than they educated. Like the long, long war and the extended period of its aftermath, often called the Reservation Era (together they spanned well over three hundred years), the Indian boarding school and its effects form a major subtext in Native American narrative. Writers publishing between 1900 and 1965 were either its products or were raised by parents and grandparents who were. Many of these institutions were reorganized in the 1970s and came under the governing authority of Native advisory boards.

In the work of the three major Native writers of the 1930s—John M. Oskison, John Joseph Mathews, and D'Arcy McNickle—its "educational" effects are evident in both subject matter and structure. The most characteristic structural feature, linearity, came about as a direct consequence of Western educational and publishing modes. These American institutions seemed as incapable of grasping the creative potential of complexity as did government and church.

Under the dual influences of education and the publishing climate, the stories and novels necessarily focus on cultural and psychic dissolution. The hero is generally portrayed as "caught between two worlds," and is inexorably drawn toward alienation and destruction. This effect is the result of a Western plot structure that is conflict-centered and in need of perceiving the Native world as near extinction.

Given the conflict with white invaders in which Native populations were heavily engaged during the period—and which they were clearly losing—and given the American public's almost obsessive interest in Dead Indians, Native writers understandably employed the conventional white plot (usually called "the well-made story") that would lead to publication.

The "Dead Indian" story line works well in American society as it appeals to unconscious psychic structures embodied in the Western Myths of the Crucified Lord and the Dying Warrior. Indeed, the success of modern epics such as *Dances with Wolves* is based in large measure on this ancient Western taste: Everybody loves a dead Indian, it seems, and an entire band of dead Indians is a guaranteed box-office winner.

Native writers who wanted to publish, and who couldn't endure the pain such plots entail, avoided (and still avoid) the subject entirely. Such a writer was John M. Oskison. Born in Oklahoma in Indian Territory, Oskison was educated at the Oklahoma prep school that the younger Will Rogers, the famed Cherokee humorist and commentator, attended several years after Oskison. Later, he graduated from Stanford University. Of his early novels only one, *Brothers Three*, features Native people as main characters.

Some Native Americans, like Black Elk, didn't have the luxury of avoidance; he lived through the war and a great deal of the Reservation Era, a practicing medicine man the whole time. Born on the northern Great Plains, Lakota Nicolas Black Elk toured England, Europe, and the eastern United States with Buffalo Bill's Wild West Show. In his old age he narrated his autobiography to the poet and writer John G. Neihardt, who came to his home in South Dakota, which like Black Elk himself, had acquired an Anglo-American name.

As Neihardt presents it, *Black Elk Speaks* is a painful narrative about the defeat of the Lakota. But its most significant portion, "The Great Vision," tells of the eventual triumph of the power of Spirits in the modern world.

Black Elk didn't avoid the circus or the wars, but he did avoid boarding school, unlike his sister Sioux Gertrude Bonnin, who as a young woman named herself Zitkala-Ša. The problem of names, common in Indian Country, is an extension of the general problem of identity for people who are overwhelmed by alien invaders who not only rename the human beings but the land and all its features. It is said that the conquerors write the histories: They determine the "facts" as well. The question of facts and of identity, be it personal or political, concerns Zitkala-Ša in her narrative. The ability to prove identity to the satisfaction of the white bureaucracy becomes a matter of life and death, not only for her character Blue-Star Woman but for all Indian people. During the period of engulfment, identity and power were used to dispossess traditional people. This was terribly perplexing to traditional people and comprised a wide-spread enigma indeed.

Zitkala-Ša, like many Native people, was the product of a mixed racial heritage. Daughter of a Sioux mother and a white father, she wanted to go away to school because the white recruiter promised to give her an apple. Her mother, believing that her mixed-blood daughter deserved familiarity with both of her source cultures, agreed. When she tried to return home after several years away, Zitkala-Ša learned what too many of her contemporaries discovered when their schooling was done: She couldn't go home again. Her writings and her work as an Indian rights activist represent a lifelong attempt to come to terms with this devastating loss.

John Joseph Mathews, another journalist and author from Indian Territory, Oklahoma, was raised on the oil-rich Osage reservation. His family's share of oil income afforded Mathews a fine education, which he completed at Oxford University. His novel, *Sundown*, centers on the decline of the Osage people as a consequence of their wealth and the predatory capitalists it attracts. *Sundown* confronts the twin horrors of community dissolution and loss of identity, but is structured in a distinctly Native manner. The novel doesn't end with the destruction of the protagonist so much as stop, leaving the clear impression that Challenge Windzer's story goes on and on. In addition, the protagonist's name, Challenge Windzer, shows a hint of "Indi'n humor" and is a sly reference to the psychological and social ruling center of Anglo-American culture.

At about the time Mathews and Oskison were publishing their Oklahoma-based work, the Cree/Salish writer from the Northwest, D'Arcy McNickle, was writing his novel *The Surrounded*. Profoundly northwestern in scope, and reminiscent of *Cogewea* in a number of aspects, McNickle's novel conforms to the Western conflict-crisis-resolution fictional mode. Perhaps worse, the structure determines the message: *The Surrounded* is a deeply depressing novel, satisfying readers who believe in ultimate destruction of Native peoples and traditions however grieved they might be at our passing. McNickle's original novel was quite different from the version that saw print because it ran afoul of the publisher's knife: In the interests of profit, audience potential, and promulgation of Anglo-American normative standards, which depend in large measure on the destruction of the Other as a result of rousing conflict, the published version exemplified America's favorite story.

During much of the 20th century, the old ways seemed to be dying. But they were, it seems, drawing a new breath. They were, in a word, transformed, in ways outlined in Black Elk's vision, however Sioux-specific his Spirits and symbols might have been. It is clear that the Spirits have taken a keen interest in this Great Transformational process, even getting directly involved from time to time.

In *Sun Chief*, the autobiography of Dan C. Talayesva first published in 1942, their involvement surfaces as a narrative thread, heretofore almost as quiet and unseen as Spider Grandmother weaving her Web. Away at boarding school and torn between the promise of white standards and his Hopi traditions, Talayesva was brought up short by the Spirits. He nearly died, and "in extremis" they were able to get through to him. Years later they got through to an ever-growing audience by way of his autobiography. In that narrative, the transformational nature of the preceding centuries was made plain; the near hopelessness of Johnson, Pretty-shield, McNickle, and the rest was transformed within the ancient narrative web that extends from Time Immemorial into the Mythic Now. Chronology, like linear plot structure, fell aside, and the devastation of change was revealed as the liminal, danger-filled, near-death process common in all events of transformation.

A quarter of a century after the publication of *Sun Chief*, and a half century after the publication of *Cogewea: The Half-*

Blood, the diverse threads of history, politics, and the Native spiritist tradition achieved their most integrated realization in N. Scott Momaday's *House Made of Dawn*. There the subtle web, sometimes prominent, sometimes all but hidden, begins to reveal its profound depth and ancient resonance. We didn't die, after all. Surrounded, engulfed, but not surrendered, the Native Narrative Tradition reveals itself transformed and stronger than ever before. In breathtaking beauty but not without anguish, the ancient web stands forth, renewed, vital, and splendid.

The Great Transformation that began in the Western Hemisphere in the sixteenth century and continues through the present was signaled by the coming of the Anglo-Europeans in numbers far larger than such encounters had previously engendered. This Transformation, like all that derive from the Other Realms or the Great Mystery, was not a one-way affair. Careful perusal of historic chronicles of the interchange between New World and Old World peoples clearly demonstrate that the Transformation of Anglo-European, Asian, and African life and thought has been at least as great as that experienced by Native Americans, though the exchange has been overwhelmingly in favor of Old World systems. Only in the latter part of the twentieth century has the voice of Turtle Island been heard.

The work of Ronald Rogers, Grey Cohoe, and Simon J. Ortiz with which this volume ends represent the closing pages of a major chapter in the Narrative Tradition. Their stories appeared in *The American Indian Speaks*, published by South Dakota University in 1969, the same year Momaday received the Pulitzer Prize for *House Made of Dawn*. Rogers, a Cherokee writer, follows what has become a narrative convention; he was attending San Francisco State University when the story, located in an institutional setting, was published. In theme, structure, and significance, as well as in setting, "The Angry Truck" is something of a recapitulation of the eighty years of Native writing preceding him.

Navajo writer Grey Cohoe's "The Promised Visit" is innocent of overt political or historical content, yet it betrays the legacy of colonization in the values and views the protagonist holds toward his Navajo world. In the midst of the narrator's scorn for "uneducated" superstition—boarding school lessons assimilated—he reveals his profound connection to tradition and, in employing a traditionalist structure, invites the reader to share it.

New Mexico poet and writer Simon J. Ortiz, an Acoma Pueblo man who has since published a number of books in a variety of genres, took as his earliest themes the restoration of tradition's voice in the lives of modern Indians. "Woman Singing" is written from a solidly Native point of view, and though there is no mistaking the pain experienced by the story's Native characters or the bleakness of their condition, there is also no mistaking their orientation. They are centered in their tradition, their Native identity, and their home. The reader might notice the almost poignant way the narrator views the Navajo family; the narrator embodies the alienation factor, while the family represents the traditional.

By the end of the 1960s, Native writers could almost cavalierly take for granted a freedom to use all aspects of the Native Narrative Tradition in rendering a Native work. After a long, long winter, the flowers began to bloom, and the voice of the turtle, of the people of Turtle Island, so long silenced, was heard again in the land.

The story doesn't end here, nor does it end with the second volume of *Voice of the Turtle*. The division of the stories into two volumes is best perceived as a pause, like the one that occurs between story-telling sessions in Indian Country, part of that wondrous web of life that finds expression not only in words but in blankets, baskets, pots, needlework, beadwork, paintings, sculpture, and song. The stories have neither beginning nor end; they just go on and on, as McNickle described it:

He had the vivid imagery of a song which went back and back into mistiness, like a living thread of water which you might watch from a grassy hilltop inlaying its silvered course in the prairie and disappearing with a final gleam on the horizon's uncertain edge. So it was a song, *En roulant ma boule, roulant* [roll along my ball, roll on], rather than a connected narrative, which he knew so intimately. Yet it was a song which gave him a full sense of the narrative. Words would never fill out any more vividly the passages which he knew by knowing images alone. *En roulant ma boule, roulant* was four hundred years of history captured in a phrase as no book would ever catch it, and Dieudonné was but a stripling with all life before him in which to give verbiage to sensory gropings.

E. PAULINE JOHNSON

A Red Girl's Reasoning (1906)

*E. Pauline Johnson wrote poetry and fiction, engaging, as many
writers do, in a multigenre approach. She dealt with similar
themes in her work, including the status of women; the perilous
straits Native people, male or female, were required to navigate in
a predominately white world; the value of paganism; and concepts
of honor that white colonial history chronically betrayed. Her stories were straightforward, nearly florid narratives, crafted more for
social content than for elegant style, a characteristic that would
come to mark feminist writing in Canada and the United States
half a century after her death.*

*"A Red Girl's Reasoning" is one of Johnson's strongest stories.
Mr. Robinson's advice to his "brand-new son-in-law," which sets up
a story with far deeper implications than a surface reading would
suggest, might well have been given to a mate of mine. My father
often used the same words to characterize my mother—dutiful,
stubborn. "With an Indian," he'd say, "when it's tsa, it's tsa. When
your mother makes up her mind, she doesn't talk about it, she
doesn't argue. That's it."*

Christie's reasoning is impeccable, and to the point even, or especially, now: "How do I know when another nation will come and conquer you as you white men conquered us?" she asks her status-conscious white husband. In every particular, "A Red Girl's Reasoning" is a clear analog for the false marriage between Indian and white in the political and social sense. In the way of the Native Narrative Tradition, it counsels and cautions: Any honorable relationship must be based on honor, dignity, and mutual respect. Any other footing seeds disaster.

"Be pretty good to her, Charlie, my boy, or she'll balk sure as shooting."

That was what old Jimmy Robinson said to his brand-new son-in-law, while they waited for the bride to reappear.

"Oh, you bet, there's no danger of much else. I'll be good to her, help me Heaven," replied Charlie McDonald, brightly.

"Yes, of course you will," answered the old man, "but don't you forget, there's a good big bit of her mother in her, and"—closing his left eye significantly—"you don't understand these Indians as I do."

"But I'm just as fond of them, Mr. Robinson," Charlie said assertively, "and I get on with them too, now, don't I?"

"Yes, pretty well for a town boy; but when you have lived forty years among these people, as I have done; when you have had your wife as long as I have had mine—for there's no getting over it, Christine's disposition is as Native as her mother's, every bit—and perhaps when you've owned for eighteen years a daughter as dutiful, as loving, as fearless, and, alas, as obstinate as that little piece you are stealing away from me today—I tell you, youngster, you'll know more than you know now. It is kindness for kindness, bullet for bullet, blood for blood. Remember, what you are, she will be," and the old Hudson Bay trader scrutinized Charlie McDonald's face like a detective.

It was a happy, fair face, good to look at, with a certain

ripple of dimples somewhere about the mouth, and eyes that laughed out the very sunniness of their owner's soul. There was not a severe nor yet a weak line anywhere. He was a well-meaning young fellow, happily dispositioned, and a great favorite with the tribe at Robinson's Post, whither he had gone in the service of the Department of Agriculture, to assist the local agent through the tedium of a long census-taking.

As a boy he had had the Indian relic-hunting craze, as a youth he had studied Indian archaeology and folklore, as a man he consummated his predilections for Indianology by loving, winning, and marrying the quiet little daughter of the English trader, who himself had married a Native woman twenty years ago. The country was all backwoods, and the Post miles and miles from even the semblance of civilization, and the lonely young Englishman's heart had gone out to the girl who, apart from speaking a very few words of English, was utterly uncivilized and uncultured, but had withal that marvelously innate refinement so universally possessed by the higher tribes of North American Indians.

Like all her race, observant, intuitive, having a horror of ridicule, consequently quick at acquirement and teachable in mental and social habits, she had developed from absolute pagan indifference into a sweet, elderly Christian woman whose broken English, quiet manner, and still handsome copper-colored face, were the joy of old Robinson's declining years.

He had given their daughter Christine all the advantages of his own learning—which, if truthfully told, was not universal; but the girl had a fair common education, and the Native adaptability to progress.

She belonged to neither and still to both types of the cultured Indian. The solemn, silent, almost heavy manner of the one so commingled with the gesticulating Frenchiness and vivacity of the other, that one unfamiliar with Native Canadian life would find it difficult to determine her nationality.

She looked very pretty to Charles McDonald's loving eyes, as she reappeared in the doorway, holding her mother's hand and saying some happy words of farewell. Personally she looked much the same as her sisters, all Canada through, who are the offspring of red and white parentage—olive-complexioned, gray-eyed, black-haired, with figure slight and delicate, and the wistful, unfathomable expression in her whole face that turns one so heart-sick as they glance at the young Indians of today—it is the forerunner too frequently of "the white man's disease," consumption—but McDonald was pathetically in love, and thought her the most beautiful woman he had ever seen in his life.

There had not been much of a wedding ceremony. The priest had cantered through the service in Latin, pronounced the benediction in English, and congratulated the "happy couple" in Indian, as a compliment to the assembled tribe in the little amateur structure that did service at the Post as a sanctuary.

But the knot was tied as firmly and indissolubly as if all Charlie McDonald's swell city friends had crushed themselves up against the chancel to congratulate him, and in his heart he was deeply thankful to escape the flower-pelting, white-gloved, rice-throwing, and ponderous stupidity of a breakfast, and indeed all the regulation gimcracks of the usual marriage celebrations, and it was with a hand trembling with absolute happiness that he assisted his little Indian wife into the old muddy buckboard that, hitched to an underbred-looking pony, was to convey them over the first stages of their journey. Then came more adieus, some handclasping, old Jimmy Robinson looking very serious just at the last, Mrs. Jimmy, stout, stolid, betraying nothing of visible emotion, and then the pony, roughshod and shaggy, trudged on, while mutual hand-waves were kept up until the old Hudson Bay Post dropped out of sight, and the buckboard with its lightsome load of hearts, deliriously happy, jogged on over the uneven trail.

• • •

She was "all the rage" that winter at the provincial capital. The men called her a "deuced fine little woman." The ladies said she was "just the sweetest wildflower." Whereas she was really but an ordinary, pale, dark girl who spoke slowly and with a strong accent, who danced fairly well, sang acceptably, and never stirred outside the door without her husband.

Charlie was proud of her; he was proud that she had "taken" so well among his friends, proud that she bore herself so complacently in the drawing-rooms of the wives of pompous government officials, but doubly proud of her almost abject devotion to him. If ever a human being was worshipped, that being was Charlie McDonald; it could scarcely have been otherwise, for the almost godlike strength of his passion for that little wife of his would have mastered and melted a far more invincible citadel than an already affectionate woman's heart.

Favorites socially, McDonald and his wife went everywhere. In fashionable circles she was "new"—a potent charm to acquire popularity, and the little velvet-clad figure was always the center of interest among all the women in the room. She always dressed in velvet. No woman in Canada has she but the faintest dash of Native blood in her veins but loves velvets and silks. As beef to the Englishman, wine to the Frenchman, fads to the Yankee, so are velvet and silk to the Indian girl, be she wild as prairie grass, be she on the borders of civilization, or, having stepped within its boundary, mounted the steps of culture even under its superficial heights.

"Such a dolling little appil blossom," said the wife of a local M.P., who brushed up her etiquette and English once a year at Ottawa. "Does she always laugh so sweetly, and gobble you up with those great big gray eyes of hers, when you are togetheah at home, Mr. McDonald? If so, I should think youah pooah brothah would feel himself terribly *de trop*."

He laughed lightly. "Yes, Mrs. Stuart, there are not two of

Christie; she is the same at home and abroad, and as for Joe, he doesn't mind us a bit; he's no end fond of her."

"I'm very glad he is. I always fancied he did not care for her, d'you know."

If ever a blunt woman existed it was Mrs. Stuart. She really meant nothing, but her remark bothered Charlie. He was fond of his brother, and jealous for Christie's popularity. So that night when he and Joe were having a pipe he said:

"I've never asked you yet what you thought of her, Joe." A brief pause, then Joe spoke. "I'm glad she loves you."

"Why?"

"Because that girl has but two possibilities regarding humanity—love or hate."

"Humph! Does she love or hate *you*?"

"Ask her."

"You talk bosh. If she hated you, you'd get out. If she loved you I'd *make* you get out."

Joe McDonald whistled a little, then laughed.

"Now that we are on the subject; I might as well ask—honestly, old man, wouldn't you and Christie prefer keeping house alone to having me always around?"

"Nonsense, sheer nonsense. Why, thunder, man, Christie's no end fond of you, and as for me—you surely don't want assurances from me?"

"No, but I often think a young couple—"

"Young couple be blowed! After a while when they want you and your old surveying chains, and spindle-legged tripod telescope kickshaws farther west, I venture to say the little woman will cry her eyes out—won't you, Christie?" This last in a higher tone, as through clouds of tobacco smoke he caught sight of his wife passing the doorway.

She entered. "Oh, no, I would not cry; I never do cry, but I would be heart-sore to lose you, Joe, and apart from that"—a little wickedly—"you may come in handy for an exchange some day, as Charlie does always say when he hoards up duplicate relics."

"Are Charlie and I duplicates?"

"Well—not exactly"—her head a little to one side, and eyeing them both merrily, while she slipped softly onto the arm of her husband's chair—"but, in the event of Charlie's failing me"—everyone laughed then. The "some day" that she spoke of was nearer than they thought. It came about in this wise.

There was a dance at the Lieutenant-Governor's, and the world and his wife were there. The nobs were in great feather that night, particularly the women, who flaunted about in new gowns and much splendor. Christie McDonald had a new gown also, but wore it with the utmost unconcern, and if she heard any of the flattering remarks made about her she at least appeared to disregard them.

"I never dreamed you could wear blue so splendidly," said Captain Logan, as they sat out a dance together.

"Indeed she can, though," interposed Mrs. Stuart, halting in one of her gracious sweeps down the room with her husband's private secretary.

"Don't shout so, captain. I can hear every sentence you uttah—of course Mrs. McDonald can wear blue—she has a morning gown of cadet blue that she is a picture in."

"You are both very kind," said Christie. "I like blue; it is the color of all the Hudson's Bay posts, and the factor's residence is always decorated blue."

"Is it really? How interesting—do tell us some more of your old home, Mrs. McDonald; you so seldom speak of your life at the post, and we fellows so often wish to hear it all," said Logan eagerly.

"Why do you not ask me of it, then?"

"Well—er, I'm sure I don't know; I'm fully interested in the Ind—in your people—your mother's people, I mean, but it always seems so personal, I suppose; and—a—a—"

"Perhaps you are, like all other white people, afraid to mention my nationality to me."

The captain winced, and Mrs. Stuart laughed uneasily. Joe McDonald was not far off, and he was listening, and chuckling, and saying to himself, "That's you, Christie, lay 'em out; it won't hurt 'em to know how they appear once in a while."

"Well, Captain Logan," she was saying, "what is it you would like to hear—of my people, or my parents, or myself?"

"All, all, my dear," cried Mrs. Stuart clamorously. "I'll speak for him—tell us of yourself and your mother—your father is delightful, I am sure—but then he is only an ordinary Englishman, not half as interesting as a foreigner, or—or, perhaps I should say, a Native."

Christie laughed. "Yes," she said, "my father often teases my mother now about how *very* Native she was when he married her; then, how could she have been otherwise? She did not know a word of English, and there was not another English-speaking person besides my father and his two companions within sixty miles."

"Two companions, eh? One a Catholic priest and the other a wine merchant, I suppose, and with your father in the Hudson Bay, they were good representatives of the pioneers in the New World," remarked Logan, waggishly.

"Oh, no, they were all Hudson Bay men. There were no rum-sellers and no missionaries in that part of the country then."

Mrs. Stuart looked puzzled. *"No missionaries?"* she repeated with an odd intonation.

Christie's insight was quick. There was a peculiar expression of interrogation in the eyes of her listeners, and the girl's blood leapt angrily up into her temples as she said hurriedly, "I know what you mean; I know what you are thinking. You are wondering how my parents were married—"

"Well—er, my dear, it seems peculiar—if there was no

priest, and no magistrate, why—a—" Mrs. Stuart paused awkwardly.

"The marriage was performed by Indian rites," said Christie.

"Oh, do tell me about it; is the ceremony very interesting and quaint—are your chieftains anything like Buddhist priests?" It was Logan who spoke.

"Why, no," said the girl in amazement at that gentleman's ignorance. "There is no ceremony at all, save a feast. The two people just agree to live only with and for each other, and the man takes his wife to his home, just as you do. There is no ritual to bind them; they need none; an Indian's word was his law in those days, you know."

Mrs. Stuart stepped backwards. "Ah!" was all she said. Logan removed his eye-glass and stared blankly at Christie. "And did McDonald marry you in this singular fashion?" he questioned.

"Oh, no, we were married by Father O'Leary. Why do you ask?"

"Because if he had, I'd have blown his brains out tomorrow."

Mrs. Stuart's partner, who had hitherto been silent, coughed and began to twirl his cuff stud nervously, but nobody took any notice of him. Christie had risen, slowly, ominously—risen, with the dignity and pride of an empress.

"Captain Logan," she said, "what do you dare to say to me? What do you dare to mean? Do you presume to think it would not have been lawful for Charlie to marry me according to my people's rites? Do you for one instant dare to question that my parents were not as legally—"

"Don't, dear, don't," interrupted Mrs. Stuart hurriedly; "it is bad enough now, goodness knows; don't make—" Then she broke off blindly. Christie's eyes glared at the mumbling woman, at her uneasy partner, at the horrified captain. Then they rested on the McDonald brothers, who stood within earshot, Joe's face scarlet, her husband's white as ashes, with something in his eyes she had never seen before. It was Joe who saved the situation. Stepping quickly across towards his sister-in-law, he offered her his arm, saying, "The next dance is ours, I think, Christie."

Then Logan pulled himself together, and attempted to carry Mrs. Stuart off for the waltz, but for once in her life that lady had lost her head. "It is shocking!" she said, "outrageously shocking! I wonder if they told Mr. McDonald before he married her!" Then looking hurriedly round, she too saw the young husband's face—and knew that they had not.

"Humph! Deuced nice kettle of fish—and poor old Charlie has always thought so much of honorable birth."

Logan thought he spoke in an undertone, but "poor old Charlie" heard him. He followed his wife and brother across the room. "Joe, he said, "will you see that a trap is called?" Then to Christie, "Joe will see that you get home all right." He wheeled on his heel then and left the ballroom.

Joe *did* see.

He tucked a poor, shivering, pallid little woman into a cab, and wound her bare throat up in the scarlet velvet cloak that was hanging uselessly over her arm. She crouched down beside him, saying, "I am so cold, Joe; I am so cold," but she did not seem to know enough to wrap herself up. Joe felt all through this long drive that nothing this side of Heaven would be so good as to die, and he was glad when the poor little voice at his elbow said, "What is he so angry at, Joe?"

"I don't know exactly, dear," he said gently, "but I think it was what you said about this Indian marriage."

"But why should I not have said it? Is there anything wrong about it?" she asked pitifully.

"Nothing that I can see—there was no other way; but Charlie is very angry, and you must be brave and forgiving with him, Christie, dear."

"But I did never see him like that before, did you?"

"Once."

"When?"

"Oh, at college, one day, a boy tore his prayer-book in half, and threw it into the grate, just to be mean, you know. Our mother had given it to him at his confirmation."

"And did he look so?"

"About, but it all blew over in a day—Charlie's tempers are short and brisk. Just don't take any notice of him; run off to bed, and he'll have forgotten it by the morning."

They reached home at last. Christie said goodnight quietly, going directly to her room. Joe went to his room also, filled a pipe and smoked for an hour. Across the passage he could hear her slippered feet pacing up and down, up and down the length of her apartment. There was something pantherlike in those restless footfalls, a meaning velvetyness that made him shiver, and again he wished he were dead—or elsewhere.

After a time the hall door opened, and someone came upstairs, along the passage, and to the little woman's room. As he entered, she turned and faced him.

"Christie," he said harshly, "do you know what you have done?"

"Yes," taking a step nearer him, her whole soul springing up into her eyes, "I have angered you, Charlie, and—"

"Angered me? You have disgraced me; and, moreover, you have disgraced yourself and both your parents."

"*Disgraced?*"

"Yes, *disgraced*; you have literally declared to the whole city that your father and mother were never married, and that you are the child of—what shall we call it—love? certainly not legality."

Across the hallway sat Joe McDonald, his blood freezing; but it leapt into every vein like fire at the awful anguish in the little voice that cried simply, "Oh! Charlie!"

"How could you do it, how could you do it, Christie, without shame either for yourself or for me, let alone your parents?"

The voice was like an angry demon's—not a trace was there in it of the yellow-haired, blue-eyed, laughing-lipped boy who had driven away so gaily to the dance five hours before.

"Shame? Why should I be ashamed of the rites of my people any more than you should be ashamed of the customs of yours—of a marriage more sacred and holy than half of your white man's mockeries."

It was the voice of another nature in the girl—the love and the pleading were dead in it.

"Do you mean to tell me, Charlie—you who have studied my race and their laws for years—do you mean to tell me that, because there was no priest and no magistrate, my mother was not married? Do you mean to say that all my forefathers, for hundreds of years back, have been illegally born? If so, you blacken my ancestry beyond—beyond—beyond all reason."

"No, Christie, I would not be so brutal as that; but your father and mother live in more civilized times. Father O'Leary has been at the post for nearly twenty years. Why was not your father straight enough to have the ceremony performed when he *did* get the chance?"

The girl turned upon him with the face of a fury. "Do you suppose," she almost hissed, "that my mother would be married according to your *white* rites after she had been five years a wife, and I had been born in the meantime? *No*, a thousand times I say, *no*. When the priest came with his notions of Christianizing, and talked to them of remarriage by the Church, my mother arose and said, 'Never—never—I have never had but this one husband; he has had none but me for wife, and to have you remarry us would be to say as much to the whole world as that we had never been married before. You go away; *I* do not ask that *your* people be remarried; talk not so to me. I *am* married, and you or the Church cannot do or undo it.' "

"Your father was a fool not to insist upon the law, and so was the priest."

"Law? *My* people have *no* priest, and my nation cringes not to law. Our priest is purity, and our law is honor. Priest? Was there a *priest* at the most holy marriage known to humanity—that stainless marriage whose offspring is the God you white men told my pagan mother of?"

"Christie—you are *worse* than blasphemous; such a profane remark shows how little you understand the sanctity of the Christian faith—"

"I know what I *do* understand; it is that you are hating me because I told some of the beautiful customs of my people to Mrs. Stuart and those men."

"Pooh! Who cares for them? It is not them; the trouble is they won't keep their mouths shut. Logan's a cad and will toss the whole tale about at the club before tomorrow night; and as for the Stuart woman, I'd like to know how I'm going to take you to Ottawa for presentation and the opening, while she is blabbing the whole miserable scandal in every drawing-room, and I'll be pointed out as a romantic fool, and you—as worse; I *can't* understand why your father didn't tell me before we were married; I at least might have warned you to never mention it." Something of recklessness rang up through his voice, just as the pantherlikeness crept up from her footsteps and couched herself in hers. She spoke in tones quiet, soft, deadly.

"Before we were married! Oh! Charlie, would it have—made—any—difference?"

"God knows," he said, throwing himself into a chair, his blond hair rumpled and wet. It was the only boyish thing about him now.

She walked toward him, then halted in the center of the room. "Charlie McDonald," she said, and it was as if a stone had spoken, "look up." He raised his head, startled by her tone. There was a threat in her eyes that, had his rage been less courageous, his pride less bitterly wounded, would have cowed him.

"There was no such time as that before our marriage, for we *are not married now.* Stop," she said, outstretching her palms against him as he sprang to his feet, "I tell you we are not married. Why should I recognize the rites of your nation when you do not acknowledge the rites of mine? According to your own words, my parents should have gone through your church ceremony as well as through an Indian contract; according to *my* words, *we* should go through an Indian contract as well as through a church marriage. If their union is illegal, so is ours. If you think my father is living in dishonor with my mother, my people will think I am living in dishonor with you. How do I know when another nation will come and conquer you as you white men conquered us? And they will have another marriage rite to perform, and they will tell us another truth, that you are not my husband, that you are but disgracing and dishonoring me, that you are keeping me here, not as your wife, but as your—your—*squaw.*"

The terrible word had never passed her lips before, and the blood stained her face to her very temples. She snatched off her wedding ring and tossed it across the room, saying scornfully, "That thing is as empty to me as the Indian rites to you."

He caught her by the wrists; his small white teeth were locked tightly, his blue eyes blazed into hers.

"Christine, do you dare to doubt my honor towards you? *You*, whom I should have died for; do you *dare* to think I have kept you here, not as my wife, but—"

"Oh, God! You are hurting me; you are breaking my arm," she gasped.

The door was flung open, and Joe McDonald's sinewy hands clinched like vices on his brother's shoulders.

"Charlie, you're mad, mad as the devil. Let go of her this minute."

The girl staggered backwards as the iron fingers loosed her wrists.

"Oh! Joe," she cried, "I am not his wife, and he says I am born—nameless."

"Here," said Joe, shoving his brother towards the door. "Go downstairs till you can collect your senses. If ever a being acted like an infernal fool, you're the man."

The young husband looked from one to the other, dazed by his wife's insult, abandoned to a fit of ridiculously childish temper. Blind as he was with passion, he remembered long afterwards seeing them standing there, his brother's face darkened with a scowl of anger—his wife, clad in the mockery of her ball dress, her scarlet velvet cloak half covering her bare brown neck and arms, her eyes like flames of fire, her face like a piece of sculptured graystone.

Without a word he flung himself furiously from the room, and immediately afterwards they heard the heavy hall door bang behind him.

"Can I do anything for you, Christie?" asked her brother-in-law calmly.

"No, thank you—unless—I think I would like a drink of water, please."

He brought her up a goblet filled with wine; her hand did not even tremble as she took it. As for Joe, a demon arose in his soul as he noticed she kept her wrists covered.

"Do you think he will come back?" she said.

"Oh, yes, of course; he'll be all right in the morning. Now go to bed like a good little girl, and—and, I say, Christie you can call me if you want anything; I'll be right here, you know."

"Thank you, Joe; you are kind—and good."

He returned then to his apartment. His pipe was out, but he picked up a newspaper instead, threw himself into an armchair, and in a half-hour was in the land of dreams.

When Charlie came home in the morning, after a six-mile walk into the country and back again, his foolish anger was dead and buried. Logan's "Poor old Charlie" did not ring so distinctly in his ears. Mrs. Stuart's horrified expression had faded considerably from his recollection. He thought only of that surprisingly tall, dark girl, whose eyes looked like coals, whose voice pierced him like a flint-tipped arrow. Ah, well, they would never quarrel again like that, he told himself. She loved him so, and would forgive him after he had talked quietly to her, and told her what an ass he was. She was simpleminded and awfully ignorant to pitch those old Indian laws at him in her fury, but he could not blame her; oh, no, he could not for one moment blame her. He had been terribly severe and unreasonable, and the horrid McDonald temper had got the better of him; and he loved her so. *Oh!* he loved her so! She would surely feel that, and forgive him, and— He went straight to his wife's room. The blue velvet evening dress lay on the chair into which he had thrown himself when he doomed his life's happiness by those two words, "God knows." A bunch of dead daffodils and her slippers were on the floor, everything—but Christie.

He went to his brother's bedroom door.

"Joe," he called, rapping nervously thereon. "Joe, wake up; where's Christie, d'you know?"

"Good Lord, no," gasped that youth, springing out of his armchair and opening the door. As he did so a note fell from off the handle. Charlie's face blanched to his very hair while Joe read aloud, his voice weakening at every word:

> Dear Old Joe,—I went into your room at day-
> light to get that picture of the Post on your book-
> shelves. I hope you do not mind, but I kissed your

hair while you slept; it was so curly, and yellow, and soft, just like his. Good-bye, Joe.

                                                              Christie.

And when Joe looked into his brother's face and saw the anguish settle in those laughing blue eyes, the despair that drove the dimples away from that almost girlish mouth; when he realized that this boy was but four-and-twenty years old, and that all his future was perhaps darkened and shadowed forever, a great, deep sorrow arose in his heart, and he forgot all things, all but the agony that rang up through the voice of the fair, handsome lad as he staggered forward, crying, "Oh! Joe—what shall I do—what shall I do!"

It was months and months before he found her, but during all that time he had never known a hopeless moment; discouraged he often was, but despondent, never. The sunniness of his ever-boyish heart radiated with a warmth that would have flooded a much deeper gloom than that which settled within his eager young life. Suffer? Ah! yes, he suffered, not with locked teeth and stony stoicism, not with the masterful self-command, the reserve, the conquered bitterness of the still-water sort of nature that is supposed to run to such depths. He tried to be bright, and his sweet old boyish self. He would laugh sometimes in a pitiful, pathetic fashion. He took to petting dogs, looking into their large, solemn eyes with his wistful, questioning blue ones; he would kiss them, as women sometimes do, and call them "dear old fellow," in tones that had tears; and once in the course of his travels, while at a little way station, he discovered a huge St. Bernard imprisoned by some mischance in an empty freight car; the animal was nearly dead from starvation, and it seemed to salve his own sick heart to rescue back the dog's life. Nobody claimed the big starving creature, the train hands knew nothing of its owner, and gladly handed it over to its deliverer.

"Hudson," he called it, and afterwards when Joe McDonald would relate the story of his brother's life he invariably terminated it with, "And I really believe that big lumbering brute saved him." From what, he was never known to say.

But all things end, and he heard of her at last. She had never returned to the Post, as he at first thought she would, but had gone to the little town of B——, in Ontario, where she was making her living at embroidery and plain sewing.

The September sun had set redly when at last he reached the outskirts of the town, opened up the wicket gate, and walked up the weedy, unkept path leading to the cottage where she lodged.

Even through the twilight, he could see her there, leaning on the rail of the veranda—oddly enough she had about her shoulders the scarlet velvet cloak she wore when he had flung himself so madly from the room that night.

The moment the lad saw her his heart swelled with a sudden heat, burning moisture leapt into his eyes and clogged his long, boyish lashes. He bounded up the steps—"Christie," he said, and the word scorched his lips like audible flame.

She turned to him, and for a second stood magnetized by his passionately wistful face; her peculiar grayish eyes seemed to drink the very life of his unquenchable love, though the tears that suddenly sprang into his seemed to absorb every pulse in his body through those hungry, pleading eyes of his that had, oh, so often been blinded by her kisses when once her whole world lay in their blue depths.

"You will come back to me, Christie, my wife? My wife, you will let me love you again?"

She gave a singular little gasp, and shook her head. "Don't, oh, don't," he cried piteously. "You will come to me, dear? It is all such a bitter mistake—I did not understand. Oh! Christie, I did not understand, and you'll forgive me, and love me again, won't you—won't you?"

"No," said the girl with quick, indrawn breath.

He dashed the back of his hand across his wet eyelids. His lips were growing numb, and he bungled over the monosyllable "Why?"

"I do not like you," she answered quietly.

"God! Oh! God, what is there left?"

She did not appear to hear the heartbreak in his voice; she stood like one wrapped in somber thought; no blaze, no tear, nothing in her eyes; no hardness, no tenderness about her mouth. The wind was blowing her cloak aside, and the only visible human life in her whole body was once when he spoke the muscles of her brown arm seemed to contract.

"But, darling, you are mine—*mine*—we are husband and wife! Oh, heaven, you *must* love me, you *must* come to me again."

"You cannot *make* me come," said the icy voice, "neither church, nor law, nor even"—and the voice softened—"nor even love can make a slave of a red girl."

"Heaven forbid it," he faltered. "No, Christie, I will never claim you without your love. What reunion would that be? But oh, Christie, you are lying to me, you are lying to yourself, you are lying to heaven."

She did not move. If only he could touch her he felt as sure of her yielding as he felt sure there was a hereafter. The memory of times when he had but to lay his hand on her hair to call a most passionate response from her filled his heart with a torture that choked all words before they reached his lips; at the thought of those days he forgot she was unapproachable, forgot how forbidding were her eyes, how stony her lips. Flinging himself forward, his knee on the chair at her side, his face pressed hardly in the folds of the cloak on her shoulder, he clasped his arms about her with a boyish petulance, saying, "Christie, Christie, my little girl wife, I love you, I love you, and you are killing me."

She quivered from head to foot as his fair, wavy hair brushed her neck, his despairing face sank lower until his cheek, hot as fire, rested on the cool, olive flesh of her arm. A warm moisture oozed up through her skin, and as he felt its glow he looked up. Her teeth, white and cold, were locked over her under lip, and her eyes were as gray stones.

Not murderers alone know the agony of a death sentence.

"Is it all useless? All useless, dear?" he said, with lips starving for hers.

"All useless," she repeated. "I have no love for you now. You forfeited me and my heart months ago, when you said *those two words*."

His arms fell away from her wearily, he arose mechanically, he placed his little gray checked cap on the back of his yellow curls, the old-time laughter was dead in the blue eyes that now looked scared and haunted, the boyishness and the dimples crept away forever from the lips that quivered like a child's; he turned from her, but she had looked once into his face as the Law Giver must have looked at the land of Canaan outspread at his feet. She watched him go down the long path and through the picket gate, she watched the big yellowish dog that had waited for him lumber up on to its feet—stretch—then follow him. She was conscious of but two things, the vengeful lie in her soul, and a little space on her arm that his wet lashes had brushed.

It was hours afterwards when he reached his room. He had said nothing, done nothing—what use were words or deeds? Old Jimmy Robinson was right; she had "balked" sure enough.

What a bare, hotelish room it was! He tossed off his coat and sat for ten minutes looking blankly at the sputtering gas jet. Then his whole life, desolate as a desert, loomed up before him with appalling distinctness. Throwing himself on the floor beside his bed, with clasped hands and arms outstretched on the white counterpane, he sobbed. "Oh! God, dear God, I thought you loved me; I thought you'd let me have her again, but you must be tired of me, tired of loving me too. I've nothing left now, nothing! It doesn't seem that I even have you tonight."

He lifted his face then, for his dog, big and clumsy and yellow, was licking at his sleeve.

CHARLES A. EASTMAN (OHIYESA)

The War Maiden (1906)

In the winter of 1890, three hundred unarmed, starving Minneconjou and Hunkpapa Sioux, two-thirds of them women and children, were surrounded and murdered by the U.S. Cavalry at Wounded Knee. Dr. Eastman, then serving as the government doctor at Pine Ridge Agency (in South Dakota), was one of the first to reach the scene. Testimony of Native people holds that the soldiers cut off women's genitals and mounted them on the crowns of their cavalry hats.

In the words of American historian William Brandon, Eastman "described, quite dispassionately, the way young girls had knelt and covered their faces with their shawls so they would not see the troopers come up to shoot them." (The Last Americans, 426) That incident, identified by historians as the official end of the "Indian Wars," was one of hundreds, reminding us that terrorism in the United States did not begin with the bombing of the World Trade Center in 1993.

Perhaps in commemoration of the women of Wounded Knee, as well as in keeping with Native attitudes of respect toward women, Eastman began his collection of short stories, Old Indian

Days: *"I Dedicate these Stories of the Old Indian Life, and especially of the Courageous and Womanly Indian Woman, to my Daughters."* His account of a woman's bravery in "The War Maiden" is topical in our time: The "problem" of women in combat is a male problem. Indian humor gleams through this story about the true nature of courage.

The old man, Smoky Day, was for many years the best-known storyteller and historian of his tribe. He it was who told me the story of the War Maiden. In the old days it was unusual but not unheard of for a woman to go upon the war-path—perhaps a young girl, the last of her line, or a widow whose well-loved husband had fallen on the field—and there could be no greater incentive to feats of desperate daring on the part of the warriors.

"A long time ago," said old Smoky Day, "the Unkpapa and the Cut-Head bands of Sioux united their camps upon a vast prairie east of the Minnie Wakan (now called Devil's Lake). It was midsummer, and the people shared in the happiness of every living thing. We had food in abundance, for bison in countless numbers overspread the plain.

"The tipi village was laid out in two great rings, and all was in readiness for the midsummer entertainments. There were ball games, feasts, and dances every day and late into the night. You have heard of the festivities of those days; there are none like them now," said the old man, and he sighed heavily as he laid down the red pipe which was to be passed from hand to hand during the recital.

"The head chief of the Unkpapas then was Tamákoche (His Country). He was in his time a notable warrior, a hunter, and a feast-maker, much beloved by his people. He was the father of three sons, but he was so anxious to make them warriors of great reputation that they had all, despising danger, been killed in battle.

"The chief had also a very pretty daughter, whose name was Makátah. Since all his sons were slain he had placed his affections solely upon the girl, and she grew up listening to the praises of the brave deeds of her brothers, which her father never tired of chanting when they were together in the lodge. At times Makátah was called upon to dance to the 'Strong-Heart' songs. Thus even as a child she loved the thought of war, although she was the prettiest and most modest maiden in the two tribes. As she grew into womanhood she became the belle of her father's village, and her beauty and spirit were talked of even among the neighboring bands of Sioux. But it appeared that Makátah did not care to marry. She had only two ambitions. One was to prove to her father that, though only a maid, she had the heart of a warrior. The other was to visit the graves of her brothers—that is, the country of the enemy.

"At this pleasant reunion of two kindred peoples one of the principal events was the Feast of Virgins, given by Makátah. All young maidens of virtue and good repute were invited to be present, but woe to her who should dare to pollute the sacred feast! If her right to be there were challenged by any it meant a public disgrace. The two arrows and the red stone upon which the virgins took their oath of chastity were especially prepared for the occasion. Every girl was beautifully dressed, for at that time the white doeskin gowns, with a profusion of fringes and colored embroidery, were the gala attire of the Sioux maidens. Red paint was added, and ornaments of furs and wampum. Many youths eagerly surveyed the maiden gathering, at which the daughter of Tamákoche outshone all the rest.

"Several eligible warriors now pressed their suits at the chieftain's lodge, and among them were one or two whom he would have gladly called son-in-law; but no! Makátah would not listen to words of courtship. She had vowed, she said, to the spirits of her three brothers—each of whom fell in the country of the Crows—that she would see that country before she became a wife.

"Red Horn, who was something of a leader among the young men, was a persistent and determined suitor. He had urged every influential friend of his and hers to persuade her to listen to him. His presents were more valuable than those of any one else. He even made use of his father's position as a leading chief of the Cut-Head band to force a decision in his favor; and while the maiden remained indifferent her father seemed inclined to countenance this young man's pretensions.

"She had many other lovers, as I have said," the old man added, "and among them was one Little Eagle, an orphan and a poor young man, unknown and unproved as a warrior. He was so insignificant that nobody thought much about him, and if Makátah regarded him with any favor the matter was her secret, for it is certain that she did not openly encourage him.

"One day it was reported in the village that their neighbors, the Cut-Head Sioux, would organize a great attack upon the Crows at the mouth of the Redwater, a tributary of the Missouri. Makátah immediately inquired of her male cousins whether any of them expected to join the war-party.

" 'Three of us will go,' they replied.

" 'Then,' said the girl, 'I beg that you will allow me to go with you! I have a good horse, and I shall not handicap you in battle. I only ask your protection in camp as your kinswoman and a maid of the war-party.'

" 'If our uncle Tamákoche sanctions your going,' they replied, 'we shall be proud to have our cousin with us, to inspire us to brave deeds!'

"The maiden now sought her father and asked his permission to accompany the war-party.

" 'I wish,' said she, 'to visit the graves of my brothers! I shall carry with me their war-bonnets and their weapons, to give to certain young men on the eve of battle, according to the ancient custom. Long ago I resolved to do this, and the time is now come.'

"The chief was at this time well advanced in years, and had been sitting quite alone in his lodge, thinking upon the days of his youth, when he was noted for daring and success in battle. In silence he listened as he filled his pipe, and seemed to meditate while he smoked the fragrant tobacco. At last he spoke with tears in his eyes.

" 'Daughter, I am an old man! My heart beats in my throat, and my old eyes cannot keep back the tears. My three sons, on whom I had placed all my hopes, are gone to a far country! You are the only child left to my old age, and you, too, are brave—as brave as any of your brothers. If you go I fear that you may not return to me; yet I cannot refuse you my permission!'

"The old man began to chant a war song, and some of his people, hearing him, came in to learn what was in his mind. He told them all, and immediately many young men volunteered for the war-party, in order to have the honor of going with the daughter of their chief.

"Several of Makátah's suitors were among them, and each watched eagerly for an opportunity to ride at her side. At night she pitched her little tipi within the circle of her cousins' camp-fires, and there she slept without fear. Courteous youths brought to her every morning and evening fresh venison for her repast. Yet there was no courting, for all attentions paid to a maiden when on the war-path must be those of a brother to a sister, and all must be equally received by her.

"Two days later, when the two parties of Sioux met on the plains, the maiden's presence was heralded throughout the camp, as an inspiration to the young and untried warriors of both bands to distinguish themselves in the field. It is true that some of the older men considered it unwise to allow Makátah to accompany the war-party.

" 'The girl,' said they to one another, 'is very ambitious as well as brave. She will surely risk her own life in battle, which will make the young men desperate, and we shall lose many of them!'

"Nevertheless they loved her and her father; therefore they did not protest openly.

"On the third day the Sioux scouts returned with the word that the Crows were camping, as had been supposed, at the confluence of the Redwater and the Missouri rivers. It was a great camp. All the Crow tribe were there, they said, with their thousands of fine horses.

"There was excitement in the Sioux camp, and all of the head men immediately met in council. It was determined to make the attack early on the following morning, just as the sun came over the hills. The councilors agreed that in honor of the great chief, her father, as well as in recognition of her own courage, Makátah should be permitted to lead the charge at the outset, but that she must drop behind as they neared the enemy. The maiden, who had one of the fleetest ponies in that part of the country, had no intention of falling back, but she did not tell anyone what was in her mind.

"That evening every warrior sang his war song, and announced the particular war charm or 'medicine' of his clan, according to the custom. The youths were vying with one another in brave tales of what they would do on the morrow. The voice of Red Horn was loud among the boasters, for he was known to be a vain youth, although truly not without reputation. Little Eagle, who was also of the company, remained modestly silent, as indeed became one without experience in the field. In the midst of the clamor there fell a silence.

" 'Hush! hush!' they whispered. 'Look, look! The War Maiden comes!'

"All eyes were turned upon Makátah, who rode her fine buckskin steed with a single lariat. He held his head proudly, and his saddle was heavy with fringes and gay with colored embroidery. The maiden was attired in her best and wore her own father's war-bonnet, while she carried in her hands two which had belonged to two of her dead brothers. Singing in a clear voice the songs of her clan, she completed the circle, according to custom, before she singled out one of the young braves for special honor by giving him the bonnet which she held in her right hand. She then crossed over to the Cut-Heads, and presented the other bonnet to one of their young men. She was very handsome; even the old men's blood was stirred by her brave appearance!

"At daybreak the two war-parties of the Sioux, mounted on their best horses, stood side by side, ready for the word to charge. All of the warriors were painted for the battle—prepared for death—their nearly nude bodies decorated with their individual war-totems. Their well-filled quivers were fastened to their sides, and each tightly grasped his oaken bow.

"The young man with the finest voice had been chosen to give the signal—a single high-pitched yell. This was an imitation of the one long howl of the gray wolf before he makes the attack. It was an ancient custom of our people.

" 'Woo-o-o-o!'—at last it came! As the sound ceased a shrill war whoop from five hundred throats burst forth in chorus, and at the same instant Makátah, upon her splendid buckskin pony, shot far out upon the plain, like an arrow as it leaves the bow. It was a glorious sight! No man has ever looked upon the like again!"

The eyes of the old man sparkled as he spoke, and his bent shoulders straightened.

"The white doeskin gown of the War Maiden," he continued, "was trimmed with elk's teeth and tails of ermine. Her long black hair hung loose, bound only with a strip of otter skin, and with her eagle-feather war-bonnet floated far behind. In her hand she held a long coup-staff decorated with eagle feathers. Thus she went forth in advance of them all!

"War cries of men and screams of terrified women and children were borne upon the clear morning air as our warriors neared the Crow camp. The charge was made over a wide plain, and the Crows came yelling from their lodges, fully armed, to meet the attacking party. In spite of the surprise they easily held their own, and even began to press us hard, as their number was much greater than that of the Sioux.

"The fight was a long and hard one. Toward the end of the day the enemy made a countercharge. By that time many of our ponies had fallen or were exhausted. The Sioux retreated, and the slaughter was great. The Cut-Heads fled womanlike, but the people of Tamákoche fought gallantly to the very last.

"Makátah remained with her father's people. Many cried out to her, 'Go back! Go back!' but she paid no attention. She carried no weapon throughout the day—nothing but her coup-staff—but by her presence and her cries of encouragement or praise she urged on the men to deeds of desperate valor.

"Finally, however, the Sioux braves were hotly pursued and the retreat became general. Now at last Makátah tried to follow, but her pony was tired, and the maiden fell farther and farther behind. Many of her lovers passed her silently, intent upon saving their own lives. Only a few still remained behind, fighting desperately to cover the retreat, when Red Horn came up with the girl. His pony was still fresh. He might have put her up behind him and carried her to safety, but he did not even look at her as he galloped by.

"Makátah did not call out, but she could not help looking after him. He had declared his love for her more loudly than any of the others, and she now gave herself up to die.

"Presently another overtook the maiden. It was Little Eagle, unhurt and smiling.

" 'Take my horse!' he said to her. 'I shall remain here and fight!'

"The maiden looked at him and shook her head, but he sprang off and lifted her upon his horse. He struck him a smart blow upon the flank that sent him at full speed in the direction of the Sioux encampment. Then he seized the exhausted buckskin by the lariat, and turned back to join the rear guard.

"That little group still withstood in some fashion the all but irresistible onset of the Crows. When their comrade came back to them, leading the War Maiden's pony, they were inspired to fresh endeavor, and though few in numbers they made a countercharge with such fury that the Crows in their turn were forced to retreat!

"The Sioux got fresh mounts and returned to the field, and by sunset the day was won! Little Eagle was among the first who rode straight through the Crow camp, causing terror and consternation. It was afterward remembered that he looked unlike his former self and was scarcely recognized by the warriors for the modest youth they had so little regarded.

"It was this famous battle which drove that warlike nation, the Crows, to go away from the Missouri and to make their home up the Yellowstone River and in the Bighorn country. But many of our men fell, and among them the brave Little Eagle!

"The sun was almost over the hills when the Sioux gathered about their campfires, recounting the honors won in battle, and naming the brave dead. Then came the singing of dirges and weeping for the slain! The sadness of loss was mingled with exultation.

"Hush! Listen! The singing and wailing have ceased suddenly at both camps. There is one voice coming around the circle of campfires. It is the voice of a woman! Stripped of all her ornaments, her dress shorn of its fringes, her ankles bare, her hair cropped close to her neck, leading a pony with mane and tail cut short, she is mourning as widows mourn. It is Makátah!

"Publicly, with many tears, she declared herself the widow of the brave Little Eagle, although she had never been his wife! He it was, she said with truth, who had saved her people's honor and her life at the cost of his own. He was a true man!

" 'Ho, ho!' was the response from many of the old warriors; but the young men, the lovers of Makátah, were surprised and sat in silence.

"The War Maiden lived to be a very old woman, but she remained true to her vow. She never accepted a husband; and all her lifetime she was known as the widow of the brave Little Eagle."

CHARLES A. EASTMAN (OHIYESA)

The Singing Spirit (1907)

In "The Singing Spirit," Eastman reflects his deep connection to the spiritual traditions of his people. In it we see how identity slips and changes as readily in a short story as it does in the oral tradition, and how humor informs both. Stories of the Little People abound in Native American lore, as they do among the modern-day Celts of Ireland, Scotland, and Wales. In "The Singing Spirit," Eastman deftly combines two traditions, and adds a couple of twists to his intricately designed combination.

I

"Ho my steed, we must climb one more hill! My reputation depends upon my report!"

Anookasan addressed his pony as if he were a human companion, urged on like himself by human need and human ambition. And yet in his heart he had very little hope of sighting any buffalo in that region at just that time of the year.

The Yankton Sioux were ordinarily the most farsighted of

their people in selecting a winter camp, but this year the late fall had caught them rather far east of the Missouri bottoms, their favorite camping ground. The upper Jim River, called by the Sioux the River of Gray Woods, was usually bare of large game at that season. Their store of jerked buffalo meat did not hold out as they had hoped, and by March it became an urgent necessity to send out scouts for buffalo.

The old men at the tiyo tipi (council lodge) held a long council. It was decided to select ten of their bravest and hardiest young men to explore the country within three days' journey of their camp.

"Anookasan, uyeyo-o-o, woo, woo!" Thus the ten men were summoned to the council lodge early in the evening to receive their commission. Anookasan was the first called and first to cross the circle of the tipis. A young man of some thirty years, of the original Native type, his massive form was wrapped in a fine buffalo robe with the hair inside. He wore a stately eagle feather in his scalp-lock, but no paint about his face.

As he entered the lodge all the inmates greeted him with marked respect, and he was given the place of honor. When all were seated the great drum was struck and a song sung by four deep-chested men. This was the prelude to a peculiar ceremony.

A large red pipe, which had been filled and laid carefully upon the central hearth, was now taken up by an old man, whose face was painted red. First he held it to the ground with the words: "Great Mother, partake of this!" Then he held it toward the sky, saying: "Great Father, smoke this!" Finally he lighted it, took four puffs, pointing it to the four corners of the earth in turn, and lastly presented it to Anookasan. This was the oath of office, administered by the chief of the council lodge. The other nine were similarly commissioned, and all accepted the appointment.

It was no light task that was thus religiously enjoined

upon these ten men. It meant at the least several days and nights of wandering in search of signs of the wily buffalo. It was a public duty, and a personal one as well; one that must involve untold hardship; and if overtaken by storm the messengers were in peril of death!

Anookasan returned to his tipi with some misgiving. His old charger, which had so often carried him to victory, was not so strong as he had been in his prime. As his master approached the lodge the old horse welcomed him with a gentle whinny. He was always tethered near by, ready for any emergency.

"Ah, Wakan! We are once more called upon to do duty! We shall set out before daybreak."

As he spoke, he pushed nearer a few strips of the poplar bark, which was oats to the Indian pony of the olden time.

Anookasan had his extra pair of buffalo-skin moccasins with the hair inside, and his scanty provisions of dried meat neatly done up in a small packet and fastened to his saddle. With his companions he started northward, up the River of the Gray Woods, five on the east side and a like number on the west.

The party had separated each morning, so as to cover as much ground as possible, having agreed to return at night to the river. It was now the third day; their food was all but gone, their steeds much worn, and the signs seemed to indicate a storm. Yet the hunger of their friends and their own pride impelled them to persist, for out of many young men they had been chosen, therefore they must prove themselves equal to the occasion.

The sun, now well toward the western horizon, cast over snow-covered plains a purplish light. No living creature was in sight and the quest seemed hopeless, but Anookasan was not one to accept defeat.

"There may be an outlook from yonder hill which will

turn failure into success," he thought, as he dug his heels into the sides of his faithful nag. At the same time he started a "Strong Heart" song to keep his courage up!

At the summit of the ascent he paused and gazed steadily before him. At the foot of the next coteau he beheld a strip of black. He strained his eyes to look, for the sun had already set behind the hilltops. It was a great herd of buffalo, he thought, which was grazing on the foothills.

"Hi, hi, uncheedah! Hi, hi, tunkasheedah!" he was about to exclaim in gratitude, when, looking more closely, he discovered his mistake. The dark patch was only timber.

His horse could not carry him any farther, so he got off and ran behind him toward the river. At dusk he hailed his companions.

"Ho, what success?" one cried.

"Not a sign of even a lone bull," replied another.

"Yet I saw a gray wolf going north this evening. His direction is propitious," remarked Anookasan, as he led the others down the slope and into the heavy timber. The river just here made a sharp turn, forming a densely wooded semicircle, in the shelter of a high bluff.

The braves were all downhearted because of their ill-luck, and only the sanguine spirit of Anookasan kept them from utter discouragement. Their slight repast had been taken and each man had provided himself with abundance of dry grass and twigs for a bed. They had built a temporary wigwam of the same material, in the center of which there was a generous fire. Each man stretched himself out upon his robe in the glow of it. Anookasan filled the red pipe, and, having lighted it, he took one or two hasty puffs and held it up to the moon, which was scarcely visible behind the cold clouds.

"Great Mother, partake of this smoke! May I eat meat tomorrow!" he exclaimed with solemnity. Having uttered this prayer, he handed the pipe to the man nearest him.

For a time they all smoked in silence, then came a distant call.

"Ah, it is Shunkmanito, the wolf! There is something cheering in his voice tonight," declared Anookasan. "Yes, I am sure he is telling us not to be discouraged. You know that the wolf is one of our best friends in trouble. Many a one has been guided back to his home by him in a blizzard, or led to game when in desperate need. My friends, let us not turn back in the morning; let us go north one more day!"

No one answered immediately, and again silence reigned, while one by one they pulled the reluctant whiffs of smoke through the long stem of the calumet.

"What is that?" said one of the men, and all listened intently to catch the delicate sound. They were familiar with all the noises of the night and voices of the forest, but this was not like any of them.

"It sounds like the song of a mosquito, and one might forget while he listens that this is not midsummer," said one.

"I hear also the medicine man's single drumbeat," suggested another.

"There is a tradition," remarked Anookasan, "that many years ago a party of hunters went up the river on a scout like this of ours. They never returned. Afterward, in the summer, their bones were found near the home of a strange creature, said to be a little man, but he had hair all over him. The Isantees call him Chanotedah. Our old men give him the name Oglugechana. This singular being is said to be no larger than a newborn babe. He speaks an unknown tongue.

"The home of Oglugechana is usually a hollow stump, around which all of the nearest trees are felled by lightning. There is an open spot in the deep woods wherever he dwells. His weapons are the plumes of various birds. Great numbers of these variegated feathers are to be found in the deserted lodge of the little man.

"It is told by the old men that Oglugechana has a weird music by which he sometimes bewitches lone travelers. He leads them hither and thither about his place until they have lost their senses. Then he speaks to them. He may make of them great war prophets or medicine men, but his commands are hard to fulfill. If anyone sees him and comes away before he is bewildered, the man dies as soon as he smells the campfire, or when he enters his home his nearest relative dies suddenly."

The warrior who related this legend assumed the air of one who narrates authentic history, and his listeners appeared to be seriously impressed. What we call the supernatural was as real to them as any part of their lives.

"This thing does not stop to breathe at all. His music seems to go on endlessly," said one, with considerable uneasiness.

"It comes from the heavy timber north of us, under the high cliff," reported a warrior who had stepped outside of the rude temporary structure to inform himself more clearly of the direction of the sound.

"Anookasan, you are our leader—tell us what we should do! We will follow you. I believe we ought to leave this spot immediately. This is perhaps the spirit of some dead enemy," suggested another. Meanwhile, the red pipe was refilled and sent around the circle to calm their disturbed spirits.

When the calumet returned at last to the one addressed, he took it in a preoccupied manner, and spoke between labored pulls on the stem.

"I am just like yourselves—nothing more than flesh—with a spirit that is as ready to leave me as water to run from a punctured water bag! When we think thus, we are awake. Let us rather think upon the brave deeds of our ancestors! This singing spirit has a gentle voice; I am ready to follow and learn if it be an enemy or no. Let us all be found together next summer if need be!"

"Ho, ho, ho!" was the full-throated response.

"All put on your war paint," suggested Anookasan. "Have your knives and arrows ready!"

They did so, and all stole silently through the black forest in the direction of the mysterious sound. Clearer and clearer it came through the frosty air, but it was a foreign sound to the savage ear. Now it seemed to them almost like a distant waterfall, then it recalled the low hum of summer insects and the drowsy drone of the bumblebee. Thump, thump, thump! was the regular accompaniment.

Nearer and nearer to the cliff they came, deeper into the wild heart of the woods. At last out of the gray, formless night a dark shape appeared! It looked to them like a huge buffalo bull standing motionless in the forest, and from his throat there apparently proceeded the thump of the medicine drum, and the song of the beguiling spirit!

All of a sudden a spark went up into the air. As they continued to approach, there became visible a deep glow about the middle of the dark object. Whatever it was, they had never heard of anything like it in all their lives!

Anookasan was a little in advance of his companions, and it was he who finally discovered a wall of logs laid one upon another. Halfway up there seemed to be stretched a parfleche (rawhide), from which a dim light emanated. He still thought of Oglugechana, who dwells within a hollow tree, and determined to surprise and if possible to overpower this wonder-working old man.

All now took their knives in their hands and advanced with their leader to the attack upon the log hut. "Wa-wa-wa-wa, woo, woo!" they cried. Zip, zip! went the parfleche door and window, and they all rushed in!

There sat a man upon a roughly hewn stool. He was attired in wolfskins and wore a foxskin cap upon his head. The larger portion of his face was clothed with natural fur. A rudely made cedar fiddle was tucked under his furred chin. Supporting it with his left hand, he sawed it vigorously with a bow that was not unlike an Indian boy's miniature weapon, while his moccasined left foot came down upon the sod floor in time with the music. When the shrill war whoop came, and the door and window were cut in strips by the knives of the Indians, he did not even cease playing, but instinctively he closed his eyes, so as not to behold the horror of his own end.

II

It was long ago, upon the rolling prairie south of the Devil's Lake, that a motley body of hunters gathered near a mighty herd of the bison, in the Moon of Falling Leaves. These were the first generation of the Canadian mixed-bloods, who sprang up in such numbers as to form almost a new people. These semi-wild Americans soon became a necessity to the Hudson Bay Company, as they were the greatest hunters of bison, and made more use of this wonderful animal than even their aboriginal ancestors.

A curious race of people this, in their makeup and their customs! Their shaggy black hair was allowed to grow long, reaching to their broad shoulders, then cut off abruptly, making their heads look like a thatched house. Their dark faces were in most cases well covered with hair, their teeth large and white, and their eyes usually liquid black, although occasionally one had a tiger-brown or cold-gray eye. Their costume was a buckskin shirt with abundance of fringes, buckskin pantaloons with short leggins, a gay sash, and a cap of fox fur. Their arms consisted of flintlock guns, hatchets, and butcher knives. Their ponies were small but as hardy as themselves.

As these men gathered in the neighborhood of an immense herd of buffalo, they busied themselves in adjusting the girths of their beautifully beaded pillowlike saddles. Among them there were exceptional riders and hunters. It was said that few could equal Antoine Michaud in feats of riding into and through the herd. There he stood, all alone, the observed of many others. It was his habit to give several Indian yells when the onset began, so as to ensure a successful hunt.

In this instance, Antoine gave his usual whoops, and when they had almost reached the herd, he lifted his flintlock over his head and plunged into the black moving mass. With a sound like the distant rumbling of thunder, those tens of thousands of buffalo hooves were pounding the earth in retreat. Thus Antoine disappeared!

His wild steed dashed into the midst of the vast herd. Fortunately for him, the animals kept clear of him; but alas!, the gap through which he had entered instantly closed again.

He yelled frantically to secure an outlet, but without effect. He had tied a red bandanna around his head to keep the hair off his face, and he now took this off and swung it crazily about him to scatter the buffalo, but it availed him nothing.

With such a mighty herd in flight, the speed could not be great; therefore the "Bois Brule" settled himself to the situation, allowing his pony to canter along slowly to save his strength. It required much tact and presence of mind to keep an open space, for the few paces of obstruction behind had gradually grown into a mile.

The mighty host moved continually southward, walking and running alternately. As the sun neared the western horizon, it fired the sky above them, and all the distant hills and prairies were in the glow of it, but immediately about them was a thick cloud of dust, and the ground appeared like a fire-swept plain.

Suddenly Antoine was aware of a tremendous push from behind. The animals smelled the cool water of a spring which formed a large bog in the midst of the plain. This solitary pond or marsh was a watering place for the wild animals. All pushed and edged toward it; it was impossible for anyone to withstand the combined strength of so many.

Antoine and his steed were in imminent danger of being pushed into the mire and trampled upon, but a mere chance brought them upon solid ground. As they were crowded across the marsh, his pony drank heartily, and he, for the first time, let go his bridle, put his two palms together for a dipper, and drank greedily of the bitter water. He had not eaten since early morning, so he now pulled up some bulrushes and ate of the tender bulbs, while the pony grazed as best he could on the tops of the tall grass.

It was now dark. The night was well-nigh intolerable for Antoine. The buffalo were about him in countless numbers, regarding him with vicious glances. It was only by reason of the natural offensiveness of man that they gave him any space. The bellowing of the bulls became general, and there was a marked uneasiness on the part of the herd. This was a sign of approaching storm, therefore the unfortunate hunter had this additional cause for anxiety. Upon the western horizon were seen some flashes of lightning.

The cloud which had been a mere speck upon the horizon had now increased to large proportions. Suddenly the wind came, and lightning flashes became more frequent, showing the ungainly forms of the animals like strange monsters in the white light. The colossal herd was again in violent motion. It was a blind rush for shelter, and no heed was paid to buffalo wallows or even deep gulches. All was in the deepest of darkness. There seemed to be groaning in heaven and earth— millions of hooves and throats roaring in unison!

As a shipwrecked man clings to a mere fragment of wood, so Antoine, although almost exhausted with fatigue, still stuck to the back of his equally plucky pony. Death was imminent for them both. As the mad rush continued, every flash displayed heaps of bison in death struggle under the hooves of their companions.

From time to time Antoine crossed himself and whispered a prayer to the Virgin, and again he spoke to his horse after the fashion of an Indian:

"Be brave, be strong, my horse! If we survive this trial, you shall have great honor!"

The stampede continued until they reached the bottom lands, and, like a rushing stream, their course was turned aside by the steep bank of a creek or small river. Then they moved more slowly in wide sweeps or circles, until the storm ceased, and the exhausted hunter, still in his saddle, took some snatches of sleep.

When he awoke and looked about him again it was morning. The herd had entered the strip of timber which lay on both sides of the river, and it was here that Antoine conceived his first distinct hope of saving himself.

"Waw, waw, waw!" was the hoarse cry that came to his ears, apparently from a human being in distress. Antoine strained his eyes and craned his neck to see who it could be. Through an opening in the branches ahead he perceived a large grizzly bear, lying along an inclined limb and hugging it desperately to maintain his position. The herd had now thoroughly pervaded the timber, and the bear was likewise hemmed in. He had taken to his unaccustomed refuge after making a brave stand against several bulls, one of which lay dead near by, while he himself was bleeding from many wounds.

Antoine had been assiduously looking for a friendly tree, by means of which he hoped to effect his escape from captivity by the army of bison. His horse, by chance, made his way directly under the very box elder that was sustaining the bear and there was a convenient branch just within his reach. The Bois Brule was not then in an aggressive mood, and he saw at a glance that the occupant of the tree would not interfere with him. They were, in fact, companions in distress. Antoine tried to give a war whoop as he sprang desperately from the pony's back and seized the cross limb with both his hands.

The hunter dangled in the air for a minute that to him seemed a year. Then he gathered up all the strength that was in him, and with one grand effort he pulled himself up on the limb.

If he had failed in this, he would have fallen to the ground under the hooves of the buffalo, and at their mercy.

After he had adjusted his seat as comfortably as he could, Antoine surveyed the situation. He had at least escaped from sudden and certain death. It grieved him that he had been forced to abandon his horse, and he had no idea how far he had come nor any means of returning to his friends, who had, no doubt, given him up for lost. His immediate needs were rest and food.

Accordingly he selected a fat cow and emptied into her sides one barrel of his gun, which had been slung across his chest. He went on shooting until he had killed many fat cows, greatly to the discomfiture of his neighbor, the bear, while the bison vainly struggled among themselves to keep the fatal spot clear.

By the middle of the afternoon the main body of the herd had passed, and Antoine was sure that his captivity had at last come to an end. Then he swung himself from his limb to the ground, and walked stiffly to the carcass of the nearest cow, which he dressed and prepared himself a meal. But first he took a piece of liver on a long pole to the bear!

Antoine finally decided to settle in the recesses of the heavy timber for the winter, as he was on foot and alone, and not able to travel any great distance. He jerked the meat of all the animals he had killed, and prepared their skins for bedding and clothing. The Bois Brule and Ami, as he called the bear, soon became necessary to one another. The former considered the bear very good company, and the latter had learned that man's business, after all, is not to kill every animal he meets. He had been fed and kindly treated, when helpless from his wounds, and this he could not forget.

Antoine was soon busy erecting a small log hut, while the other partner kept a sharp lookout, and, after his hurts were healed, often brought in some small game. The two had a perfect understanding without many words; at least, the speech was all upon one side! In his leisure moments Antoine had occupied himself with whittling out a rude fiddle of cedarwood, strung with the guts of a wild cat that he had killed. Every evening that winter he would sit down after supper and play all the old familiar pieces, varied with improvisations of his own. At first, the music and the incessant pounding time with his foot annoyed the bear. At times, too, the Canadian would call out the figures for the dance. All this Ami became accustomed to in time, and even showed no small interest in the buzzing of the little cedar box. Not infrequently, he was out in the evening, and the human partner was left alone. It chanced, quite fortunately, that the bear was absent on the night that the red folk rudely invaded the lonely hut.

The calmness of the strange being had stayed their hands. They had never before seen a man of other race than their own!

"Is this Chanotedah? Is he man, or beast?" the warriors asked one another.

"Ho, wake up, koda!" exclaimed Anookasan. "Maybe he is of the porcupine tribe, ashamed to look at us!"

At this moment they spied the haunch of venison which swung from a cross-stick over a fine bed of coals, in front of the rude mud chimney.

"Ho, koda has something to eat! Sit down, sit down!" they shouted to one another.

Now Antoine opened his eyes for the first time upon his unlooked-for guests. They were a haggard and hungry-looking set. Anookasan extended his hand, and Antoine gave it a hearty shake. He set his fiddle against the wall and began to cut up the smoking venison into generous pieces and place it before them. All ate like famished men, while the firelight intensified the red paint upon their wild and warlike faces.

When he had satisfied his first hunger, Anookasan spoke in signs. "Friend, we have never before heard a song like that of your little cedar box! We had supposed it to be a spirit, or some harmful thing, hence our attack upon it. We never saw any people of your sort. What is your tribe?"

Antoine explained his plight in the same manner, and the two soon came to an understanding. The Canadian told the starving hunters of a buffalo herd a little way to the north, and one of their number was dispatched homeward with the news. In two days the entire band reached Antoine's place. The Bois Brule was treated with kindness and honor, and the tribe gave him a wife. Suffice it to say that Antoine lived and died among the Yanktons at a good old age; but Ami could not brook the invasion upon their hermit life. He was never seen after that first evening.

ARTHUR C. PARKER

The Coming of Death (1923)

It is said that the Druidic bards could sing only about love and death. While the Native Narrative Tradition is more inclusive, stories about death, the dead, and the afterworld and afterlife occur widely over Native America. The Seneca's origins are connected with death; their progenetrix was counseled by her dead father to contract a marriage that resulted in her downfall. Her precipitous descent through the void in turn caused her to create the earth. According to the Myth, her father was the first dead person the people of the world from which she fell had ever seen.

It is likely that Parker's account is a version of the great Myth that can be told to children and outsiders without fear of violation of the Sacred. As such stories do, it explains the situation, gives the history, and suggests appropriate attitudes under the circumstances, all common features of stories for the young and uninformed.

When the world was first made men-beings did not know that they must die sometime.

In those days everyone was happy and neither men and

women nor children were afraid of anything. They did not think of anything but doing what pleased them. At one time, in those days, a prominent man was found prone upon the grass. He was limp and had no breath. He did not breathe. The men-beings that saw him did not know what had happened. The man was not asleep because he did not awaken. When they placed him on his feet he fell like a tanned skin. He was limp. They tried many days to make him stand but he would not. After a number of days he became offensive.

A female man-being said that the man must be wrapped up and put in the limbs of a tree. So the men did so and after a while the flesh dropped from the bones and some dried on. No one knew what had happened to cause such a thing.

Soon afterward a child was found in the same condition. It had no breath. It could not stand. It was not asleep, so they said. The men-beings thought it was strange that a girl man-being should act this way. So she was laid in a tree.

Now many others did these things and no one knew why. No one thought that he himself would do such a thing.

There was one wise man who thought much about these things and he had a dream. When he slept the Good Minded Spirit came to him and spoke. He slept a long time, but the other men-beings noticed that he breathed slowly. He breathed (nevertheless). Now after a time this man rose up and his face was very solemn. He called the people together in a council and addressed the people. The head men all sat around with the people.

The wise man spoke and he said, "The Good Minded Spirit made every good thing and prepared the earth for men-beings. Now it appears that strange events have happened. A good word has come to me from the Good Minded Spirit. He says that every person must do as you have seen the other persons do. They have died. They do not breathe. It will be the same with all of you. Your minds are strong. The Good Minded

Spirit made them that way so that you could endure everything that happened. So then do not be downcast when I tell you all must die. Listen further to what I say. The name of the one that steals away your breath is Shondowekowa. He has no face and does not see anyone. You cannot see him until he grasps you. He comes sometimes for a visit and sometimes he stays with us until many are dead. Sometimes he takes away the best men and women and passes by the lesser ones. I was not told why he does this thing. He wants to destroy every person. He will continue to work forever. Everyone who hears me and everyone not yet born will die. There is more about you than living. Any moment you may be snatched by Shondowekowa, he who works in the thick darkness.

"You must now divide yourselves into nine bands, five to sit on one side of the fire and four on the other and these bands shall care for its members. You must seek out all good things and instruct one another, and those who do good things will see the place where the Maker of all things lives when their breath goes out of their body."

ARTHUR C. PARKER

The Coming of Spring (1923)

Just as death follows birth, birth follows death. This story, re-counted to Parker by Aurelia Miller, bears strong resemblance to the Laguna Pueblo account, though the two communities are separated by about two thousand miles. The Pueblo story, however, is a narrative rendition of a ritual, danced in early spring, and it is about love as much as about death. Parker's account seems to be a "men's" story—one of those belonging to the male rather than the female side of the oral tradition, as all of the Spirits in the tale are male.

In the ancient times when this world was new an old man wandered over the land in search of a suitable camping spot. He was a fierce old man and had long white flowing hair. The ground grew hard like flint where his footsteps fell, and when he breathed the leaves and grasses dropped and dried up red, and fell. When he splashed through the rivers the water stopped running and stood solid.

On and on the old man journeyed until at last on the shores

of a great lake by a high mountain he halted. He gathered the trees that had been uprooted by hurricanes and made a framework for a dwelling. He built the walls of ice and plastered the crevices with branches and snow. Then, to guard his lodge against the intruder, he placed uprooted stumps about on every side. Not even bad animals cared to enter this house. Everything living passed by it at a distance. It was like a magician's house.

The old man had but one friend. It was North Wind, and it was he alone who might enter the door of the stronghold and sit by the fire. Very wonderful was this fire and it gave flames and light but no heat! But even North Wind found little time to enter and smoke with the old man, for he took greater pleasure in piling high the snow and driving hail, like flints, against the shivering deep or hungry stormbound hunter. He liked to kill them. There came times, however, when North Wind needed new tricks and so he sought the advice of the old man— how he might pile up the snow banks higher, how he might cause famine or make great snowslides to bury Indian villages.

One very dismal night both North Wind and the old man sat smoking, half awake and half dreaming. North Wind could think of nothing new and the old man could give no more advice. So, sitting before the fire, both fell asleep. Towards morning each sprang to his feet with a cry. Not their usual cries, either, were their startled yells, for instead of a shrill "agēē! agēē! agēē!" the North Wind only gasped hoarsely and the old man's jaw opened with a smack and his tongue, thick and swollen, rolled out on his chin. Then spoke the North Wind.

"What warm thing has bewitched me? The drifts are sinking, the rivers breaking, the ice is steaming, the snow is smoking!"

The old man was silent, too sleepy to speak. He only thought, "My house is strong, very strong." Still the North Wind called loudly:

"See, the rivers are swelling full, the drifts are getting smaller."

Then he rushed from the lodge, and he flew to the mountain top where snow made him brave again. So he was happy and sang a war song as he danced on snow crust.

At the lodge of the old man a stranger struck the doorpost. The old man did not move, but dozing, thought, "oh some prank of North Wind." The knocking continued and the old man grew more sleepy. The door rattled on its fastenings but the old man's head did not raise to listen but dropped on his chest and his pipe fell down to his feet.

The logs of the lodge frame shook—one fell from the roof. The old man jumped to his feet with a war yell.

"Who is it that dares come to my house in this way? Only my friend North Wind enters here. Go away, no loafers here!"

In answer the door fell down and a stranger stood in the opening. He entered and hung the door upright again. His face was smiling and as he stirred the fire, it grew warmer inside. The old man looked at the stranger but did not answer his pleasant words, but his heart was very angry. Finally when he could no longer keep silent he burst forth:

"You are a stranger to me and have entered my lodge, breaking down my door. Why have you broken down my door? Why have your eyes a fire? Why does light shine from your skin? Why do you go about without skins when the wind is sharp? Why do you stir up my fire when you are young and need no warmth? Why do you not fall on my wolf skins and sleep? Did not North Wind blow the sun far away? Go away now before he returns and blows you against the mountains. I do not know you. You do not belong in my lodge!"

The younger stranger laughed and said, "Oh, why not let me stay a little longer and smoke my pipe?"

"Then listen to me," yelled the old man in anger. "I am mighty! All snows and ice and frosts are my making. I tell the North Wind to cut the skins of men to let the blood through to make war paint on the drifts. I tell him to freeze things that are food. Birds and animals run away from the North Wind. I pile the drifts on the rocks on the mountains and when it gets very high the North Wind knocks it off to crush the villages beneath."

Listlessly the stranger viewed the raving old man, and only smiled and said, "I like to be sociable, let me stay a little longer and we will smoke together."

So, shaking with fear, the old man took the pipe and drew a breath of smoke and then the warrior sang.

"Continue to smoke for me, I am young and warm, I am not afraid of boasting, I am young and strong. Better wrap up, you are old. I am here. I am here, keep on smoking. I am Dedio'sʻnwineqʻdoⁿ, the Spring. Look at your hair, it is falling out; look at the drifts, they are melting. My hair is long and glossy, see—the grasses are sprouting! I want to smoke with you. I like smoking. See—the ground is smoking! My friend Dăgāʻĕⁿ''dă, the South Wind, is coming. I guess your friend is dead. You had better wrap up and go away. There is a place. You cannot own all things always. See—the sun is shining. Look out now!"

As the young warrior sang the old man shrank very small and shriveled up smaller until his voice only whispered, "I don't know you!"

And so the young warrior sang, "I am the Spring. I am the chief now. The South Wind is coming. Don't be late. You can go yet while I sing."

A rushing wind made the lodge tremble, the door fell in and an eagle swooped down and carried Hăʻtʻhowāʻneʻ away toward the north.

The lodge fire was out and where it had burned a plant was growing and where the provisions were buried in a hole a tree was starting to have buds.

The sun was shining and it was warm. The swollen rivers carried away the ice. So the winter went away and in the morning it was springtime.

MOURNING DOVE (HUMISHUMA)

Coyote Juggles His Eyes (1933)

Coyote, trickster figure among western Native nations, embodies the capricious, sometimes very selfish creative force. Coyote is ever renewable, and is seen among many Native peoples as Old Man who holds almost as much Power as the Creator. Among Mourning Dove's people, Colville-Okanogan of Washington State, Coyote stories are part of the Creation cycle. We are reminded by these narratives that life is shaped by mysterious forces; that death itself is transitory; and that a good sense of humor in the face of the inexplicable is a necessity.

In "Coyote Juggles His Eyes," Old Man, ever curious, ever self-centered, sees a trick he wants to learn; but as often happens in Coyote stories, his trick turns on him. Since the story revolves around Sun Dance, a central ceremony among a great number of Native Nations, the reader is put on notice that the elements of this story verge on the Sacred.

One note of interest: Mourning Dove was often shy about writing the stories as they were originally told. In "Coyote Juggles His Eyes," Bluebird and Bluejay keep dropping Old Man because he makes himself an awkward burden. In the original version, it's be-

cause he is sexually assaulting them. In certain ways this story re-
volves around themes Mourning Dove repeats in her novel,
Cogewea: The Half-Blood; *in a couple of instances it echoes, in a*
deliberate act of cross-cultural humor, a well-known EuroAmerican
children's tale.

As he was walking through the timber one morning, Coyote heard someone say: "I throw you up and you come
down in!"

Coyote thought that was strange talk. It made him curious. He wanted to learn who was saying that, and why. He followed the sound of the voice, and he came upon little
Zst-skaká-na—Chickadee—who was throwing his eyes into the
air and catching them in his eye sockets. When he saw Coyote
peering at him from behind a tree, Chickadee ran. He was afraid
of Coyote.

"That is my way, not yours," Coyote yelled after him.

Now, it wasn't Coyote's way at all, but Coyote thought he
could juggle his eyes just as easily as Chickadee juggled his, so
he tried. He took out his eyes and tossed them up and repeated
the words used by the little boy: "I throw you up and you come
down in!" His eyes plopped back where they belonged. That
was fun. He juggled the eyes again and again.

Two ravens happened to fly that way. They saw what Coyote was doing, and one of them said: "Sin-ka-lip' is mocking
someone. Let us steal his eyes and take them to the Sun-dance.
Perhaps then we can find out his medicine power."

"Yes, we will do that," agreed the other raven. "We may
learn something."

As Coyote tossed his eyes the next time, the ravens
swooped, swift as arrows from a strong bow. One of them
snatched one eye and the other raven caught the other
eye.

"Quoh! Quoh! Quoh!" they laughed, and flew away to the Sun-dance camp.

Oh, but Coyote was mad! He was crazy with rage. When he could hear the ravens laughing no longer, he started in the direction they had gone. He hoped somehow to catch them and get back his eyes. He bumped into trees and bushes, fell into holes and gullies, and banged against boulders. He soon was bruised all over, but he kept on going, stumbling along. He became thirsty, and he kept asking the trees and bushes what kind they were, so that he could learn when he was getting close to water. The trees and bushes answered politely, giving their names. After a while he found he was among the mountain bushes, and he knew he was near water. He came soon to a little stream and satisfied his thirst. Then he went on and presently he was in the pine timber. He heard someone laughing. It was Kok'-qhi Shi'-kaka—Bluebird. She was with her sister, Kwas'-kay—Bluejay.

"Look, sister," said Bluebird. "There is Sin-ka-lip' pretending to be blind. Isn't he funny?"

"Do not mind Sin-ka-lip'," advised Bluejay. "Do not pay any attention to him. He is full of mean tricks. He is bad."

Coyote purposely bumped into a tree and rolled over and over toward the voices. That made little Bluebird stop her laughing. She felt just a little bit afraid.

"Come, little girl," Coyote called. "Come and see the pretty star that I see!"

Bluebird naturally was very curious, and she wanted to see that pretty star, but she hung back, and her sister warned her again not to pay attention to Coyote. But Coyote used coaxing words, told her how bright the star looked.

"Where is the star?" asked Bluebird, hopping a few steps toward Coyote.

"I cannot show you while you are so far away," he replied. "See, where I am pointing my finger!"

Bluebird hopped close, and Coyote made one quick bound and caught her. He yanked out her eyes and threw them into the air, saying:

"I throw you up and you come down in!" and the eyes fell into his eye sockets.

Coyote could see again, and his heart was glad. "When did you ever see a star in the sunlight?" he asked Bluebird, and then ran off through the timber.

Bluebird cried, and Bluejay scolded her for being so foolish as to trust Coyote. Bluejay took two of the berries she had just picked and put them into her sister's eye sockets, and Bluebird could see as well as before. But as the berries were small, her new eyes were small, too. That is why Bluebird has such berry-like eyes.

While his new eyes were better than none at all, Coyote was not satisfied. They were too little. They did not fit very well into his slant sockets. So he kept on hunting for the ravens and the Sun-dance camp. One day he came to a small tipi. He heard someone inside pounding rocks together. He went in and saw an old woman pounding meat and berries in a stone mortar. The old woman was Su-see-wass—Pheasant. Coyote asked her if she lived alone.

"No," she said, "I have two granddaughters. They are away at the Sun-dance. The people there are dancing with Coyote's eyes."

"Aren't you afraid to be here alone?" Coyote asked. "Isn't there anything that you fear?"

"I am afraid of nothing but the *stet'-chee-hunt* (stinging-bush)," she said.

Laughing to himself, Coyote went out to find a stinging-bush. In a swamp not far away he found several bushes of that kind. He broke off one of those nettle bushes and carried it back to the tipi. Seeing it, Pheasant cried:

"Do not touch me with the *stet'-chee-hunt*! Do not touch me! It will kill me!"

But Coyote had no mercy in his heart, no pity. He whipped poor Pheasant with the stinging-bush until she died. Then, with his flint knife, he skinned her, and dressed himself in her skin. He looked almost exactly like the old woman. He hid her body and began to pound meat in the stone mortar. He was doing that when the granddaughters came home. They were laughing. They told how they had danced over Coyote's eyes. They did not recognize Coyote in their grandmother's skin, but Coyote knew them. One was little Bluebird and the other was Bluejay. Coyote smiled. "Take me with you to the Sun-dance, Granddaughters," he said in his best old-woman's voice.

The sisters looked at each other in surprise, and Bluejay answered: "Why, you did not want to go with us when the morning was young."

"Grandmother, how strange you talk!" said Bluebird.

"That is because I burned my mouth with hot soup," said Coyote.

"And, Grandmother, how odd your eyes look!" Bluejay exclaimed. "One eye is longer than the other!"

"My grandchild, I hurt that eye with my cane," explained Coyote.

The sisters did not find anything else wrong with their grandmother, and the next morning the three of them started for the Sun-dance camp. The sisters had to carry their supposed grandmother. They took turns. They had gone part way when Coyote made himself an awkward burden and almost caused Bluejay to fall. That made Bluejay angry, and she threw Coyote to the ground. Bluebird then picked him up and carried him. As they reached the edge of the Sun-dance camp, Coyote again made himself an awkward burden, and Bluebird let him fall. Many of the people in the camp saw that happen. They thought the sisters were cruel, and the women scolded Bluebird and Bluejay for treating such an old person so badly.

Some of the people came over and lifted Coyote to his feet

and helped him into the Sun-dance lodge. There the people were dancing over Coyote's eyes, and the medicine-men were passing the eyes to one another and holding the eyes up high for everyone to see. After a little, Coyote asked to hold the eyes, and they were handed to him.

He ran out of the lodge, threw his eyes into the air, and said: "I throw you up and you come down in!"

His eyes returned to their places, and Coyote ran to the top of a hill.

There he looked back and shouted: "Where are the maidens who had Coyote for a grandmother?"

Bluejay and Bluebird were full of shame. They went home, carrying Pheasant's skin, which Coyote had thrown aside. They searched and found their grandmother's body and put it back in the skin, and Pheasant's life was restored. She told them how Coyote had killed her with the stinging-bush.

MOURNING DOVE (HUMISHUMA)

from *Cogewea: The Half-Blood*
(1916; published 1927)

Cogewea is a young mixed-blood woman who lives on the Horseshoe Bend cattle ranch on the Pend d'Oreille River. The ranch is owned by Cogewea's sister Julia's white husband, John Carter, a family man with a big heart, for not only does Cogewea live there but, as the novel opens, her grandmother (the Stemteemä) and her younger sister Mary, usually called "shy girl," move to the ranch. The Stemteemä, however, prefers traditional quarters, so she occupies a tipi set up near the main house. There are the usual complement of ranch hands—the "buckaroos" in the parlance of the West, among them Frenchie, the camp cook who hails from France, and the foreman Jim LaGrinder, a mixed-blood who is deeply in love with Cogewea.

Cogewea, however, prefers the dashing Easterner Alfred Densmore, who is a true scoundrel. For his part, Densmore believes that Cogewea is wealthy, due to the machinations of the buckaroos. In true Western style, their deceit is a joke, but the Easterner doesn't get it. He woos Cogewea for her money, although he has no intention of marrying her. He has ambitions toward marriage with a wealthy Eastern woman, and he needs a considerable sum to court her. Cogewea has ambitions of her own: She longs for a life of philosophy, music, delicate china, and art, and her youthful romanticism betrays her. The novel turns on the question of identity—a question peculiarly American. Cogewea's conflict between traditional family values and the siren call of city life and modern values very nearly costs her her life.

This selection comprises three chapters from Cogewea, *including the final one.*

Swa-lah-kin: The Frog Woman

With her moods of shade and sunshine
Eyes that smiled and frowned alternate,
Feet as rapid as the river,
Tresses flowing like the water,
And as musical a laughter;

—*HIAWATHA*

A week had passed since the roundup outfit left the ranch. The lengthening days brought with them the indubitable evidence of an early and short-lived autumn. The deep green leaves were transforming to mellow golden and the blaze of crimson glory. The grass was sere, with no indications of the usually short, velvety after-crop so peculiar to the arid range. The songbirds no longer trilled among the pines of the Pend d'Oreille. Flown to the South land, their notes were supplanted by the discordant honk and scream of the migratory waterfowl, echoing along the winding shore.

Densmore often went shooting on the big flats where numerous small lakes were in evidence. To the surprise of all, he proved a successful hunter and bagged a goodly number of both ducks and prairie chickens along with an occasional goose.

Badger, a noted wolfhound, and Bringo were his constant companions on these excursions, ofttimes chasing down the wily coyote and the fleet-footed jackrabbit. Densmore had also become handy with the rod, bringing home fine strings of fish. Stemteemä was kept bountifully supplied with these delicacies, nor did the sportsman forego an opportunity of ingratiating himself in her favor. But the ancient woman received the gifts with stoic indifference and with doubtful gratitude. Perhaps it was more to please Cogewea that she accepted the offerings, regarding them as part of her daily food supply. The girl sometimes accompanied the donor in these presentation visits, acting as interpreter. The keen witted grandmother discerned that her grandchild was growing more fond of the hated Shoyahpee, and that she was also endeavoring to win her to regard him with greater favor. These symptoms she noticed with increased perturbation and had spoken to Julia on the subject. But the older sister, who had given the situation but scant or no thought during the press of summer work, was inclined to regard the possible alliance in a different light. She, herself, had married a white man who was good and kind to her, and consequently her racial prejudices were not so strongly pronounced.

Cogewea, in walking habit, stood gazing pensively from the window. She saw Julia, leading little Denny, enter the low doorway of the smoke-browned tipi just as the well-proportioned form of Densmore emerged from the bunkhouse. He carried two fishing rods and had a trap slung over his shoulder. Coming up the path, he stopped at the gate, turning toward the house.

•   •   •

Densmore was discoursing on the charms of city life as they passed the tipi door. Inside, Stemteemä was crooning an Indian lullaby, which intoned musically with the sleepy baby prattle of Denny. The song was hushed suddenly. No bird carols greeted them as they approached the stream, and the squirrels and chipmunks appeared too busy storing their winter hoards to notice the intrusion. Following the bank for a mile or so, they came to a promising pool, deep and clear, at the base of an overhanging cliff. Here they prepared to cast.

"The kale that I land the first one," challenged Cogewea as the two flies struck the water simultaneously.

"Taken!" was the quick acceptance.

Scarcely had Densmore spoken when his line cut the water in a straight drive, the reel spinning yard after yard of singing cord. Far out in the stream a silvery form leaped, scintillating in a radiant curve, sending up a shower of sparkling spray as the fish clove the water. The played-out line slacked and the fisherman reeled in, minus hook and fly.

"King of the Pend d'Oreille!" exclaimed Cogewea. "How gamy! You . . ."

Her own line spun with a musical purr, and deftly handling the reel, she slowly brought the stampeding salmonoid too, in a wide, sweeping circle. The battle was on, but with a skill attained only through experience she finally landed a shimmering beauty of rare size.

"Lost! Shoyahpee!" she taunted. "Lost two ways: your trout and your wager."

"I will lay an even five thousand against your hand that the next is mine," bantered the Easterner as he adjusted a new fly.

"I fade you!" was the prompt acceptance.

Again they cast and again she won.

"Please ante!" laughed the girl, as with a dextrous movement of thumb and fingers, the catch was rendered unconscious before removed from the hook.

"Would you have been as prompt in delivering, had I won?"

"An *honest* gambler is supposed to meet all obligations unequivocally," was the evasive answer.

"Nor will the *true* sport deny to an unfortunate loser the opportunity of retrieving," came the ready counter.

"Certainly! My digits and winnings against an even ten thousand."

"You are mine!" was the confident response as the fly was twirled over the water for "luck." "Now listen for the wedding chimes."

The game was growing wild and fascinating. This time the Easterner lost only by the fraction of a minute.

"Betting is off!" declared Cogewea when Densmore proposed a still higher wager. "Those chimes are remote, for I don't believe that you could redeem even now."

"There is where your reckoning is faulty," a crafty light in his eyes. "I am nothing near my limit. I can make good several such doubles."

"Well, I make no more wagers today," in a tone of finality. "My *tahmahnawis* tells me that the signs are bad. Besides, we have enough fish already. There are still a few left of your yesterday's catch and it is wrong and wasteful to hook them just for misconceived sport. Indians take only enough for food and no more."

"Wait a moment! I think there is a big shiner by that rock and I want him."

"Aw! come on and don't be selfish. Leave a few for the next fellow who may really need them. Let's rest on this mossy log and watch the river as it glides on its way to the ocean. You can tell me something of interest."

No further urging was required, and Densmore, reeling his line, joined her on the fallen forest giant. Spying a small land toad, with the end of his pole he mischievously turned it over and over toward her. Noting the action, the girl exclaimed in agitation:

"Oh! Alfred! Don't do that to the poor little helpless thing. Besides, it will bring a storm sure. Indians claim that if you place a frog on its back, it will cause a storm without doubt. There is an old legend which tells the story of Swa-lah-kin the 'frog woman.' It is in connection with the sun; that if you turn the frog thus, she will look up at the sun and flirt with him as in the beginning. He hates her so badly that he will wrinkle his brow and a tempest gathers which wets the earth. This forces her odious flippancy to find shelter out of his sight."

Densmore picked up a fragment of bark and getting the Batrachian on it, threw both into the stream with the observation:

"I guess with that cold bath the little miss will do no more flirting for a while. Anyhow, it is too clear for rain today."

Cogewea glanced upward. The sky was blue and limpid with the exception of a single diminutive cloud which appeared to draw nearer to the hot, blazing orb of day. Pointing to it, she admonished:

"I told you that she would bring rain. See that little cloud? It will unfold and spread until the heavens are covered in no time. It is her! the Swah-lah-kin of the myth. She has flirted with the Sun and we will get soaked. There will be a downpour swift and without warning. You have done the mischief and spoiled our afternoon."

"I supposed that you were enough educated to know better than to believe all those ridiculous signs of your people," chided the Easterner.

"What if I am slightly educated!" came the retort with a tinge of resentment. "The true American courses my veins and *never* will I cast aside my ancestral traditions. I was born to them!"

•   •   •

"To the truly high minded there are no racial barriers. Why should you care to remain exclusively Indian? What is the incentive?"

"I have my Stemteemä and my sisters, besides other kindred ties. Then, there are the traditions of my ancient race."

"But you cannot exist on sentiment alone. With no vested or property interests to demand your continued presence, you should feel at freedom to see something of the world. I take it that there are no such bonds."

"Sure! Not only my allotment of eighty acres of the finest of land, but I have— Why do you ask?" she broke off suddenly, lifting inquiring eyes.

He stood the scrutiny with calculating coolness. She had very unexpectedly increased in value. Taking her shapely hand in his, he answered with apparent sincerity:

"I meant nothing. I am only anxious to make you happy. Listen! my little Injun sweetheart! I have plenty, all that you could wish for. I want to share my wealth with you. You won the wagers at fishing. Suppose we form a partnership and call it settled by me doubling your winnings?"

"I would not sell myself!" was the scornful reply. "Money cannot bring happiness. Too often its heritage is one of unfathomed misery."

Densmore, realizing his mistake, retrenched hastily.

"You misunderstood me. I am but endeavoring to show you that I care deeply and am anxious to be to you all that a husband should. If I could only hear you say that you care for me—that you love me ever so little."

He was straining her to his breast and he felt her responsive form quiver. He attempted to lift her warm lips to his own, but she held aloof.

"Cogewea!" he whispered, smoothing her raven tresses. "I love you to distraction! I am willing to meet you in every way that you desire. I will be Indian. Tell me more about your tribal customs. That marriage ceremony—"

The girl, struggling free, started up in sudden fright. With arm outflung, she exclaimed in terror:

"Look! See how the frown of the Sun-god darkens the earth! He bends his shaggy brow over the portals of the West Wind and hurls his anger along the sky! He breathes! and the air is thick with anguish! It is the Swa-lah-kin! *You* did this!" she cried angrily. "You should not have turned the frog! Come! let us hurry home! We will be fortunate if we escape with only a drenching."

Densmore's eyes followed her outstretched arm and he leaped to his feet in amazement. The western heavens were overcast with a mighty canopy of black, billowing clouds, hurtling upward toward the zenith with appalling rapidity. The onslaught was swift and terrible in its silence. Only the faintest hum, like the smothered chords of an Aeolian harp struck by the softest zephyr, was audible. Never had the Easterner witnessed an elemental conflict of such awe-inspiring grandeur. Seizing their effects, they hurriedly started for home.

Gathering momentum, the storm came sweeping onward with lowering front; the chaotic cloud-rack, a sable wall blotting out the universe. The low, indistinct murmur increased in volume until the cadence became a mournful dirge in the pine tops. This was but a prelude. Murky with misty shadows, the wind, in one fell swoop, enveloped the fugitives, nearly carrying them off their feet. Clasping hands, they struggled in the face of the gale now shrieking like a thousand Harpies about their bursting ears. Densmore's hat went sailing out over the river, while Cogewea's broad-brim fluttering, was held secure by feminine anchorage. Bracing hard, they made but slow progress and were still a considerable distance from home when the first spattering raindrops, like the skirmish shots of a hostile army, struck them. When within a hundred paces of Stemteemä's lodge, the anguished heavens were rent by a lurid tongue of lightning, followed by a crash which seemed to rock the very earth's foundations. The dreaded Thunder-bird was abroad on the storm and at the gleaming flash of his eye and the booming crash of his ponderous wing, the rain descended in torrents.

"The tipi! The tipi!" screamed Cogewea above the roar of the tempest.

Densmore tore back the door-flap and completely soaked they stumbled through the opening. The interposition of the canvas walls against the sudden gale was most grateful. It was solace to hear the deluge beating against the swaying roof. The wings of the smoke-flue had been closed and the seemingly frail structure made entirely proof against the onslaughts of Thor. Not only Julia, but Mary was there and, what, with the two children sleeping among the blankets, the wigwam was well crowded.

Stemteemä spoke to Cogewea, her tone sharp and emphatic. The girl answered at length in Okanogan and without her accustomed blithesomeness. The little audience gave rapt attention as she narrated the frog incident on the river bank. The grandmother and Mary cast looks of displeasure at the Shoyahpee, but Julia appeared less impressed. The conversation was necessarily loud, because of the howling of the warring elements without, which seemed to increase in momentary violence. However, the storm ceased as suddenly as it began and the sun shone upon a drenched world.

After a futile attempt at gayety, Densmore departed for the bunkhouse, and the aged woman requested Cogewea to go change her clothing and then return to the tipi. She had a story of the past which she desired to tell her three grandchildren.

•   •   •

The Sentinel at the Rock

But she heeded not the warning,
Heeded not those words of wisdom,
—*HIAWATHA*

The streets of Polson bore an air of desertion, as Cogewea wended her way down the boardwalk in the early morn, nodding to an occasional chance acquaintance. Indecision and anxiety suffused her usually serene face. The girl felt at a loss and the question had come to her often:

"Why did you weaken to the importunities of the Shoyahpee against your better judgment?"

She seemed to accede to his overtures however ridiculous. The shame of the past evening when she agreed to loan him money for the proposed elopement trip haunted her, but now it appeared too late to recede. She half wished that she had pointedly refused even though it broke her heart.

Thus meditating, Cogewea came opposite the bank as it opened its doors for the day. Crossing the street, she entered and, stepping to the side desk, produced from an Indian beaded handbag a cheque book and wrote feverishly. Glancing cautiously around, she handed the slip of paper to the cashier at the cage window. The official scanned it, then read it the second time, before looking up in surprise to ask:

"A thousand dollars? Do you mean to draw all this—all this amount at one time?"

"Yes, that was my intention," was the courteous reply. "Haven't I enough on deposit to cover that cheque made payable to myself?"

.   .   .

Cogewea left the bank with a heavier mind than she dared admit. She hurried to her companionable, though at times erratic, cayuse, left standing unhitched. Wanawish whinnied as she approached, and Bringo came forward to greet her. But for once the girl gave slight notice to her dumb friends.

Cogewea mounted and scaled the steep Polson Hill. There she paused and gazed longingly back at the little town nestling by the shimmering lake. She wondered when she would be permitted to see it again. Her feelings were altogether different from those supposedly of the happy bride-to-be. As if to smother a rising sensibility of her present questionable course, she abruptly turned Wanawish and raced down the sharp slope with reckless speed. She galloped over the smooth prairie until in sight of the Pablo Buffalo Ranch. The pasture and the high coral were alike empty. These recalled to her days passed, when she rode the range a carefree girl with no "sweet love" weighing her down, when her heart leaped at the sensation of thundering on the flank of the stampeding herd. But now, the vision of the dust cloud rolling up from the vast expanse brought only a pang of regret.

Reaching Mud Creek—a misnomer of a truly clear stream—Wanawish showed thirst and Cogewea gave him the rein as he turned from the wooden bridge. While watching the horse take in the cool, mountain water, the girl realized that she, too, was thirsty. Dismounting, she knelt and drank. As she rose, she spied two riders on the lofty ridge overlooking the Buffalo Ranch. Mechanically she felt for her glass, only to find that in her haste it had been left at home. Although the atmosphere was clear, the distance was too great to make out with the naked eye who the horsemen were. They sat their mounts motionless and facing towards her. As she turned to Wanawish, the thought of the money in her handbag at the saddle-bow came to her. Removing her gauntlets and gazing cautiously around that no one was observing, she made a rent in her paddled saddle blanket. Into the opening she shoved the crisp bills and then deftly closed it with a hair pin. Remounting, she swung into a steady lope for Ronan. Before passing from view, she glanced at the ridge where the two riders had been observed. Only one, sentinel-like, was to be seen. Both the horse and the rider appeared as immobile as though cast in bronze. Apprehensive of the missing horseman, the girl gave rein to Wanawish and sped furiously over the smooth-packed road.

Ronan was still some distance away when Cogewea came in sight of the tall elevator of the flour mill, with its gray roof and the smoke belching up in a dark column through the clear air.

· · ·

Wanawish sped across the bridge, pressing hard on the bit as he was reined in at the hostelry. Cogewea sprang to the ground and was met by Densmore. Ordering her horse stalled next to his own, he accompanied her to the dining hall. He selected an isolated table and sat so as to command the door. His nervous movements and unusual self-interest drew the attention of diners and there were low whisperings of:

"Somethin' doin' with them there couple!"

The meal over, Cogewea thought that Densmore exhibited unusual haste in mounting and being again off. They galloped through the "Lane"; nor did they slacken pace until near Crow Creek, where they met a train of "freighters" from Ravalli. The high seated wagons were piled with merchandise, and were strung along the road for a considerable distance. Some had "trailers" and were drawn by six and eight horses. Passing these, the elopers again quickened pace, coming to the big flat. Small lakes, where wild geese and ducks disported, enlivened the scene. The long necks of the birds would momentarily disappear under the surface, as they groped for food along the shallows. "Shacks," the initial domicile of the energetic homesteaders, dotted the landscape. Herds of cattle and bands of horses grazed about the plain; the latter sometimes disturbed by the flying pair.

•   •   •

Down the lower road to Post Creek, the two rode at a slower pace. Densmore was far from being a perfect rider, although greatly improved over the stranger who had come to the ranch some months previous. As the wind blew aside his coat, Cogewea noticed for the first time the heavy six-gun holstered at his hip. A sun glint on the polished grip had first caught her eye.

"Why, Alfred!" she exclaimed in surprise. "I did not know that you carried a gun. I thought you were a man who never sported a weapon of any kind."

"I—I thought we might need it," he answered in embarrassment, drawing his coat in place. "Can never tell what might happen."

"That is true! I had never thought of that! I came away so hurriedly that I brought only my little thirty-two in my hand-bag."

"Let me see your gun!"

Cogewea handed Densmore her pistol. He examined it minutely and then put it in his own pocket. Cogewea laughed uneasily as she remonstrated:

"What do you mean? You are not a two-gun man, are you?"

"Now little girl," he returned lightly, "you do not want to carry this thing! It might get you hurt."

"I will bet that I can handle a gun far better than you can!"

"Don't be too sure of that, my conceited young lady! I hope that I have not practiced target shooting all summer to no avail."

"But Alfred! Please give me back my gun! I do not like to be without it, especially at this time. It is hard telling what may happen—and me with all the kale."

"I will protect you!" he volunteered with a laugh. "And as head of the family, I am really supposed to handle the purse, am I not?"

Seemingly to meet his banter, Cogewea spoke nonchalantly as the memory of the vanished horseman at the rock
flashed through her mind:

"Let me have both guns! I believe that I will be willing to
trade you my handbag for the brace, even though they do not
balance properly."

"That would depend! How much did you bring?"

"Oh! I can buy several such toys and still be a long ways
from bankruptcy. Is it a go?"

"Why do you so want both guns?"

"Jim—he might follow us! You can never tell!"

"No danger! He and the boys had gone out for stray horses
when I left the ranch. My excuse was that I was going to Ronan
and would not be back until late. They think that you are in
Polson visiting friends. Nobody will dream that we have eloped
and after we are married, what's the difference who cries?"

"Well, I do hope that they may not know until it is too
late. I'm afraid there would be hell to pay if Jim gets wise before
we find a priest."

"But why should you want both guns in case he did follow?" he questioned suspiciously. "You seem to think more of
that savage than you do of me."

"I want your gun simply to prevent likely trouble should
Jim trail us. He is too manly to ever shoot an unarmed man in
any personal altercation. He may be a savage," she continued
spiritedly, "but he has a great big heart and that is a whole lot
more than a goodly part of this highly civilized nation can
boast. Too many of the so-called *white* men are afflicted with
the worst of *black-heart*."

Densmore flushed deeply at this thrust, but he rejoined
with an attempt at pleasantry:

"You may still maintain your torture stake if you will, but
I prefer holding on to my gun so long as there is such manifest
danger of Injuns going on the war-path."

Though ill at ease, Cogewea accepted the situation without further protest. So deeply engrossed had they been in discussion, that their mounts took advantage and stopped at the creek to allay their thirst. After crossing the stream, Densmore dismounted and drank. Leading his horse, he walked along the road for a short distance, to a stock trail breaking into the brush. Here he paused, proposing that they stop among the trees and let their horses rest for a time. Cogewea, still envisioning the horsemen at the rock, demurred; but when her companion pointed out that the west bound train through Ravalli was not due until near seven o'clock and that it would be far better for them to remain in semi-seclusion until near that time than chance detection and possible detention at the station, she reluctantly acquiesced. Accordingly a grassy plot was sought just within the woods, where they drew the saddles and, leaving the horses to graze at the end of the trailing ropes, sat down in the shade.

No definite plans had been agreed upon as to their future course, further than boarding the evening train west at Ravalli. Densmore was for going to San Francisco, while Cogewea named a nearer coast city as their immediate destination. Their ideas also differed as to time of return to the ranch. Cogewea was most anxious about the Stemteemä; to get back and make an early peace with her ancient parent was her deepest concern. Densmore, scoffing at this, interposed:

"The Stemteemä should be the least of our worries. Old age, like childhood, is susceptible of petting. I am afraid," he added with a short laugh, "of being shot up by a disappointed foreman."

"You have nothing to dread from Jim once we are united," assured the girl. "I know him to be a man, and he will never place a stumble in our way."

From this, the conversation drifted again to the topic of destination; disclosing the amount of money which Cogewea had brought. The Easterner expressed surprise that she had ventured to openly draw that amount and carry it alone from Polson. Cogewea assured him that all the cowpunchers were her friends and that there had been nothing to fear.

"Look!" she exclaimed, procuring her saddle blanket and removing the hairpin. "Nobody would have thought to look there for money, even had they staged a holdup."

Densmore agreed that the hiding place would most likely have proven effective had he attempted the role of bandit. He soon learned of her balance in the bank, which opened the subject of his deepest interest. He casually asked about her livestock on both ranch and range and was astounded when informed that aside from the two cayuses they were riding, she had none. Not fully grasping the import of this appalling declaration, he fairly gasped:

"Why, don't you own most of the stock at the ranch, and all the horses and cattle of the roundup, and those sold? Were they not yours? Are not the boys working for you?"

"Those hooves all mine? Boys working for me? Who has been stuffing you, man?"

"Celluloid Bill and Rodeo Jack told me that you were a rich woman; that you owned practically all the stock on the range and had vast tracts of land."

"Bill and Rodeo? It was some of their wild pranks! They have lied to you! I am far from being a rich woman. All the stock you saw at the ranch, belongs to my brother-in-law, John Carter. The 'H-B' brand is also his property. The three thousand dollars I recently came in possession of, was inherited. Aside from my eighty-acre allotment, which hardly counts for much, this three thousand is all that I have."

For several moments the Easterner remained speechless, scarce able to realize the full force of this astounding revelation. After all, was his dream of golden wealth to be disenchanted as a mere halo of the rainbow of myth? Surely the Indian girl was joking, merely testing his fidelity of purpose. His voice was husky when he again spoke:

"Cogewea, you cannot mean that I believe all this, can you? This is hardly a time for jesting."

It was Cogewea's turn to be puzzled. What was the riddle? Was this polite and polished Shoyahpee after all, a mere adventurer, a gross money hunter? This passed through her mind before she answered rather tersely:

"I am not jesting! You would not want me to deceive you, would you? I do not understand!"

"Then, if you are telling the truth, I have already been woefully deceived and that through you," was the savage retort. "Those boys never hatched such fabrications of themselves. They were made at your instance and the only puzzle is just why you are now blocking your own game by thus prematurely disclosing facts. Your obtuse intellect, being able to contain but the one idea, has been your undoing. But what else could be expected from a nest of coppery vipers? Brazen blackmail, and I am tempted to turn you over to the proper authorities to be dealt with according to the just laws of our land! You may be thankful that I am letting you off so easy."

He had risen to his feet and before the astounded girl could divine his action, he had seized her saddle blanket and ripping out the folded bank bills, pocketed them. With stunning effect the truth dawned upon her that she had not only been betrayed, but was also being openly robbed by her professed lover and supposed protector. Enraged and smarting with humiliation at such duplicity, she sprang up, laying a detaining hand on his arm. With an oath he freed himself, dealing her a blinding blow in the face. Grasping her by the shoulders, he shook her viciously as he warned in a low, menacing tone:

"You had as well understand at once that I am standing no foolishness from you? The more quiet you are the better it is going to be for you. I am giving you unwarranted consideration. Many a man would deal with you differently and my ultimate actions are going to be governed by your own. You can always depend on a desperate man doing desperate things and perhaps if the truth was known you would find that I have not been too squeamish on other occasions."

"But you do not dare take my money like this! Liar! Thief! Robber! Blackguard that you are! The law—"

"Is absolutely helpless to help you!" he scoffed. "The law is of the white man's make, interpreted by the white man, made to talk by the white man's money. With a comparatively small amount of this which you have so generously bestowed upon me, I can make the law talk! You have no witnesses! It would be my word against yours, a white gentleman's against an Injun squaw's. What would you do? Don't think that I am not going to take advantage of the situation."

"I will have you arrested at Ravalli!"

"No, I hardly think so! If your horse should happen to have his leg broke—"

"Oh, please Alfred! Take the money and go but do not hurt my Wanawish! I will promise not to attempt following you. I will be only too glad to see you go! Oh, the ways of the Shoyahpee!"

"Your word would be great guarantee!" he snarled mockingly. "I am taking no chance nor am I going to waste further time in any palaver with you. Come on, and see how cleverly I can disable that fine steed of yours."

With this, he jerked her rudely about and started toward the two horses, still grazing. Cogewea, apparently resigned, moved unresistingly. Unaccustomed to the approach of man, Wanawish lifted his head in the air, and with forward-pricked ears, emitted a shrill snort of alarm. Cogewea, alert, snatched Densmore's hat with her one free hand and hurled it at the animal, emitting at the same time a shrill scream. The startled

95

horse whirled and darted into a nearby thicket, where he was lost to view. Cogewea laughed aloud.

"You damned ed—!"

Choking with rage, Densmore supplemented the vile epithet with another brutal blow in the face. Dragging the now dazed girl, he secured his own horse, returning with it and his captive to where the saddles were lying. His eyes were those of the murderer as he again addressed her:

"Now, my fine lady! another screech out of you and I do not promise what might not happen. Your little trick has saved that horse of yours, but there is another way of playing safe. Maybe by the time you rest here a few hours, perhaps a few days, in seclusion, you will have had time to ponder on the absurdity of contending against your betters. You are in my power and I am certainly going to use it effectively."

"Yes, you have me in your power, but how have you accomplished that boast? Give me back my gun! You may keep your big one but I will not fear you, though I am a woman."

Craven as he was, Densmore winced at this challenge. All the venom of his perverted nature found vent in his retort:

"Bosh! you squaw! And to think that I was ordered from a smoke-dinged lair of your 'breed'! I am but half squaring accounts; and when you get back to that dear old grandmother of yours, you can tell her how nice the white man was in his dealings with you. You may then feel like talking, for that tongue of yours is now going to have a rest, if I meet my guess."

Cogewea loftily disdained reply to this tirade of abuse. Knowing the futility of resistance, she submitted without a word of protest as he securely bound her to a cottonwood, twining the rope about her from neck to foot. An effective gag was made from her own scarf. Completing his task to his own satisfaction, Densmore again addressed her, assuming a mock air of apologetic politeness:

"Goodbye! little sweetheart! O statuette in bronze with a

wild-wood setting! How superb! And the sun fast sinking to rest. A merry time and pleasant dreams as you hear the coyotes squalling tonight. I tried to give you a good time the past summer, and I feel that I am really entitled to this small pittance which you have so kindly permitted me to appropriate. I hope that you are generous spirited enough to concede that you have had value received. I am placing your toy gun here in your own pocket, the cartridges considerately extracted of course. Give my regards to that coppery-hided lover of yours—should you ever see him—and know that with your opportunity to convey this last message for me, I will be far out of the state and among really civilized folks. After all, Densmore the 'tenderfoot' has not fared so badly financially, considering the few months that he has sojourned in the wilds, do you think? Goodbye! Goodbye!"

Then hastily saddling his horse, he mounted and turned toward the highway, calling back over his shoulder:

"That you may retain your deep respect for my integrity, you will find this horse, which you have so graciously loaned me, at the livery in Ravalli. Of course this is considerate of me and I know that you will appreciate the courtesy. So long!"

Cogewea, her limbs already aching from the cut of the overdrawn lariat, heard the clatter of pounding hooves, as the false Shoyahpee fled from the scene of his most hellish duplicity.

. . .

A Voice from the Buffalo Skull

As unto the bow the cord is,
So unto the man is woman,
Though she bends him, she obeys him,
Though she draws him, yet she follows,
Useless each without the other!

—*HIAWATHA*

Two snows had passed and the birds, again returned from the warm-land, filled the river pines with their old-time melody, while the buttercups flowered in radiance. The wild rose peeped coquettishly from its bud, and the tender grass clothed plain and upland with shimmering green. The ermine cloak of winter, pursued by the melting breeze, retreated still farther into the higher altitudes of the majestic Rockies. Earth was taking on new life and the joy of living seemed with all— save one whose heart was emptiness—whose face was but a reflection of her former self.

Jim stood at the door of the bunkhouse and watched the familiar figure on Wanawish ride over the ridge to her favorite haunt. He muttered an oath as the cause of the blighted life came into his mind. He glanced at the sun now past the meridian and going to the barn, threw the saddle on Bay Devil. He had determined to go to the village for the week's mail in the hope of hearing from his mother, whom he had not seen for three years.

The foreman did not loiter on the way. Reaching the little town, he went directly to the post office where he received a heavy ranch mail, but no missive from his mother. There was one, however, addressed to Cogewea, from the Indian Agent of her old home in the Okanogan country. Some of the "boys" endeavored to prevail on Jim to engage in a game of pool, or try monte at the Kootenai camp, but to all entreaties he turned a deaf ear. He thought of the lonely, unhappy girl out on the solitary butte and the letter was an excuse for going to her. He had never intruded on her sorrow, as much as he loved her. Aside from a tribal custom, he had felt that her grief was sacred and that time was the only balm. But now, well, he would carry the letter to her, and if opportunity afforded perhaps—

Cogewea lingered on Buffalo Butte, thinking of the days when all was happiness, of the many pleasant hours she had spent on this isolated height. At her feet lay the old gray buffalo skull and broken arrow point. The towering mountains greeted her vision, but not with the soul-awakening emotions of the past. Life seemed to hold but little for her. Friends were not so familiar as of yore, and Jim held strangely aloof. Somehow she yearned for his old-time companionship. She realized now that it was something more than a "sister's love" which she had borne for him. This new awakening was gnawing her very life away. He surely did not understand the true cause of her despondency. After the first pangs of humiliating disappointment, her only feelings for the false Shoyahpee were of remorse and bitter regret that their paths had ever crossed. In her generous heart, she pitied Densmore's weakness but detested his duplicity, and above all she devoutly thanked the Great Spirit for her timely deliverance.

She recalled Jim's many considerate attentions; his unselfish protective care for her, his fearless interference in her behalf at the races, his graceful and manly acceptance of humiliating defeat at the social, the refusal of his hand on this same spot, and the chivalry of his coming to her rescue among the cottonwoods, all came crowding in upon her memory. She could not help wishing that he would—

The fall of an unshod hoof on the stony ground and the jingle of spurs broke upon Cogewea's ears. She did not look up, but intuitively knew who the horseman was. Her eyes dropped to the old skull. She started visibly! *Could* she be deceived? A voice seemed to issue from its cavernous depths in the Indian tongue, a laudation of—

"*The Man! The Man! The Man!*"

Then it was accusing; a plea of pity that such deep and honorable love should be requited with nothing more than insipid friendship.

The voice ceased as suddenly and as mysteriously as it came.

Jim was at Cogewea's side silently holding the outstretched letter. She missed the cheery old-time: "Hell-o Sis!" With no word of greeting, she took the missive and broke the seal. Jim stood, arms folded and leaning against the rock, gazing at the splendid panorama of the Rockies. She read the letter and he heard her murmur:

"The lust of gold and the mockery of money! The toil amid glaciers and the ghastly snowfields of the North! The daddy we scarcely knew! The Shoyahpee barters his life, his very soul, for a heritage of death!"

Jim turned to see the old-time dream in the girl's eyes, otherwise her face showed no emotion save that of the sorrow to which he had grown accustomed.

"What is it, Sis?" he asked kindly.

"Nothing," was the reply, "except that I have escaped a lot of trouble."

"Some settlement of reservation of 'lotment 'fairs?"

"Not exactly! You know that we had not heard from daddy for over fourteen years. He was in Alaska and we thought long ago that he was dead. This letter informs me that he only recently died, leaving money and mining property worth several millions of dollars."

"But you don't call that missin' a lot of trouble do you?" asked Jim, his eyes showing slight astonishment.

"Daddy had remarried, made a will bequeathing his three

daughters twenty dollars each, and the remainder of his fortune to his widow, a young white woman from New York!"

"Well, I bedam'! Your daddy, Sis, but a Shoyahpee to the last. My own father the same, only we don't know where he is or what became of him. He left my Indian mother many years ago, coverin' his tracks completely. Too bad that you and your sisters couldn't a had some of that there dough."

"It was all right!" Cogewea rejoined smiling, although her eyes were swimming in tears. "I don't know that I care! The curse of the Shoyahpee seems to go with everything that he touches. We despised *breeds* are in a zone of our own and when we break from the corral erected about us we meet up with trouble. I only wish that the fence could not be scaled by the soulless creatures who have ever preyed upon us."

"I wish I had a killed that there da—"

"Don't Jim! Do not refer to the past! It never was! It's only an impossible fearfulness! a dreadful hallucination! a nightmare of lies! It is dead! buried and forgotten!"

Cogewea's countenance had changed to something of her former self. Jim thought that she never had appeared quite so beautiful and captivating. For a time he was silent and then exclaimed earnestly:

"Sis! I always did love you some, and now I like you like hell! S'pose we remain together in that there corral you spoke of as bein' built 'round us by the Shoyahpee? I ain't never had no ropes on no gal but you."

"Aw, Jim, quit yo' kiddin'!" she answered, dropping into the easy vocabulary of the range. "I've tol' yo' that I would be yo' sister, but if yo' don't behave I'll quit likin' yo as—as a *brother*! Savey?"

There was a banter in her tone which Jim could not mistake.

"Yes! I think I savey all right!" and he slipped an arm

about the yielding form. "By gollies! little squ—Sis! Oh, hell! That there don't sound right to me no more. I—"

"Call me Cogewea! Your own little Cogewea!" she exclaimed, nestling her head on his deep chest like a weary child.

For a long minute the transported Westerner held the girl closely and in silence. Then releasing her, he said simply:

"Guess we better be hittin' the trail! It's late and night's goin' be chilly for you without no shawl."

"Do not hurry! See how magnificent those grand old mountains are in the moonlight. *Isn't* this a splendid world?"

"Yes, it is jus' 'bout right—when not too cold nor too hot—nor nothin' wrong with the corral fencin'. But the best rider of the Flathead ain't a worryin' 'bout this durn' old world no more! And I sure do b'lieve in them there hot rock signs of the sweat-house!"

"So do I!" laughed Cogewea, feeling the blood suffuse her cheeks. "But do let up on that 'best rider' stunt. Maybe you will not want to ride anymore, only for fun. I forgot to tell you all that is in this letter. It transpired that owing to a technical flaw in daddy's will, we girls come in for a share in some of his fortune, amounting to a quarter million dollars each. And say! Jim! Stemteemä will now let me have that brooch, I told you I would wear."

"Well! I bedam'!" ejaculated Jim, as they turned to go.

Cogewea paused, gazing intensely at the gray skull—listening! She heard the Voice as it comes only to the Indian:

"The Man! The Man! The Man!"

The moon, sailing over the embattled Rockies, appeared to smile down on the dusky lovers despite the ugly Swah-lah-kin clinging to his face.

In a cheap boarding house in an eastern city a few weeks later, a young man with a selfish mouth suddenly turned pale as he read in a western paper an account of the settling of the great McDonnald mining estate in Alaska, and the marriage of his two half-blood daughters. One of them a graduate of Carlisle, to the "Best Rider of the Flathead," also a half-blood. The younger daughter known as the "Shy girl," had departed with her husband, Eugene LaFleur, a polished and wealthy Parisian scholar, on a honeymoon tour of Europe.

> *The trail's a lane! the trail's a lane!*
> *Dead is the branding fire.*
> *The Prairies wild are tame and mild,*
> *All close-corraled with wire.*
>
> —*BADGER CLARK*

PRETTY-SHIELD AND FRANK B. LINDERMAN

Pretty-shield's Medicine (1932)

Sometime in the late 1920s or early 1930s, Frank B. Linderman, a Montana writer, instituted conversations with Pretty-shield, a Crow elder and wise woman. He was particularly interested in "women's stories," and she obliged him, telling him a number of spiritual stories about her "medicine" and that of other women she had known, both older and younger than herself. In her mid-seventies at the time, and responsible for her grandchildren, she took time out of her busy schedule to "talk" to Linderman. Pretty-shield signed her stories and with the aid of one of her women friends, Linderman recorded what she said. Their collaboration is itself an intriguing metaphor for Indian-white relations during the dreadful Reservation Era when their conversations took place. The term she uses, "Person," means a spirit or non–human being—the sort of beings many Native people see frequently or infrequently, but that whites like Linderman think are really figures in a dream and without reality. One point her story makes is that medicine power and vision do not come from chanting, feeling good, or sitting in meditation. They come from grief, loss, pain, and a willingness to open oneself, painfully, to the nonhuman forces that are a necessary, integral part of human life.

"I had lost a little girl, a beautiful baby girl," she said. "I had been mourning for more than two moons. I had slept little, sometimes lying down alone in the hills at night, and always on hard places. I ate only enough to keep me alive, hoping for a medicine-dream, a vision, that would help me to live and to help others. One morning, after a night spent on a high cliff, when I was returning to my lodge to pack things for a long move, I saw a woman ahead of me. She was walking fast, as though she hoped to reach my lodge before I could get there. But suddenly she stopped and stood still, looking down at the ground. I thought I knew her, thought that she was a woman who had died four years before. I felt afraid. I stopped, my heart beating fast. 'Come here, daughter.' Her words seemed to draw me toward her against my will.

"Walking a few steps I saw that she was not a real woman, but that she was a Person [apparition], and that she was standing beside an ant hill.

" 'Come here, daughter.' Again I walked toward her when I did not wish to move. Stopping by her side, I did not try to look into her face. My heart was nearly choking me. 'Rake up the edges of this ant hill and ask for the things that you wish, daughter,' the Person said, and then she was gone. Only the ant hill was there, and a wind was blowing. I saw the grass tremble, as I was trembling, when I raked up the edges of the ant hill, as the Person had told me. Then I made my wish, 'Give me good luck, and a good life,' I said aloud, looking at the hills.

"I was weak. In my lodge there were no bed-robes for me, because I had long ago destroyed all my comfortable things. But now, in this medicine-dream, I entered a beautiful white lodge, with a war eagle at the head. He did not speak to me, and yet I have often seen him since that day. And even now the ants help me. I listen to them always. They are my medicine, these busy, powerful little people, the ants."

PRETTY-SHIELD AND FRANK B. LINDERMAN

Women and War (1932)

Clearly a strong-minded old woman, Pretty-shield delighted in stories of women who bested men and showed singular valor in times of war. She was something of a Crow patriot, and several of the stories she "told" Linderman, using sign language for the telling, deal with intertribal skirmishes. A woman with a peerless sense of humor, she often used their sessions to obliquely acknowledge Linderman's awkward attempts to frame Native consciousness in Anglo contexts, which was, I suspect, a major reason she chose to recount several stories of women warriors to him.

"Of course the Lacota, Striped-feathered-arrows [Cheyenne], Arapahoes, Pecunnies, and other tribes never let us rest, so that there was always war. When our enemies were not bothering *us*, our warriors were bothering *them*, so there was always fighting going on somewhere. We women sometimes tried to keep our men from going to war, but this was like talking to winter-winds; and of course there was always some woman, sometimes many women, mourning for men who had been killed in war. These women had to be taken care of. Somebody had to kill meat for them. Their fathers or uncles or brothers did this until the women married again, which they did not always do, so that war made more work for everybody. There were few lazy ones among us in those days. My people used to be too proud to be lazy. Besides this, in the old days a lazy person didn't get along very well, man or woman."

"Were there always men left in your camps?" I asked, hoping that the answer might remind her of another story.

"Yes," she said, "but sometimes when war-parties were out looking for the enemy, and besides these, many hunters were on the plains after buffalo, only old men were left in camp, old ones, and a few lazy young ones. Once, a long time ago, the Lacota nearly wiped the Crows out, because all the men were gone to steal horses. Nearly all the women were killed, and all the old men that had been left in the village besides. But this was long before my time. Even in my days young men were always going to war, or to steal horses, leaving the village short of warriors, because they could not marry until they had counted coup, or had reached the age of twenty-five years. Young men do not like to wait so long," she smiled.

"My man, Goes-ahead, was a Fox [member of that secret society], and although we women had no secret societies we sided with our men, so that my heart was always strong for the Foxes. The Foxes were warlike. We women did not like war, and yet we could not help it, because our men loved war. Always there was some man missing, and always some woman was having to go and live with her relatives, because women are not hunters. And then there were the orphans that war made. They had to be cared for by somebody. You see that when we women lost our men we lost our own, and our children's, living. I am glad that war has gone forever. It was no good—*no good*!"

Here her signs were most emphatic.

"I want to go back to the time when I was eight years old,"

said Pretty-shield. "Will it be all right to do this now, after we have passed that time?"

"Yes, always when you think of a story of your girlhood I wish you would tell it."

"Well, once when we had much fat meat that had been roasted in meat-holes, and were almost lazy from eating, our village moved a long way. My mother and I let the travois go on ahead of us, because we saw some roots that we wished to dig."

Meat was often roasted in holes in the ground, hot stones being used in very much the same way as in fireless cookers of modern days.

"When at last my mother and I started to follow the people we were alone on the wide plains. My mother was riding a mare that had a colt. This colt kept lagging back, sometimes getting far behind, making the mare so nervous that she kept trying to turn around. Her whinnying made a lot of noise, and we did not like to hear it, because we were alone. At last the troublesome colt got so far behind that we had to turn back to find it. When we found it the colt wanted to nurse, but we were so far behind now that my mother would not wait for the colt to fill up. I have often wondered what might have happened to us if she had waited for that little colt to nurse," Pretty-shield said speculatively. "We might have saved ourselves a lot of trouble, and yet we might have been captured by the Lacota and enslaved.

"We were riding fast, my mother ahead and I behind, with the bothersome colt between us, when we saw Lacota coming. My heart fell to the ground. We both forgot all about the colt. Mother turned up a deep coulee, with me by her side. 'They may not have seen us,' she said, lashing her old mare that was going like the wind.

"But I thought they must have seen us. A hundred warriors with two hundred eyes must have seen as much as we two women saw with but four eyes, I felt sure.

"We began to go uphill, our horses getting slower and slower, until at last we reached the top. Here my mother stopped and got down. Her mare was breathing so fast that her sides were going in and out like a tired wolf's. We had stopped behind a juniper tree and my mother, keeping behind it, looked back. Then she called me. I got down, and went to her. 'Look,' she pointed.

"The Lacota had found the place where we had turned away from the trail the travois had made. Four of them, afoot, were following our tracks. I knew what this meant. A party of Lacota would take up our trail and ride us down.

"My mother saw that I understood. 'Daughter,' she said, softly, putting her arm around me, 'we have not always *lived* together, but before this sun touches the world we may *die* together.'

"She straightened my saddle's cinch, and that of her own. Then she took a fine wolf's skin from her saddle, and brushed the ground with it, as though wiping away our horses' tracks. 'If they come to this place they will be fooled by this,' she told me. But I was afraid.

" 'Come,' she said, and we rode again. There were two creeks far ahead of us now. Mother headed for the one that was on our left a little, singing her medicine-song, 'I'm doing as you told me to do; I'm doing as you told me to do.'

"Suddenly our horses told us that there was something bad ahead. My mother stopped so quickly that I ran against her. She put the wolf skin over her head and sang, 'I'm doing as you told me to do; I'm doing as you told me to do.'

"A black cloud, full of thunder that sounded like many guns shooting together near my ears, passed over our heads. I felt a strong wind on my shoulders. The black cloud ran back to hang over the Lacota, its thunders nearly bursting my ears.

" 'Ho!' cried my mother, above the wind. And away we

dashed again. When we came out of the wind I could hear my mother's voice singing her medicine-song.

"We got away. That wolf skin was big medicine. I have it to this day," she finished, confidentially.

"Did the Lacota attack the Crow village?" I asked.

"No," she answered. "Our warriors went out to find the Lacota. But I do not like to talk of war. The last time I did I nearly forgot my grandchildren."

"Did the Crow warriors find the Lacota?" I pressed her.

"Yes. Next morning there were many Lacota horses mixed with ours, and I saw more Lacota scalps than I had ever before seen at one time. No Crow had been killed, and but one warrior wounded. His name was Blue-scalp. We won a big fight that time. The men had a big dance, with their faces painted black [sign of victory].

"But it was not long until the Lacota got even with us. This was always the way with our wars. No matter which side won a battle, ourselves or our enemies, the loser always got even in the end. Getting even was what kept our men fighting; and this wanting to get even was what made so much mourning, too."

LUTHER STANDING BEAR

First Days at Carlisle (1928)

This chapter from Chief Standing Bear's My People, the Sioux *is all the more chilling for its reasonable, accepting tone. One wonders if the narrator comprehended the dynamics of his situation as a child; evidently he did not. Indeed, sophisticated understanding of the process called "brainwashing" did not exist in his day, though a thoroughgoing awareness of it clearly did exist. Richard Pratt's deculturation method is clear in this ingenuous account: It reads like the Sumerian goddess Inanna's mythic journey to the underworld, where at each "Gate" she is stripped of some piece of her identity until, reaching the lowest depth, she is only a desiccated corpse.*

The gates through which young Ota K'te, Plenty Kill, passes begin at the gate of the school—a place he would later call a "prison for children." There they are made to wait a long time, and he was the first Indian boy to enter. My great-grandmother was in that same class; I wonder if she was the first girl to go through that imposing gate. The point of brainwashing is to take away all sense of self, of community, of value, of worth, even of orientation, to be replaced by habits of mind and behavior that the captor finds ac-

ceptable. The boys and girls at Carlisle Indian School were trained to be cannon fodder in American wars, to serve as domestics and farm hands, and to leave off all ideas or beliefs that came to them from their Native communities, including and particularly their belief that they were entitled to land, life, liberty, and dignity.

In a short time, the child comes to love and admire his captor, as Standing Bear admired and respected Richard Pratt, a not uncommon adjustment made by those taken hostage; separated from all that is familiar; stripped, shorn, robbed of their very self; renamed.

By and large the procedure was successful, although the legacy of damaged minds and crippled souls it left in its wake is as yet untold. Psychic numbing, Post Traumatic Stress Syndrome, battered wife syndrome, suicide, alcoholism, ennui—are there any names for psychecide? A century after that exhausted little boy walked through those imposing gates into a sterile room, the great-great-grandchildren of decultured Indians struggle to find the world that was ripped away: not by war, not by disease, not by wretched poverty, although all those played a part, but by a deliberate, planned method euphemistically called education. "First Days at Carlisle" is a tale of transformation that has as its pattern myths about that dread-full process from all over the world.

A t last the train arrived at a junction where we were told we were at the end of our journey. Here we left the train and walked about two miles to the Carlisle Barracks. Soon we came to a big gate in a great high wall. The gate was locked, but after quite a long wait it was unlocked and we marched in through it. I was the first boy inside. At that time I thought nothing of it, but now I realize that I was the first Indian boy to step inside the Carlisle Indian School grounds.

Here the girls were all called to one side by Louise McCoz, the girls' interpreter. She took them into one of the big buildings, which was very brilliantly lighted, and it looked good to us from the outside.

When our interpreter told us to go to a certain building, which he pointed out to us, we ran very fast, expecting to find nice little beds like those the white people had. We were so tired and worn out from the long trip that we wanted a good long sleep. From Springfield, Dakota, to Carlisle, Pennsylvania, riding in day coaches all the way, with no chance to sleep, is an exhausting journey for a bunch of little Indians.

But the first room we entered was empty. A cast-iron stove stood in the middle of the room, on which was placed a coal-oil lamp. There was no fire in the stove. We ran through all the rooms, but they were all the same—no fire, no beds. This was a two-story building, but we were all herded into two rooms on the upper floor.

Well, we had to make the best of the situation, so we took off our leggins and rolled them up for a pillow. All the covering we had was the blanket which each had brought. We went to sleep on the hard floor, and it was so cold! We had been used to sleeping on the ground, but the floor was so much colder.

Next morning we were called downstairs for breakfast. All we were given was bread and water. How disappointed we were! At noon we had some meat, bread, and coffee, so we felt a little better. But how lonesome the big boys and girls were for their faraway Dakota homes where there was plenty to eat! The big boys seemed to take it worse than we smaller chaps did. I guess we little fellows did not know any better. The big boys would sing brave songs, and that would start the girls to crying. They did this for several nights. The girls' quarters were about a hundred and fifty yards from ours, so we could hear them crying. After some time the food began to get better, but it was far from being what we had been used to receiving back home.

At this point I must tell you how the Carlisle Indian School was started. A few years previously, four or five tribes in

Oklahoma had some trouble. They were Cheyennes, Arapahoes, Comanches, and Wichitas. There was another tribe with them, but I have forgotten the name. The Government arrested some braves from these various tribes and took them to Virginia as prisoners. Captain Pratt was in charge of them. He conceived the idea of placing these Indians in a school to see if they could learn anything in that manner. So they were put into the Hampton School, where negroes were sent. They were good-sized young men, having been on the war-path already, but old as they were, they were getting on splendidly with their studies.

That gave Captain Pratt another idea. He thought if he could get some young Indian children and educate them, it would help their people. He went to the government officials and put the proposition up to them, and asked permission to try the experiment. They told him to go ahead and see what he could do, providing he could get any Indians to educate. Captain Pratt was not at all sure he could do this.

He had nothing prepared to start such a school, but the Government gave him the use of some empty buildings at Carlisle, Pennsylvania. He brought some of the Indian prisoners from Virginia with him, and they remained in the Carlisle Barracks until Captain Pratt could go to Dakota and return with his first consignment of "scholars." Carlisle School had been a soldiers' home at one time, so at the start it was not built for the education of the Indian people.

I had come to this school merely to show my people that I was brave enough to leave the reservation and go East, not knowing what it meant and not caring.

When we first arrived at Carlisle, we had nothing to do. There were no school regulations, no rules of order, or anything of that sort. We just ran all over the school grounds and did about as we pleased.

Soon some white people began to come in from nearby towns to see us. Then we would all go up on the second floor and stand against the railings to look down at them. One of our boys was named Lone Hill. He watched the people closely, and if he saw a negro in the crowd he would run inside and put his war-shirt on. Then he would come out and chase the negro all over the grounds until he left. How the people laughed at this!

For some time we continued sleeping on the hard floor, and it was far from being as comfortable as the nice, soft beds in our tipis back home. One evening the interpreter called us all together, and gave each a big bag. He said these were to be our mattresses, but that we would have to fill them ourselves with straw. He said, "Out behind the stable is a large haystack. Go there and fill these bags all full."

So we all ran as fast as we could to the haystack and filled our sacks as quickly as possible, pushing and scuffling to see who would get finished first. When the bags were all full, we carried them to one of the big rooms on the second floor. Here the bags were all laid out in a row. We little fellows certainly did look funny, lugging those great bags across the yard and up-stairs.

That night we had the first good sleep in a long time. These bags were sewed all around, and in the center there was a slit through which they were filled with the straw; but there was nobody to sew the slit up after the bag was filled. We had no sheets and no extra blankets thus far—nothing but the blankets we had brought from the reservation.

The next day we played back and forth over these bags of straw, and soon it began to filter out through the slits. Presently it was scattered all over the floor, and as we had no brooms with which to sweep it up, you can imagine the look of the room at the starting of our school!

Although we were yet wearing our Indian clothes, the interpreter came to us and told us we must go to school. We were marched into a schoolroom where we were each given a pencil and slate. We were seated at single desks. We soon discovered that the pencils made marks on the slates. So we covered our heads with our blankets, holding the slate inside so the other fellow would not know what we were doing. Here we would draw a man on a pony chasing buffalo, or a boy shooting birds in a tree, or it might be one of our Indian games, or anything that suited our fancy to try and portray.

When we had all finished, we dropped our blankets down on the seat and marched up to the teacher with our slates to show what we had drawn. Our teacher was a woman. She bowed her head as she examined the slates and smiled, indicating that we were doing pretty well—at least we interpreted it that way.

One day when we came to school there was a lot of writing on one of the blackboards. We did not know what it meant, but our interpreter came into the room and said, "Do you see all these marks on the blackboard? Well, each word is a white man's name. They are going to give each one of you one of these names by which you will hereafter be known." None of the names were read or explained to us, so of course we did not know the sound or meaning of any of them.

The teacher had a long pointed stick in her hand, and the interpreter told the boy in the front seat to come up. The teacher handed the stick to him, and the interpreter then told him to pick out any name he wanted. The boy had gone up with his blanket on. When the long stick was handed to him, he turned to us as much as to say, "Shall I—or will you help me—to take one of these names? Is it right for me to take a white man's name?" He did not know what to do for a time, not uttering a single word, but he acted a lot and was doing a lot of thinking.

Finally he pointed out one of the names written on the blackboard. Then the teacher took a piece of white tape and wrote the name on it. Then she cut off a length of the tape and sewed it on the back of the boy's shirt. Then that name was erased from the board. There was no duplication of names in the first class at Carlisle School!

Then the next boy took the pointer and selected a name. He was also labeled in the same manner as Number One. When my turn came, I took the pointer and acted as if I were about to touch an enemy. Soon we all had the names of white men sewed on our backs. When we went to school, we knew enough to take our proper places in the class, but that was all. When the teacher called the roll, no one answered his name. Then she would walk around and look at the back of the boys' shirts. When she had the right name located, she made the boy stand up and say "Present." She kept this up for about a week before we knew what the sound of our new names was.

I was one of the "bright fellows" to learn my name quickly. How proud I was to answer when the teacher called the roll! I would put my blanket down and half raise myself in my seat, all ready to answer to my new name. I had selected the name "Luther"—not "Lutheran" as many people call me. "Lutheran" is the name of a church denomination, not a person.

Next we had to learn to write our names. Our good teacher had a lot of patience with us. She is now living in Los Angeles, California, and I still like to go and ask her any question which may come up in my mind. She first wrote my name on the slate for me, and then, by motions, indicated that I was to write it just like that. She held the pencil in her hand just so, then made first one stroke, then another, and by signs I was given to understand that I was to follow in exactly the same way.

The first few times I wrote my new name, it was scratched so deeply into the slate that I was never able to erase it. But I copied my name all over both sides of the slate until there was no more room to write. Then I took my slate up to show it to the teacher, and she indicated, by the expression of her face, that it was very good. I soon learned to write it very well; then

I took a piece of chalk downstairs and wrote "Luther" all over everything I could copy it on.

Next the teacher wrote out the alphabet on my slate and indicated to me that I was to take the slate to my room and study. I was pleased to do this, as I expected to have a lot of fun. I went up on the second floor, to the end of the building, where I thought nobody would bother me. There I sat down and looked at those queer letters, trying hard to figure out what they meant. No one was there to tell me that the first letter was "A," the next "B," and so on. This was the first time in my life that I was really disgusted. It was something I could not decipher, and all this study business was not what I had come East for anyhow—so I thought.

How lonesome I felt for my father and mother! I stayed upstairs all by myself, thinking of the good times I might be having if I were only back home, where I could ride my ponies, go wherever I wanted to and do as I pleased, and, when it came night, could lie down and sleep well. Right then and there I learned that no matter how humble your home is, it is yet home.

So it did me no good to take my slate with me that day. It only made me lonesome. The next time the teacher told me by signs to take my slate to my room, I shook my head, meaning "no." She came and talked to me in English, but of course I did not know what she was saying.

A few days later, she wrote the alphabet on the blackboard, then brought the interpreter into the room. Through him she told us to repeat each letter after her, calling out "A," and we all said "A"; then "B," and so on. This was our real beginning. The first day we learned the first three letters of the alphabet, both the pronunciation and the reading of them.

I had not determined to learn anything yet. All I could think of was my free life at home. How long would these people keep us here? When were we going home? At home we could eat anytime we wished, but here we had to watch the sun all the time. On cloudy days the waits between meals seemed terribly long.

There soon came a time when the school people fixed up an old building which was to be used as our dining-room. In it they placed some long tables, but with no cover on. Our meals were dished up and brought to each plate before we entered. I very quickly learned to be right there when the bell rang, and get in first. Then I would run along down the table until I came to a plate which I thought contained the most meat, then I would sit down and begin eating without waiting for anyone.

We soon "got wise" when it came to looking out for the biggest portion of meat. When we knew by the sun that it was near dinnertime, we would play close to the dining-room, until the woman in charge came out with a big bell in her hand to announce that the meal was ready. We never had to be called twice! We were right there when it came mealtime!

After a while they hung a big bell on a walnut tree near the office. This was to be rung for school hours and meals. One of the Indian boys, Edgar Fire Thunder, used to sneak around the building and ring the bell before it was time to eat. Of course we would all rush for the dining-room, only to find the doors locked. Nobody seemed to object to this boy playing such pranks, but we did not like it.

We were still wearing our Indian clothes. One of the Indian prisoners was delegated to teach us to march in to the dining-room and to school. Some of the boys had bells on their leggins, which helped us to keep time as we stepped off.

One day we had a strange experience. We were all called together by the interpreter and told that we were to have our hair cut off. We listened to what he had to say, but we did not reply. This was something that would require some thought, so that evening the big boys held a council, and I recall very distinctly that Nakpa Kesela, or Robert American Horse, made a serious speech. Said he, "If I am to learn the ways of the white people, I can do it just as well with my hair on." To this we all exclaimed "Hau!"—meaning that we agreed with him.

In spite of this meeting, a few days later we saw some white men come inside the school grounds carrying big chairs. The interpreter told us these were the men who had come to cut our hair. We did not watch to see where the chairs were carried, as it was schooltime, and we went to our classroom. One of the big boys, Ya Slo, or Whistler, was missing. In a short time he came in with his hair cut off. Then they called another boy out, and when he returned, he also wore short hair. In this way we were called out one by one.

When I saw most of them with short hair, I began to feel anxious to be "in style" and wanted mine cut, too. Finally I was called out of the schoolroom, and when I went into the next room, the barber was waiting for me. He motioned for me to sit down, and then he commenced work. But when my hair was cut short, it hurt my feelings to such an extent that the tears came into my eyes. I do not recall whether the barber noticed my agitation or not, nor did I care. All I was thinking about was that hair he had taken away from me.

Right here I must state how this hair-cutting affected me in various ways. I have recounted that I always wanted to please my father in every way possible. All his instructions to me had been along this line: "Son, be brave and get killed." This expression had been molded into my brain to such an extent that I knew nothing else.

But my father had made a mistake. He should have told me, upon leaving home, to go and learn all I could of the white man's ways, and be like them. That would have given a new idea from a different slant, but Father did not advise me along that line. I had come away from home with the intention of never returning alive unless I had done something very brave.

Now, after having had my hair cut, a new thought came

into my head. I felt that I was no more Indian but would be an imitation of a white man. And we are still imitations of white men, and the white men are imitations of the Americans.

We all looked so funny with short hair. It had been cut with a machine and was cropped very close. We still had our Indian clothes, but we were all "bald-headed." None of us slept well that night; we felt so queer. I wanted to feel of my head all the time. But in a short time I became anxious to learn all I could.

Next, we heard that we were soon to have white men's clothes. We were all very excited and anxious when this was announced to us. One day some wagons came in, loaded with big boxes, which were unloaded in front of the office. Of course we were all very curious, and gathered around to watch the proceedings and see all we could.

Here, one at a time, we were "sized up" and a whole suit handed to each of us. The clothes were some sort of dark heavy gray goods, consisting of coat, pants, and vest. We were also given a dark woolen shirt, a cap, a pair of suspenders, socks, and heavy farmer's boots.

Up to this time we had all been wearing our thin shirts, leggins, and a blanket. Now we had received new outfits of white men's clothes, and to us it seemed a whole lot of clothing to wear at once, but even at that, we had not yet received any underwear.

As soon as we had received our outfits, we ran to our rooms to dress up. The Indian prisoners were kept busy helping us put the clothes on. Although the suits were too big for many of us, we did not know the difference. I remember that my boots were far too large, but as long as they were "screechy" or squeaky, I didn't worry about the size! I liked the noise they made when I walked, and the other boys were likewise pleased.

How proud we were with clothes that had pockets and with boots that squeaked! We walked the floor nearly all that night. Many of the boys even went to bed with their clothes all on. But in the morning, the boys who had taken off their pants had a most terrible time. They did not know whether they were to button up in front or behind. Some of the boys said the open part went in front; others said, "No, it goes at the back." There is where the boys who had kept all their clothes on came in handy to look at. They showed the others that the pants buttoned up in front and not at the back. So here we learned something again.

Another boy and I received some money from home. His name was Waniyetula, or Winter, and he was my cousin. We concluded we might as well dress up like white men; so we took all our money to the interpreter and asked him if he would buy us some nice clothes. He promised he would.

We did not know the amount of money which we handed over to him, but we gave him all we had received, as we did not know values then. He took the money and went to town. When he returned he brought us each a big bundle. We took them and went into an empty room to dress up, as we did not want the other boys to see us until we had the clothes on. When we opened the bundles, we were surprised to see how many things we had received for our money. Each bundle contained a black suit of clothes, a pair of shoes and socks, stiff bosom shirt, two paper collars, a necktie, a pair of cuffs, derby hat, cuff buttons, and some colored glass studs for our stiff shirt fronts.

We were greatly pleased with our purchases, which we examined with great curiosity and eagerness. As it was nearly time for supper, we tied the bundles together again and took them into one of the rooms where an Indian prisoner was staying, asking him to keep the bundles for us until the next day. We had to talk to him in the sign language, as he was from a different tribe. The sign language, by the way, was invented by the Indian. White men never use it correctly.

We felt very proud of our new purchases and spent most of that evening getting off by ourselves and discussing them. We found out later that our wonderful clothes cost all together about eleven dollars. The interpreter had bought the cheapest things he could get in the town of Carlisle.

All the next day we were together. We kept our eyes on our disciplinarian, Mr. Campbell, because we wanted to see how he put on his collar. We were studying not very far away from him and we watched him constantly, trying to figure out how he had put that collar on his shirt.

When evening came at last, we carried our bundles up to the second floor where we could be alone. Here we opened the things up and started to dress up. While we were thus engaged, in came the prisoner with whom we had left the bundles the night before. We were glad, in a way, that he had come in, because he knew more about how the clothes ought to be worn than we did, and he helped us dress.

Just as we were through, the bell rang for supper. The other boys were already in line. We came down the outside stairway, and when they observed us, what a war whoop went up! The boys made all kinds of remarks about our outfits, and called us "white men." But our teachers and the other white people were greatly pleased at our new appearance.

We had only two paper collars apiece, and when they became soiled we had to go without collars. We tried our best to wear the ties without the collars, but I guess we must have looked funny.

It was now winter and very cold, so we were supplied with red flannel underwear. These looked pretty to us, but we did not like the warmth and the "itching" they produced. I soon received some more money from my father, and another boy named Knaska, or Frog, and I bought us some white underwear. This was all right, but we did not dare let any one else know it, as the rules were that we had to wear the red flannels.

So every Sunday morning we would put the red ones on, because they held inspection on Sunday morning. Captain Pratt and others always looked us over that day very carefully, but as soon as the inspection was through, we would slip into our white underclothes and get ready to attend Sunday school in town.

All the boys and girls were given permission to choose the religious denomination which appealed to them best, so they were at liberty to go where they pleased to Sunday school. Most of us selected the Episcopal church. I was baptized in that church under the name of Luther.

In our room lived a boy named Kaici Inyanke, or Running Against. While not exactly bad, he was always up to some mischief. His father's name was Black Bear, so when the boy was baptized he took his father's name, while his Christian name was Paul. He is yet living at Pine Ridge Agency, South Dakota. More than once Captain Pratt had to hold Paul up. He would play until the very last minute and then try to clean his shoes and comb his hair, all at once seemingly. On this particular Sunday, Paul rushed in and was so busy that he did not get half finished. He had combed his hair, but had applied too much water, which was running down his face, while one of his shoes was cleaned and the other was dirty.

We had been taught to stand erect like soldiers when Captain Pratt, Dr. Givens, and others entered the room for inspection. First, Captain Pratt would "size us up" from head to foot, notice if we had our hair combed nicely, if our clothes were neatly brushed, and if we had cleaned our shoes. Then he would look the room over to see if our beds were made up right, often lifting the mattresses to see that everything was clean underneath. Often they would look into our wooden boxes where we kept our clothes, to see that everything was spick and span.

Paul Black Bear had not been able—as usual—to finish getting ready for inspection, and when Captain Pratt looked at his feet, Paul tried to hide the shoe that was not polished by putting it behind the other one. Captain Pratt also noticed the water running down his face. We all expected to see Paul get a "calling down," but Captain Pratt only laughed and told Paul to do better next time.

At Carlisle it was the rule that we were not to be permitted to smoke, but Paul smoked every time he had a chance. One day he made a "long smoke" and stood by one of the big fireplaces, puffing away very fast. All at once he got sick at the stomach and fainted. We had to drag him out of the fireplace and pour water on him.

One day our teacher brought some wooden plates into the schoolroom. She told us they were to paint on. She gave me about half a dozen of them. We each received a small box of watercolors. I painted Indian designs on all my plates. On some of them I had a man chasing buffalo, shooting them with the bow and arrow. Others represented a small boy shooting at birds in the trees. When I had them all painted, I gave them back to the teacher. She seemed to be well pleased with my work, and sent them all away somewhere. Possibly some persons yet have those wooden plates which were painted by the first class of Indian boys and girls at Carlisle.

About this time there were many additions to the school from various tribes in other States and from other reservations. We were not allowed to converse in the Indian tongue, and we knew so little English that we had a hard time to get along. With these other tribes coming in, we were doing our best to talk as much English as we could.

One night in December we were all marched down to the chapel. When the doors were opened, how surprised we were! Everything was decorated with green. We all took seats, but we could not keep still. There was a big tree in the room, all trimmed and decorated. We stretched our necks to see everything. Then a minister stood up in front and talked to us, but

I did not mind a thing he said—in fact, I could not understand him anyway.

This was our first Christmas celebration, and we were all so happy. I saw the others were getting gifts from off that tree, and I was anxious to get something myself. Finally my name was called, and I received several presents, which had been put on the tree for me by the people for whom I had painted the plates. Others were from my teacher, Miss M. Burgess, and some from my Sunday school teacher, Miss Eggee. I was very happy for all the things I had received.

I now began to realize that I would have to learn the ways of the white man. With that idea in mind, the thought also came to me that I must please my father as well. So my little brain began to work hard. I thought that some day I might be able to become an interpreter for my father, as he could not speak English. Or I thought I might be able to keep books for him if he again started a store. So I worked very hard.

One day they selected a few boys and told us we were to learn trades. I was to be a tinsmith. I did not care for this, but I tried my best to learn this trade. Mr. Walker was our instructor. I was getting along very well. I made hundreds of tin cups, coffee pots, and buckets. These were sent away and issued to the Indians on various reservations.

After I had left the school and returned home, this trade did not benefit me any, as the Indians had plenty of tinware that I had made at school.

Mornings I went to the tin shop, and in the afternoon attended school. I tried several times to drop this trade and go to school the entire day, but Captain Pratt said, "No, you must go to the tin shop—that is all there is to it," so I had to go. Half school and half work took away a great deal of study time. I figure that I spent only about a year and a half in school, while the rest of the time was wasted, as the school was not started properly to begin with. Possibly you wonder why I did not remain longer, but the government had made an agreement with our parents as to the length of time we were to be away.

A short time later, some boys, myself among the number, were called into one of the schoolrooms. There we found a little white woman. There was a long table in front of her, on which were many packages tied in paper. She opened up one package and it contained a bright, shining horn. Other packages disclosed more horns, but they seemed to be different sizes.

The little white woman picked up a horn and then looked the boys over. Finally she handed it to a boy who she thought might be able to use it. Then she picked out a shorter horn and gave it to me. I learned afterward that it was a B-flat cornet. When she had finished, all the boys had horns in their hands. We were to be taught how to play on them and form a band.

The little woman had a black case with her, which she opened. It held a beautiful horn, and when she blew on it it sounded beautiful. Then she motioned to us that we were to blow our horns. Some of the boys tried to blow from the large end. Although we tried our best, we could not produce a sound from them. She then tried to talk to us, but we did not understand her. Then she showed us how to wet the end of the mouthpiece. We thought she wanted us to spit into the horns, so we did. She finally got so discouraged with us that she started crying.

We just stood there and waited for her to get through, then we all tried again. Finally, some of the boys managed to make a noise through their horns. But if you could have heard it! It was terrible! But we thought we were doing fine.

So now I had more to occupy my attention. In the morning I had one hour to practice for the band. Then I must run to my room and change my clothes and go to work in the tin shop. From there I had to run again to my room and change my clothes and get ready for dinner. After that, I had a little time to study my lessons.

Then the school bell would ring and it was time for school. After that, we played or studied our music. Then we went to bed. All lights had to be out at nine o'clock. The first piece of music our band was able to play was the alphabet, from "A" to "Z." It was a great day for us when we were able to play this simple little thing in public. But it was a good thing we were not asked to give an encore, for that was all we knew!

After I had learned to play a little, I was chosen to give all the bugle calls. I had to get up in the morning before the others and arouse everybody by blowing the morning call. Evenings at ten minutes before nine o'clock I blew again. Then all the boys would run for their rooms. At nine o'clock the second call was given, when all lights were turned out and we were supposed to be in bed. Later on I learned the mess call, and eventually I could blow all the calls of the regular army.

I did these duties all the time I was at Carlisle School, so in the early part of 1880, although I was a young boy of but twelve, I was busy learning everything my instructors handed me.

One Sunday morning we were all busy getting ready to go to Sunday school in town. Suddenly there was great excitement among some of the boys on the floor below. One of the boys came running upstairs shouting, "Luther Standing Bear's father is here!" Everybody ran downstairs to see my father. We had several tribes at the school now, many of whom had heard of my father, and they were anxious to see him.

When I got downstairs, my father was in the center of a large crowd of the boys, who were all shaking hands with him. I had to fight my way through to reach him. He was so glad to see me, and I was so delighted to see him. But our rules were that we were not to speak the Indian language under any consideration. And here was my father, and he could not talk English!

My first act was to write a note to Captain Pratt, asking if he would permit me to speak to my father in the Sioux tongue. I said, "My father is here. Please allow me to speak to him in Indian." Captain Pratt answered, "Yes, my boy; bring your father over to my house."

This was another happy day for me. I took my father over to meet Captain Pratt, who was so glad to see him, and was very respectful to him. Father was so well dressed. He wore a gray suit, nice shoes, and a derby hat. But he wore his hair long. He looked very nice in white men's clothes. He even sported a gold watch and chain. Captain Pratt gave Father a room with Robert American Horse, in the boys' quarters. He allowed the boys to talk to him in the Indian tongue, and that pleased the boys very much. Here Father remained for a time with us.

ESTELLE ARMSTRONG

The Return (1925)

In her brief story, Estelle Armstrong paints a clear picture of the horrors faced by the survivors of the Holocaust that swept some 97 percent of our population into the grave. By the 1920s, when she wrote "The Return," the abject humiliation of a race of people is scathingly depicted. It is not clear if the narrator is white or Native, but certainly she has taken on a great deal of white thought: the elders at the station are "old squaws," the generic term of disrespect for Native women. She also comments on the full-bloods who, although not too bright, "with their hands do well and faithfully what is given them to do." Thus the white concept of natural order is firmly established: mixed-bloods can aspire to loftier pursuits than one such as Jose. He hides his shame beneath an amiable, acquiescent mask; menial labor enables him to avoid his parents' abject state. Then, too, the ridicule of the people who did not take on alien ways may have been the last gate, the final step in the process of psychecide.

An undercurrent of bitter irony runs through this seemingly simple story; through its prismatic lens we see Native people as they existed at the end of the Indian Wars. And we are warned: "You may beat an Indian in a fair fight and he will respect you; you may cheat him in a horse trade, if you can, and he will be wary of you; but expose him to ridicule before his peers and he is your enemy forever...."

The old squaws, sitting squat on the platform beside their mounds of beadwork, looked at Jose as he swung himself from the day coach of the Overland and nudged each the other in derision of his uniform and close-cut hair. Sitting there with their cheap, gaudy strings of beads held up to catch some unwary tourist's eye, their hair long and dank over shapeless, ugly shoulders, their grimy faces impassive with the peculiar expressionless stare of the hopeless, the old women seemed the very incarnation of the spirit of ridicule against which nearly every returned student is pitted on his return from school to his reservation home.

The innate hatred of the older Indians for the white man's dominating activity, with its resulting absorption of their own purposeless lives, eggs them on to use in retaliation the only weapon left them, often undoing by their witless ridicule of returned students what years of study and careful training has inculcated. For you may beat an Indian in a fair fight and he will respect you; you may cheat him in a horse trade, if you can, and he will be wary of you; but expose him to ridicule before his peers and he is your enemy forever; for ridicule of his person is one thing which nature has not fitted an Indian to bear.

The evil potency of this enervating criticism is recognized by every educator of our Indian youth who had watched the returned student conquer or be conquered by it. And it is because this spirit of ridicule is not an attribute of any particular tribe or locality, but is common to every clan, whether of valley or mountain or barren plain, that I select the homecoming of Jose as typical of many such that I have witnessed, and having witnessed have marveled, not at the half failure sometimes resulting but at the optimism that dared to expect success.

Jose had been but an indifferent student at best, mastering the intricacies of the sixth grade in his nineteenth year, the fifth and last of his term at Carlisle. But balanced against his poor classroom record was his good conduct as a student, his industry in the workshop, and his ability as an officer of Company C. In fact, he was an average student among the full-bloods, who, as a rule, do not take kindly to books and abstruse problems but with their hands do well and faithfully what is given them to do.

Jose had been fourteen years old when he left the hot Arizona reservation on the Colorado and the five years had wrought many changes in the dark-skinned boy who, at nineteen, walked with head and shoulders erect and saw that his shoes were duly polished and his clothes and nails immaculate. For at fourteen Jose had slouched and shoes were unknown and clothes a concession to encroaching civilization, which he had detested. Of his early home life he had but confused memories and from his parents he had received no word in all the five years. The remembrance of the squalor and meanness of his early years had faded from his mind and his thoughts of home were a misty background of idleness and freedom against which his present life loomed portentous and grim.

And now the same forceful hand which had so deliberately taken him from his home five years before was as calmly replacing him in the groove nature had fitted him to fill, after having done all in its power to make him unsuited for it. If Jose had been given to ponder on the reason of things he might have questioned the wisdom which had separated him from his natural environment to teach him customs and habits which rendered that environment detestable, only to return him to it. Happily, Jose had no such questioning—he was going home;

home to his kindred and early playmates, to the misty memories of his boyhood home.

Home! He had come to it at last, with the tropical sun beating down upon him and a strange sinking in his heart at the sight of the leering squaws at the station.

He gripped his suitcase and elbowed his way through the crowded platform, thronged with travelers, Mexicans and men of his own tribe, the latter in corduroys and light shirts, their long hair bound at the neck with gay kerchiefs and decorated at waist and elbow with strips of calico of many colors. They turned to stare at him, insolently noting his smart uniform, his cropped hair, his general well-groomed appearance, breaking into loud guffaws at his expense as he passed them. Among their number were two of Jose's early playmates, with whom he had swam the eddying Colorado in former days, sounding each treacherous sandbar and skirting dangerously close to the seething whirlpools; but he passed them now with no sign of recognition, failing to understand that one of the boyish anticipations of his homecoming had vanished in that chorus of rude laughter.

As he climbed the steep hill which skirted the Colorado and hid from view the reservation of his people, Jose felt his pulses bounding rapidly. He had not expected his parents to meet him at the train. They were very old, had been old when Jose left five years before, and had many sons, of which he was the youngest. Without thought he took the old path which led to his father's hut, the dust which lay like powder on every bush and shrub stinging his eyes and throat. He found himself wondering if his father's home was like the open, grass-thatched hovels which he passed, around which naked children stopped their play to stare at him and mongrel dogs challenged him from a safe distance. His uncertain memories of home had been largely of the freedom and unrestraint of former years and they had dealt kindly with the poor hut and the deprivation which had also been his portion.

An old woman raised her head from the pot of soup she was tending over a small open fire and watched him as he approached, and Jose recognized his mother. Old and bent with many years, her hair matted above her sunken eyes, her only garment a shred of filth that stopped above her knees, her unhuman hands ending in talons, the mother sat and watched her son draw near. The accents of his native tongue came instinctively to Jose's lips and he spoke hesitatingly—"Mother." The sunken eyes lighted as she bent near that her dim vision might view this stranger son, and voiceless the mother held him and gazed long at his altered features and alien clothes. Then, tottering to a prone form lying in the sand by the side of the hut, she spoke, and her words roused the wasted figure of Jose's father. With palsied hands he shaded his eyes as he looked at his son, then rising slowly and with difficulty, his raiment a loin cloth, his gray locks streaming over his shoulders, and yet with dignity withal, he extended his hand in welcome.

As in a dream Jose sat down on a nearby log and gazed about him. He saw the mean hut in its squalor and poverty; the heaps of rags in the sand on which his parents slept; the open fire over which hung the kettle of soup containing the coming meal; the sand and greasewood glaring in the July sun. He saw the Colorado with its treacherous gleaming quicksand and, just beyond, the vicious frontier town, flaunting its vice so shamelessly, and then his gaze wandered back to the form of his mother as she bent again over the pot of soup.

Four years had passed and again the July sun beat down on the familiar scene as I looked from the car window as the Overland pulled in for a stop of ten minutes. We "took on water" here and as I idly watched I recognized in the stalwart figure running down the platform with a length of hose our friend Jose.

Hastily making my way outside I called to him and as soon as his work permitted, he came, doffing his cap and hesitating to give me his hand in greeting, soiled as it was from his recent labors. His overalls and working shirt were neat and whole, his hair closely cut, and his face showed no signs of dissipation beneath its grime and sweat. He looked as I believe he is, an honest youth engaged in honest work, and my heart rejoiced for him.

"Oh, yes," he replied to my question, "of course I am married. We have a child a year old and we are getting along just fine. I work over here at the railroad every day," and he called goodbye as our train got under way.

Consider, you who feel called upon to judge him, to measure him by your standards, of which he falls so far short; over against your pride of birth, your mother's prayers, the sense of honor inborn, your mental capacity of assimilation, I place the forms of Jose's parents—the squalor of the mud hut, the unbridled license of his early years, the frontier town with saloon doors always open, the pointing fingers of the leering squaws— and I challenge you to declare his education vain or to proclaim his life a failure.

JOHN M. OSKISON

The Problem of Old Harjo (1907)

This complex story explores the two-way nature of transformation. Old Harjo converts to Christianity, although church rules prevent him from being baptized. At the same time, Miss Evans' faith undergoes a parallel transformation. She learns the true meaning of spiritual life from the old pagan; it consists in the life of devotion that demands dignity, respect, and integrity. The plot Oskison hangs his deeper insights upon is ubiquitous in Indian Country. There is an old joke about an elderly chief with three wives who was ordered by the newly arrived Indian Agent to send two of them away. He thought about this for a time. "You tell them," he said. "And you say which one will stay."

The dynamics—the pain, the humor, the great gulf in perception and values—of Indian-white relations are best captured in stories like "The Problem of Old Harjo"—the title itself is an ironic comment on what the U.S. government and Anglo-European settlers were wont to call "the Indian Problem." Under that phrase a multitude of implications lurk, but they can be boiled down to one: how to get all the land and not be held accountable. It is a problem, and there were many, like Mrs. Rowell, who had what they believed was a solution.

The Spirit of the Lord had descended upon old Harjo. From the new missionary, just out from New York, he had learned that he was a sinner. The fire in the new missionary's eyes and her gracious appeal had convinced old Harjo that this was the time to repent and be saved. He was very much in earnest, and he assured Miss Evans that he wanted to be baptized and received into the church at once. Miss Evans was enthusiastic and went to Mrs. Rowell with the news. It was Mrs. Rowell who had said that it was no use to try to convert the older Indians, and she, after fifteen years of work in Indian Territory missions, should have known. Miss Evans was pardonably proud of her conquest.

"Old Harjo converted!" exclaimed Mrs. Rowell. "Dear Miss Evans, do you know that old Harjo has two wives?" To the older woman it was as if someone had said to her "Madame, the Sultan of Turkey wishes to teach one of your mission Sabbath school classes."

"But," protested the younger woman, "he is really sincere, and—"

"Then ask him," Mrs. Rowell interrupted a bit sternly, "if he will put away one of his wives. Ask him, before he comes into the presence of the Lord, if he is willing to conform to the laws of the country in which he lives, the country that guarantees his idle existence. Miss Evans, your work is not even begun." No one who knew Mrs. Rowell would say that she lacked sincerity and patriotism. Her own cousin was an earnest crusader against Mormonism, and had gathered a goodly share of that wagonload of protests that the Senate had been asked to read when it was considering whether a certain statesman of Utah should be allowed to represent his state at Washington.

In her practical, tactful way, Mrs. Rowell had kept clear of such embarrassments. At first, she had written letters of indignant protest to the Indian Office against the toleration of bigamy amongst the tribes. A wise inspector had been sent to the

mission, and this man had pointed out that it was better to ig-
nore certain things, "deplorable, to be sure," than to attempt to
make over the habits of the old men. Of course, the young Indians would not be permitted to take more than one wife each.

So Mrs. Rowell had discreetly limited her missionary efforts to the young, and had exercised toward the old and biga-
mous only that strict charity which even a hopeless sinner
might claim.

Miss Evans, it was to be regretted, had only the vaguest notions about "expediency"; so weak on matters of doctrine was
she that the news that Harjo was living with two wives didn't
startle her. She was young and possessed of but one enthusiasm—that for saving souls.

"I suppose," she ventured, "that old Harjo *must* put away
one wife before he can join the church."

"There can be no question about it, Miss Evans."

"Then I shall have to ask him to do it." Miss Evans regretted the necessity for forcing this sacrifice, but had no doubt that
the Indian would make it in order to accept the gift of salvation
which she was commissioned to bear to him.

Harjo lived in a "double" log cabin three miles from the mission. His ten acres of corn had been gathered into its fence-rail
crib; four hogs that were to furnish his winter's bacon had been
brought in from the woods and penned conveniently near to the
crib; out in a corner of the garden, a fat mound of dirt rose where
the crop of turnips and potatoes had been buried against the cor-
rupting frost; and in the hayloft of his log stable were stored many
pumpkins, dried corn, onions (suspended in bunches from the
rafters) and the varied forage that Mrs. Harjo number one and
Mrs. Harjo number two had thriftily provided. Three cows, three
young heifers, two colts, and two patient, capable mares bore the
Harjo brand, a fantastic "HH" that the old man had designed. Ma-
terially, Harjo was solvent; and if the Government had ever come
to his aid he could not recall the date.

This attempt to rehabilitate old Harjo morally, Miss Evans felt, was not one to be made at the mission; it should be undertaken in the Creek's own home, where the evidences of his sin should confront him as she explained.

When Miss Evans rode up to the block in front of Harjo's cabin, the old Indian came out, slowly and with a broadening smile of welcome on his face. A clean gray flannel shirt had taken the place of the white collarless garment, with crackling stiff bosom, that he had worn to the mission meetings. Comfortable, well-patched moccasins had been substituted for creaking boots, and brown corduroys, belted in at the waist, for tight black trousers. His abundant gray hair fell down on his shoulders. In his eyes, clear and large and black, glowed the light of true hospitality. Miss Evans thought of the patriarchs as she saw him lead her horse out to the stable; thus Abraham might have looked and lived.

"Harjo," began Miss Evans before following the old man to the covered passageway between the disconnected cabins, "is it true that you have two wives?" Her tone was neither stern nor accusatory. The Creek had heard that question before, from scandalized missionaries and perplexed registry clerks when he went to Muscogee to enroll himself and his family in one of the many "final" records ordered to be made by the government preparatory to dividing the Creek lands among the individual citizens.

For answer, Harjo called, first into the cabin that was used as a kitchen and then, in a loud, clear voice, toward the small field, where Miss Evans saw a flock of half-grown turkeys running about in the corn stubble. From the kitchen emerged a tall, thin Indian woman of fifty-five, with a red handkerchief bound severely over her head. She spoke to Miss Evans and sat down in the passageway. Presently, a clear, sweet voice was heard in the field; a stout, handsome woman, about the same age as the other, climbed the rail fence and came up to the house. She, also, greeted Miss Evans briefly. Then she carried a tin basin to the well nearby, where she filled it to the brim. Setting it down on the horse block, she rolled back her sleeves, tucked in the collar of her gray blouse, and plunged her face in the water. In a minute she came out of the kitchen freshened and smiling. 'Liza Harjo had been pulling dried bean stalks at one end of the field, and it was dirty work. At last old Harjo turned to Miss Evans and said, "These two my wife—this one 'Liza, this one Jennie."

It was done with simple dignity. Miss Evans bowed and stammered. Three pairs of eyes were turned upon her in patient, courteous inquiry.

It was hard to state the case. The old man was so evidently proud of his women, and so flattered by Miss Evans' interest in them, that he would find it hard to understand. Still, it had to be done, and Miss Evans took the plunge.

"Harjo, you want to come into our church?" The old man's face lighted.

"Oh, yes, I would come to Jesus, please, my friend."

"Do you know, Harjo, that the Lord commanded that one man should mate with but one woman?" The question was stated again in simpler terms, and the Indian replied, "Me know that now, my friend. Long time ago"—Harjo plainly meant the whole period previous to his conversion—"me did not know. The Lord Jesus did not speak to me in that time and so I was blind. I do what blind man do."

"Harjo, you must have only one wife when you come into our church. Can't you give up one of these women?" Miss Evans glanced at the two, sitting by with smiles of polite interest on their faces, understanding nothing. They had not shared Harjo's enthusiasm either for the white man's God or his language.

"Give up my wife?" A sly smile stole over his face. He leaned closer to Miss Evans. "You tell me, my friend, which one I give up." He glanced from 'Liza to Jennie as if to weigh their attractions, and the two rewarded him with their pleasantest smiles. "You tell me which one," he urged.

"Why, Harjo, how can I tell you!" Miss Evans had little sense of humor; she had taken the old man seriously.

"Then," Harjo sighed, continuing the comedy, for surely the missionary was jesting with him, " 'Liza and Jennie must say." He talked to the Indian women for a time, and they laughed heartily. 'Liza, pointing to the other, shook her head. At length Harjo explained, "My friend, they cannot say. Jennie, she would run a race to see which one stay, but 'Liza, she say no, she is fat and cannot run."

Miss Evans comprehended at last. She flushed angrily, and protested, "Harjo, you are making a mock of a sacred subject; I cannot allow you to talk like this."

"But did you not speak in fun, my friend?" Harjo queried, sobering. "Surely you have just said what your friend, the white woman at the mission [he meant Mrs. Rowell] would say, and you do not mean what you say."

"Yes, Harjo, I mean it. It is true that Mrs. Rowell raised the point first, but I agree with her. The church cannot be defiled by receiving a bigamist into its membership." Harjo saw that the young woman was serious, distressingly serious. He was silent for a long time, but at last he raised his head and spoke quietly, "It is not good to talk like that if it is not in fun."

He rose and went to the stable. As he led Miss Evans' horse up to the block it was champing a mouthful of corn, the last of a generous portion that Harjo had put before it. The Indian held the bridle and waited for Miss Evans to mount. She was embarrassed, humiliated, angry. It was absurd to be dismissed in this way by—"by an ignorant old bigamist!" Then the humor of it burst upon her, and its human aspect. In her anxiety concerning the spiritual welfare of the sinner Harjo, she had insulted the man Harjo. She began to understand why Mrs. Rowell had said that the old Indians were hopeless.

"Harjo," she begged, coming out of the passageway, "please forgive me. I do not want you to give up one of your wives. Just tell me why you took them."

"I will tell you that, my friend." The old Creek looped the reins over his arm and sat down on the block. "For thirty years Jennie has lived with me as my wife. She is of the Bear people, and she came to me when I was thirty-five and she was twenty-five. She could not come before, for her mother was old, very old, and Jennie, she stay with her and feed her.

"So, when I was thirty years old I took 'Liza for my woman. She is of the Crow people. She help me make this little farm here when there was no farm for many miles around.

"Well, five years 'Liza and me, we live here and work hard. But there was no child. Then the old mother of Jennie she died, and Jennie got no family left in this part of the country. So 'Liza say to me, 'Why don't you take Jennie in here?' I say, 'You don't care?' and she say, 'No, maybe we have children here then.' But we have no children—never have children. We do not like that, but God He would not let it be. So, we have lived here thirty years very happy. Only just now you make me sad."

"Harjo," cried Miss Evans, "forget what I said. Forget that you wanted to join the church." For a young mission worker with a single purpose always before her, Miss Evans was saying a strange thing. Yet she couldn't help saying it; all of her zeal seemed to have been dissipated by a simple statement of the old man.

"I cannot forget to love Jesus, and I want to be saved." Old Harjo spoke with solemn earnestness. The situation was distracting. On one side stood a convert eager for the protection of the church, asking only that he be allowed to fulfill the obligations of humanity and on the other stood the church, represented by Mrs. Rowell, that set an impossible condition on receiving old Harjo to itself. Miss Evans wanted to cry; prayer, she felt, would be entirely inadequate as a means of expression.

THE PROBLEM OF OLD HARJO

"Oh! Harjo," she cried out, "I don't know what to do. I must think it over and talk with Mrs. Rowell again."

But Mrs. Rowell could suggest no way out; Miss Evans' talk with her only gave the older woman another opportunity to preach the folly of wasting time on the old and "unreasonable" Indians. Certainly the church could not listen even to a hint of a compromise in this case. If Harjo wanted to be saved, there was one way and only one—unless—

"Is either of the two women old? I mean, so old that she is—an—"

"Not at all," answered Miss Evans. "They're both strong and—yes, happy. I think they will outlive Harjo."

"Can't you appeal to one of the women to go away? I dare say we could provide for her." Miss Evans, incongruously, remembered Jennie's jesting proposal to race for the right to stay with Harjo. What could the mission provide as a substitute for the little home that 'Liza had helped to create there in the edge of the woods? What other home would satisfy Jennie?

"Mrs. Rowell, are you sure that we ought to try to take one of Harjo's women from him? I'm not sure that it would in the least advance morality amongst the tribe, but I'm certain that it would make three gentle people unhappy for the rest of their lives."

"You may be right, Miss Evans." Mrs. Rowell was not seeking to create unhappiness, for enough of it inevitably came to be pictured in the little mission building. "You may be right," she repeated, "but it is a grievous misfortune that old Harjo should wish to unite with the church."

No one was more regular in his attendance at the mission meetings than old Harjo. Sitting well forward, he was always in plain view of Miss Evans at the organ. Before the service began, and after it was over, the old man greeted the young woman. There was never a spoken question, but in the Creek's eyes was always a mute inquiry.

Once Miss Evans ventured to write to her old pastor in New York, and explain her trouble. This was what he wrote in reply: "I am surprised that you are troubled, for I should have expected you to rejoice, as I do, over this new and wonderful evidence of the Lord's reforming power. Though the church cannot receive the old man so long as he is confessedly a bigamist and violator of his country's just laws, you should be greatly strengthened in your work through bringing him to desire salvation."

"Oh! it's easy to talk when you're free from responsibility!" cried out Miss Evans. "But I woke him up to a desire for this water of salvation that he cannot take. I have seen Harjo's home, and I know how cruel and useless it would be to urge him to give up what he loves—for he does love those two women who have spent half their lives and more with him. What, what can be done?"

Month after month, as old Harjo continued to occupy his seat in the mission meetings, with that mute appeal in his eyes and a persistent light of hope on his face, Miss Evans repeated the question, "What can be done?" If she was sometimes tempted to say to the old man, "Stop worrying about your soul; you'll get to Heaven as surely as any of us," there was always Mrs. Rowell to remind her that she was not a Mormon missionary. She could not run away from her perplexity. If she should secure a transfer to another station, she felt that Harjo would give up coming to the meetings, and in his despair become a positive influence for evil amongst his people. Mrs. Rowell would not waste her energy on an obstinate old man. No, Harjo was her creation, her impossible convert, and throughout the years, until death—the great solvent which is not always a solvent—came to one of them, would continue to haunt her.

And meanwhile, what?

JOHN M. OSKISON

The Singing Bird (1925)

Of the twenty-three stories included in this volume, about one-third feature strong women in central roles. Of those, an equal number are written about men and women—with perhaps a slight preponderance of male writers if one takes collaborative efforts into account. A central aspect of Native thought and consciousness is the perception of bravery and heroism as gender-free, Lakota warrior pronouncements beloved of American mass media portrayals of Native life notwithstanding. One of the more grievous effects of education in the ways of the white world has been the acceptance of patriarchal thought among Native men.

The lovely heroine of Oskison's story, small, lithe, and gay, moves with thoughtful care and determined courage to protect the weak—Lovely Daniel's sister, Betsy—and the strong—Jennie Blind-Wolfe's gigantic husband, Jim. In Jennie resides the ancient tribal value of honor, ripened in the warm blaze of devotion and respect. It is in her mind and heart, this story implies, that the sacred fire of the Kee-too-wah, the traditional center of the Cherokee, resides. More than sixty years after this story was written, the Kee-too-wah

thrive in Cherokee country and a brave and protective woman,
Wilma Mankiller, is Principal Chief of the Cherokee Nation.

"Now we talk, me and these Kee-too-wah fellows. Old
woman, go to bed!"

Thus Jim Blind-Wolfe dismissed his wife, Jennie, who was
not old. With the fleetest glancing look he pushed her gently
toward the back door of the firelit cabin, one huge outspread
hand covering both of her erect shoulders.

Big Jim, old Spring Frog, Panther, and The Miller made
up this inner, unofficial council of the Kee-too-wah organization that had met at Jim's cabin. Self-charged with the duty of
carrying out the ancient command to maintain amongst the
Cherokees the full-blood inheritance of race purity and race
ideals, they would discuss an alarming late growth of outlawry
in the tribe, an increase in crime due to idleness, drink, and certain disturbing white men who had established themselves in
the hills. Paradoxically, as they talked and planned secret pres-
sures here and there, they would pass a jug of honest
moonshine—but they would drink from it discreetly, lightly, as
full-blood gentlemen should!

"Jim," old Spring Frog opened, "I hear my friend say
something about that fellow you hit that day at Tahlequah—"

Jim's sudden, loud guffaw interrupted the old man.

"Him!" and Jim's scornful rumble summed up the case of
Lovely Daniel, a wild half-breed neighbor.

Smiling at the muffled sound of Jim's laugh, Jennie Blind-
Wolfe drew a gay shawl over the thick black hair that made a
shining crown for her cleanly modeled head and oval brown
face and went across, under the brilliant September starlight, to
the out cabin where she was to sleep. It was an inviting pine-log
room, pleasantly odorous of drying vegetables and smoked side
meat hung from rafters.

She stood for a minute on the solid adz-hewn step listening to the faint, unintelligible murmur of her husband's voice, the occasional comments of the others whom she had left crouched in front of glowing wood embers in the wide stone fireplace; to the music of Spavinaw creek racing over its rocky bed to Grand river; to the incessant, high-pitched chirring of crickets in the grass, the hysteric repetitions of katydids and the steady clamor of tree frogs yonder at the edge of the clearing.

A maddening sound, this all-night chorus of the little creatures of grass and forest! For ten nights, as she lay beside the relaxed bulk of her giant husband, she had strained her ears in the effort to hear above their din the sound of a horse's tramping at the timber edge and the sound of a man's footsteps coming across the dead grass of the clearing.

"Oh, why don't they stop! Why don't they stop!" she had cried, silently, in an agony of fear. But tonight—

No fear, no resentment of the chirring voices in the grass, the forest clatter; tonight she knew what was to happen. Tonight she would know the shivery terror, the illicit thrill of the singing bird, but she would not be afraid. Lovely Daniel had promised to come to her. Some time before dawn he would come to the edge of the clearing, repeat twice the call of the hoot-owl. He would come to the tiny window of the out cabin, and then—

Lovely had made a wonderful plan, a credit to his half-breed shrewdness, if not to his name! It had been born of his hatred of big Jim Blind-Wolfe and nourished by a growing fever of desire for Jennie. Enough of it he had revealed to Jennie to set her heart pounding, hang a fox-fire glow in her eyes.

She undressed in the streaming light of a moon just past the half and diamond bright stars that laid a brilliant oblong on the floor in front of the open door. Standing on a warm wolf rug beside the wide homemade bed, she stretched her lithe brown body. Then, comfortably relaxed, she recalled the beginning of Lovely's clever plan; a ripple of laughter, soft, enigmatic, rose to her lips.

The beginning dated from a torrid day of midsummer. The Cherokee tribal council was meeting in the box-like brick capitol, set among young oaks in a fenced square. In the shade, on the trampled grass of this capitol square, lounged a knot of councilmen, townsmen, gossips from the hill farms. Jim Blind-Wolfe—huge, smiling, dominating—was of the group, in which also stood Lovely Daniel. Alert, contentious, sharp of tongue, Lovely was sneering at the full-blood gospel that was being preached. Men grew restive under his jeers and mocking flings until at length Jim demanded the word. In slow, measured terms, as became a man of his impressive presence and bull-like voice, he summed up their drawn-out discussion:

"I tell you, Kee-too-wah fellows don't like this lease business. You lease your land to white man, and pretty soon you don't have any land; white man crowd you out! This here country is Eenyan (Indian) Country, set aside for Eenyans. We want to keep it always for Eenyans. Such is belief of Kee-too-wahs, and I am Kee-too-wah!"

These were the words Jim repeated when he told Jennie of what followed. He described Lovely Daniel's quick, angry rush toward him, and mimicked his sharp retort:

"Kee-too-wah fellows—hell! They think they run this here country." Jim could not reproduce the sneer that twisted the half-breed's mouth as he went on: "Kee-too-wahs are fools. White man goin' to come anyway. Jim Blind-Wolfe—huh! Biggest dam' fool of all!" He ended with an evil gesture, the sure insult, and Jim's sledgehammer fist swung smoothly against the side of his head. Lovely's body, lifted by the blow, was flung sprawling. He lay motionless.

"Jim!" cried old Spring Frog, "maybe so you kill that fellow. Bouff!—My God, I don't like."

Jim carried Lovely Daniel across the road to the porch of the National House, while young Hunt ran for Doctor Beavertail. That grave half-breed came, rolled up his sleeves, and set to work. His native skill, combined with his medical school knowledge, sufficed to bring Lovely back to consciousness by late afternoon.

Next morning, with the memory of Jim's devastating and widely advertised blow fresh in their minds, the councilmen—after much half-jesting and half-serious debate—passed a special Act and sent it to Chief Dennis for signature:

"It shall be unlawful for Jim Blind-Wolfe to strike a man with his closed fist!"

It was promptly signed and posted in the corridor of the capitol. Jim read it, and as he strode out into the square the thin line of his sparse mustache was lifted by a loud gust of laughter. Hailing the Chief, fifty yards away, he roared:

"Hey, Dennis, must I only slap that Lovely Daniel fellow next time?" The Chief met him at the center of the square. In an undertone, he undertook a friendly warning:

"You want to watch out for that Daniel fellow, Jim. You mighty nigh killed him, and—I kind of wish you had! He's bad. Bad—" the Chief repeated soberly, and came closer to impress Jim by his words—"We ain't got sure proof yet, but I'm satisfied it was Lovely Daniel that waylaid Blue Logan on the Fort Gibson road and killed him."

The Chief's low-toned confidences went on, and before he mounted the steps and went in to his battered old desk, he recalled:

"You have seen that Yellow Crest woman sometimes? She comes into town from the hills with stovewood and sits on her wagon, with a shawl always across her face. She was a pretty young woman six years ago, wife of Looney Squirrel. This Lovely Daniel took to hanging round, and Looney caught 'em—Yellow Crest and him. You are Kee-too-wah, Jim; you know what the old fellows do to a 'singing bird'?"

"Yes," Jim admitted, "they cut off the end of her nose!"

"Yes, they punish the woman so, and"—the Chief's face showed a shadow of passionate resentment—"they do nothing to the man! The old fellows, the Kee-too-wahs," he repeated, "still do that way. It was what Looney Squirrel did before he sent Yellow Crest from his cabin."

"Yes, I know," Jim assented.

"This Lovely Daniel is bad for women to know; a bad fellow for any woman to know, Jim!" The Chief eyed him shrewdly, pressed his piston-like arm in friendly emphasis before he walked slowly away.

On the long drive to his clearing beside Spavinaw creek, Jim weighed Chief Dennis' words. He thought of Jennie's fond care of Lovely Daniel's frail sister, Betsy, who was fighting a hopeless battle against tuberculosis in the cabin across the Spavinaw where she lived with Lovely.

"A bad fellow for any woman to know!" Jim repeated, with half-closed, contemplative eyes as he urged his tough pony team along the stony road. He would have to think about that. He would have to take more notice of his wife, too—that gay, slender, laughing young woman who kept his cabin, clung adoringly to him, her eyes dancing, and flashed into song with the sudden, clear burst of a red-bird in early spring—

Lovely as a menace to himself was one thing, he considered; foolishly, he refused to believe that he might be in serious danger from the half-breed; he believed that Lovely was a boaster, a coward, and that he would be afraid of the prompt vengeance of Jim's friends. But Lovely as a menace to Jennie—well, no friend would serve him here, either to warn, fear-ing his wrath and the tiger-swipe of his great hand, or to avenge!

In direct fashion, Jim spoke to Jennie of his encounter with the half-breed, and repeated the Chief's words of warning. A passing gleam of fear rounded her eyes as she listened; it changed to a gay, defiant smile when her man added:

"I think you better not go to see Betsy anymore."

"No?" she queried, then very gravely, "She is awful low, Jim, and I am her friend." She sat studying her husband's face for many minutes, turned to the pots hanging in the fireplace with a tiny, secret smile. "I am Betsy's best friend," she reiterated coaxingly.

"Well," Jim conceded, stretching his great bulk negligently, "you watch out for that fellow, her brother!"

Some days later, Jennie rode to the capitol, sought Chief Dennis and asked:

"Is Jim in real danger from Lovely Daniel?"

"I think maybe he is in great danger, Jennie; but Jim does not agree with me on that!" The Chief's slow smile was a tribute to her husband's careless bravery.

"Ah, that would make it easier for Lovely," she said to herself softly.

Jennie's thoughts drifted back to various occasions when she had visited Betsy Daniel. Sometimes, but not often, as she sat with her friend or busied herself sweeping and airing the cabin, preparing a bowl of hominy, putting on a pot of greens and bacon, stripping husks from roasting ears, helping on a patchwork quilt, Lovely would come in. He would squat, a thin handsome figure, in front of the fire, sniff eagerly at the cooking pots, rise, move restlessly about. He would speak with Jennie of his hunting; he would talk of the white men he knew at Vinita, some of whom came to the Spavinaw hills in the late fall to chase deer with him and encourage him to become active in tribal politics. These men wished to spur him to active opposition to the reactionary full-bloods, the Kee-too-wahs, who bitterly resented white intrusion.

When Jennie was ready to leave, he would bring her pony to the door, hold his hand for her to step on as she mounted, and he would turn glittering black eyes and grinning face up to her as she gathered the reins to ride away. She had known of Yellow Crest's punishment; she knew that the full-bloods called the deceiving wife a "singing bird," with notes to lure others than her mate; and in Lovely Daniel's eyes she had read an invitation to sing!

When Jim had thrashed the half-breed, she wondered if that invitation would still hold good. The end of her wondering and weighing was a resolve to find out.

Two weeks she waited and planned before riding across Spavinaw creek, and during that time news of Lovely Daniel drifted to her ears. He had crossed the line into Arkansas with one of the reckless Pigeon boys. They had secured whisky, had rioted in the streets of a border town, had been chased home to the hills by peace officers. The half-breed had brought back a new pistol from Maysville, and up and down the Illinois river and amongst his friends on Flint creek he had sprinkled ugly treats against Jim. In mid-August, when she knew that he was at home, Jennie rode across to Betsy.

For half an hour, as Jim Blind-Wolfe's wife made Betsy comfortable in a big chair beside the doorway and put the cabin to rights, Lovely sat on the doorstep digging at its worn surface with a pocket knife, saying nothing. Then he disappeared in the brush, to return presently with his saddle horse. At sunset, after Jennie had cleared away the early supper dishes and tucked Betsy into bed, he was waiting to ride with her. Eyes lowered, fingers nervously caressing her pony's mane, Jennie rode in silence. They crossed Spavinaw at the lonely ford, where she had often seen deer come down to drink, and went slowly up the steep, pine-covered slope. Near Jim's clearing she stopped. Without raising her eyes, she put out her hand.

"Now you go back," she half whispered. "I see you again." Lovely crowded his horse close, took her hand, muttered:

"Look up, Jennie, let me see what is in your eyes!" But she turned her head away and answered:

"I am afraid of you, Lovely—goodbye." She pressed his supple, eager fingers, urged her pony forward. He dared not pursue, and turned back; at the ford he whooped, uttering the primitive burst of sound that expressed for him hatred, lust, exultation. His wildcat eyes glowed. Back at his cabin, when he had loosed his hobbled horse to browse in the brush, he sat in the doorway conjuring up pictures of the evil he meant to do Jim Blind-Wolfe and his young and foolish wife. First, he would make Jennie a sinister, branded outcast in the sight of the tribe, and then after Jim had tasted that bitterness he would lay for him. There would be a shot. Someone would find him a stiffening corpse, beside a lonely road! Until long after the new moon had sunk he sat, at times crooning fragments of old Cherokee songs, or flinging an occasional gay word to Betsy.

At Jennie's next visit, Betsy sent her brother to the Eucha settlement store for medicine. He had scarcely gone when Betsy called Jennie to her side, looking searchingly into her face.

"You are very dear to me, Jennie," she said in Cherokee, her hand stroking the other's face, fever-glowing eyes and a strain of telltale red on her thin cheeks emphasizing her anxiety. "Will you promise me that you will be wise, and careful— with Lovely? I do not want to lose you for the little time left to me!"

Jennie put her arm about her friend's wasted shoulders and leaned to whisper:

"My sister, you will not lose me."

"But Lovely—he is wild—he is Jim Blind-Wolfe's enemy—and I am afraid." Her words were hesitant, but suggestive.

"You are my friend," Jennie assured her quickly. "What I do will be best for both of us—and Lovely, too! You will trust me?"

Betsy nodded, fell quiet under Jennie's gentle caresses.

Again Lovely rode across the ford with Jennie, rode close, begging for the promise that seemed to hang upon her lips, and before they parted she gave it, in a soft rush of speech:

"That will be hard, what you ask, Lovely, but sometime when Jim is not with me I will let you know!" The half-breed's whoop at the ford punctuated a snatch of song.

Jennie was committed now. She quieted Jim's vague uneasiness at her visits to the cabin, by emphasizing Betsy's need of her care and asserting that Lovely's behavior was correct. By cunning degrees, she led the half-breed to reveal his plan for squaring accounts with her husband—that is, the part involving Jim's assassination. To Lovely's passionate outburst of hate she replied crooningly:

"Yes, I know. He hurt you, Lovely!"

By late August, when dying summer had released upon the night myriad insect sounds, above whose clamorous fiddling and chirring casual noises were hard to distinguish, she had stirred Lovely to a very frenzy of impatience. More than the desire of vengeance drew him now. He wanted Jennie for herself. He had sworn to come to her when the new moon was as wide, at the center of its crescent, as the red ribbon that bound her hair. He would come to the edge of the clearing sometime before dawn—Jim would be asleep—and twice he would utter the hoot-owl's cry. She must slip out to him. If she did not, he swore that he would cross the clearing cat-footedly, open the door very slowly and quietly, come in and shoot Jim as he lay asleep. And then—

"Oh, no, not blood!" she cried, fighting desperately to al-ter his determination. He raved, boasted. She held out, pleading:

"No, no, not blood, in my sight! Wait until I come to you." As he persisted, she threatened: "If I hear you coming to the door, I will scream and Jim will rise up and kill you!"

Night after night she lay, sleeping fitfully, listening for the double owl cry, straining her ears to catch, above the high-pitched monotone of the insects' singing, the sound of footsteps in the dead grass. Twice during that time of waiting she visited Betsy and fought off Lovely's importunate advances with the warning:

"It must be safe—no blood. I will let you know."

The moon had filled its crescent, was swelling to fullness, before the opportunity Jennie had waited for arrived. Then Jim told her of the coming secret council in his cabin of the leaders of the Kee-too-wahs. They would eat supper and talk all night. She would prepare a pot of coffee for them, set it beside the fire, and go to sleep in the out cabin. She weighed the peril, decided, and slipped across to Spavinaw to tell Lovely Daniel:

"Come to the out cabin before dawn, as you have said. Come to the little window that looks toward the creek. Tap, and I will open and say if all is safe." In a quick upward glance from her lowered eyes, Jennie saw the half-breed's grin of triumph. Trembling, she sent him back to the ford and his whooping rush up the opposite slope. In his eyes she had read—love of her? Yes; and death for Jim! Lovely's hatred of the giant who had all but killed him with a blow of his fist had become a crackling blaze in his breast.

Ten days of strain and nights of broken sleep had fined the edges of Jennie's nerves. She lay quite wide awake now, certain of herself, confident, and now she did not care about the foolish insect noises. She leaned out of bed to place her deerskin slippers at just the spot she desired to have them and hang a warm shawl over a chair where she could seize it with one movement of her hand. Fingers clasped behind her head, she lay watching a little square of starlit and moonlit sky through the window.

A rooster's crowing announced midnight; a little later she heard Jim's heavy step on the east porch of the main cabin as he emerged to sniff the fresh air, and then the slam of the door as he went in; she was aware of the pleasantly nipping coolness of the period before daybreak; again there was a stir on the east porch.

Cold, passionless men's business Jim and his three companions were busy about now. Impersonal, free from individual angers, jealousies, attachments, they sat, like remote, secret gods, in judgment on the conduct of a community, the policy of a tribe. Kee-too-wah tradition, the old conception of tribal integrity, the clean spirit of ancestors who had successfully fought against race deterioration and the decay of morale in the long years of contact with the whites in Georgia and Tennessee—these were their preoccupations. They harked back to legendary days, to the very beginning, when the Great Spirit had handed over to the tribe a sacred fire, with the injunction to keep it burning forever; and they strove to keep alive in the minds of an easy-living, careless generation the memory of that road of Calvary over which their fathers and mothers had been driven when the then new Indian country was settled.

Jennie could understand but vaguely the purpose which dominated the four. It seemed shadowy, very different from the flaming, heart-stirring enterprise that concerned her! She lay taut-strung, like a bow made ready, thinking, feeling. Soon now, perhaps when the talk in the cabin had thinned and sleep was close to the eyelids of the four, she would hear a tapping at the window. She began to listen, to watch for a shadow at the little opening.

It came. Lovely's head and shoulders made a blur against

the small luminous square; his tapping was as light as the flick of a bird's wing, insistent as the drumming of the male partridge in spring. Jennie stepped into her slippers, flung the shawl about her shoulders, flitted silently to the window.

She would not let him in at once. She knew the steps which she must take in order to test his ardor, stir him to impetuous frenzy. She knew the privilege of her who turned singing bird to savor the preliminary delights of song! She pushed the tiny sliding window aside a crack and whispered:

"Who has come?" At Lovely's fatuous answer, she laughed a faint ghost laugh and breathed, "Why have you come?" Then, before he could speak, "No, don't tell me; wait and let me talk with you here for a time."

In throaty whispers, only half coherent, the man pressed his suit. Jennie went silent in the midst of his jumbled speeches, so stirred by inner turmoil that she scarcely heard his pleading. Then her trembling voice insisted:

"You must wait a little while longer, Lovely. I am afraid. But I will let you come in before it is light. I promise!" Her shawl was drawn across her face, and as she put timid fingers in his reaching hand he felt them shake. Again, in maddening repetition, she sang the refrain:

"Wait; and tell me once more what it is that you and I will do after tonight. Wait a little. I will not be afraid to let you in after a time." When he threatened to leave the window and go round to the door, she protested in great agitation:

"No, no. The bar is up against you, and if you rattle the door Jim will hear. He will come and spoil everything. He would"—her voice all but faded in her throat—"he would kill you, Lovely!"

At length the last note of the singing bird had been sounded, and Jennie answered to Lovely's frantic entreaty:

"Come now to the door swiftly and silently, in bare feet.

Leave your coat there." She pointed, and stood breathless, watching his movements. He dropped shoes, coat, belt, and pistol holster in a heap. With a gasp of relief, she ran to unbar the door.

"Quick!" she urged, pulling him into the blinding darkness. Then, close to his ear, "wait for me here!" She flashed by him, stepped through the doorway, closed him in, and reached up to trip the stout greased bar that she had prepared. It slid noiselessly across to engage iron stirrups fixed in the heavy door and the massive logs of the door frame. Clasping her shawl tightly about her body, she ran to the cabin where Jim and his three friends sat in silence, cross-legged in front of the fireplace. She opened the door and called:

"Jim!" He jerked his head up, rose. "Don't be troubled," she told the others. "Jim will be back soon." She shut the door as the great bulk of her husband emerged.

"Quick, Jim, come with me." She seized his big paw and dragged at it. "Quick! quick!" He followed at a lumbering trot, dazed and uttering fragments of questions. To the back of the out cabin she led him, ran to the dark heap of Lovely Daniel's clothes, seized belt, holster, and pistol and thrust them into Jim's hands.

"Here, what's this!" he bellowed. Inside there was the sound of bare feet rushing across the floor, an ineffectual yank at the door, a snarl of disappointed rage—then silence.

"Jim!" His wife was on tiptoe in the effort to bring her lips nearer to his ear.

"In there is Lovely Daniel. He came to kill you, Jim— Listen, Jim; he came to kill you, do you understand? I knew why he was coming and I—I made him believe I was a—a singing bird, Jim! And he came to me first. But I did not, Jim—I put down the outside bar that I had fixed, as soon as he came in, and ran to you. Come and see. Come and see how I fixed it." She pulled him round to the door, showed him the bar firm in its place. "See, I fixed it so to trap him. You see, Jim?"

A faint glimmer of daylight had come, and big Jim stooped to look into the shining eyes of his wife. His gaze was like a downthrust knife, cutting clean and deep into her soul. It found there only a turbulent fear for him, a sunburst of adoration that excited in him a surge of primitive joy. He came erect.

"Ah, you Lovely Daniel!" he shouted savagely. "You try to make singing bird out of my wife!" He broke into the old Cherokee killer's dread warning, the wild turkey's gobble.

With his hand on the door, and before he could lift the bar, he saw his friends emerge from the main cabin. Old Spring Frog peered round the corner from the east porch. He had heard the turkey gobbler signal! Jim thought swiftly; these men must not know that Lovely Daniel was in the out cabin, where his wife had slept. In a voice forced to calmness, he called to Spring Frog:

"I just now hear a big old gobbler, yonder." He pointed across the clearing toward the creek. The three returned to their places in front of the fire.

Jim flung up the outer bar, swung the door wide, and struck aside the knife-armed hand that leaped toward his breast. The weapon dropped, and Jim grabbed Lovely by the shirt to drag him forth.

"Put on your clothes," he ordered. With one hand helpless from the force of Jim's blow, the half-breed made slow progress with his dressing, and Jim had time to think, to make a little plan of his own. With shawl drawn closely about her body and over her head, Jennie stood waiting at the corner of the out cabin, watching the dawn change from gray to pink-shot silver.

Dressed, Lovely Daniel stood still, in a sort of frozen apathy, awaiting he wondered what terrible retribution. Jim grasped his arm, turned his head to speak to Jennie:

"Stay in here until I come." She disappeared into the shad-

owy cabin, closed the door, ran to crouch against the thick pillow and the rude headboard of the bed—and waited.

Jim led the half-breed round to the east porch of the main
cabin, opened the door and thrust him into view of his friends.
They looked up, curious, expectant.

"Ah," muttered Old Spring Frog, "I did hear what I
heard!"—Jim's warning gobble.

"This fellow"—Jim shoved Lovely Daniel close to the
cross-legged group—"come to kill me. My wife, she hear him
coming and she run to tell me just now." He fell silent, waited
for a minute, then:

"You know this fellow, what I done to him. You know
this fellow, how he kill Blue Logan, how he make Yellow Crest
outcast woman, how he make Looney Squirrel a man
ashamed— We get rid of this fellow?" The last words were more
a statement than a question, but his friends nodded assent.

"Let that be done." Old Spring Frog, staunch Kee-too-wah
defender of Indian probity, made a sign; it was repeated by Panther and The Miller. The three rose to stand beside Jim Blind-
Wolfe. Sure of his friends now, Jim's face framed a smile, a kind
of savage radiance. He spoke rapidly for a minute, reached for
the brown whisky jug that was a blob of darkness on the wide,
lighted hearth—the jug from which the four had drunk spar-
ingly throughout the night. Still smiling, he handed it to the
half-breed.

"This fellow like whisky—drink!" Lovely Daniel took the
jug, tilted it, and drank deep, the Adam's apple in his lean
throat working rhythmically as he gulped the raw, hot liquor.
When at last he removed the jug from his lips he shook it to
show how little remained. They would not say that he had been
afraid to drink! Jim's smile turned to a low laugh as he spoke
to his friends:

"I take this fellow outside now; you wait here for me few
minutes."

The two stepped out to the east porch, facing a fast-mounting radiance that presaged the coming of sunrise. Jim carried the half-breed's pistol. He led Lovely Daniel to the end of the porch; they stood in silence, Jim's eyes fixed on the other's face. At the edge of the clearing they heard a crow's awakening "caw! caw!" and the jarring call of a jaybird.

Jim spoke musingly, earnestly:

"Listen, Lovely Daniel: If you want to do that, you can go away from here—clear away from all Cherokee people, and I will not kill you!" Jim's stunning speech hung suspended, and Lovely's eyes sought his face; he resumed: "If you go away, it must be for all time. You must be outcast always. You try to come back, Kee-too-wah will know and I will then kill you. You know that?" The other nodded somberly. Jim spoke again, his gaze boring into eyes that wavered. "But I don't think you want to go away, like that, to stay always, lost man. Well, then?

"Listen, I will tell you one other way. Like this, Lovely Daniel—you can go up yonder, if you are brave man"—solemnly Jim pointed to the crimson-streaked sky—"on the back of the sun! Old Cherokee folks tell about how Eenyans go home to Great Spirit on the back of the sun. I don't know; maybe so; you can try. You try?" His face had become stern now, and menacing; he bent close to peer into the drink-flushed face of the half-breed.

Lovely Daniel weighed the alternatives swiftly. Reeling, aflame with the fiery liquid he had drunk, his mind seized upon Jim's suggestion.

"I go with the sun!" he cried, swaying toward the edge of the porch. Boastfully, exultantly, he demanded, "Give me my gun." Jim handed him the pistol, stepped backwards noiselessly, his eyes holding Lovely. His hand on the latch, he stopped.

Lovely Daniel's uninjured hand, loosely gripping the pistol, hung at his side as he watched the full daylight spread down to the edge of the clearing. Out of some deep, long-hidden spring of memory rose a fragment of wild song, a chant of death. It mounted to a fervid burst, as the sharp red edge of the sun appeared; it ended in a triumphant whoop—and the roar of the pistol, pressed against his temple, sent a perching crow whirling upwards with a startled "caw!"

Jim stepped inside.

"What was that?" Spring Frog questioned perfunctorily.

"Lovely Daniel was making answer," Jim responded enigmatically.

"Making answer? To what?"

"Oh, a singing bird, I think—early morning singing bird, I think." He looked into the faces of his friends until he knew that they understood, then turned to go out. He lingered to say:

"If you fellows go look out for that which was Lovely Daniel, I get my wife to come and cook breakfast for us."

He found Jennie still crouched on the bed, hands still clapped tight against her ears. He gathered her into his arms, a vast tenderness and a fierce pride in her courage thrilling through him. With her face buried beneath his cheek and her arms tight about his neck, he sat on the bed and whispered:

"All is well now, all is well!" Her convulsive hold on him tightened.

"Oh, my Jim!" she breathed fiercely and, after a minute, "I can go now and care for Betsy without fear."

"Yes." Jim's eyes sought the brilliant oblong of daylight that was the doorway, and his voice was tender and solemn as he added:

"You can go to Betsy now, and tell her that Lovely went home without fear, on the back of the sun. I think she will understand what you say—Pretty soon you come and cook breakfast?"

"Pretty soon, I come," she echoed and, shivering, settled even closer to the great bulk of her husband.

BLACK ELK AND JOHN G. NEIHARDT

The Great Vision (1932)

Born before the invading Anglo-Europeans had made deep incursions into his homelands on "the Great Sioux Reservation," Black Elk grew to manhood during the chaotic period when the Plains Native peoples were all but destroyed. Nearly forty years after the nineteenth-century version of nuclear winter hit the Plains, Black Elk shared the story of his boyhood and of those terrible times of war, dislocation, and reservation life with the white poet and writer John G. Neihardt.

Embarking upon one of the stranger of the many collaborations that have shaped Native literature in this century, the old holy man and the old poet worked: the one recounting, the other writing. But it was not quite so straightforward an exchange, for Black Elk's son Ben and Neihardt's daughter Enid were also involved in the process. The story went from Black Elk to Ben, from Ben to Enid's stenographer's pad, and from there to Neihardt. Dialogue became a sacred conversation, there on the windswept Plains of the early 1930s.

The narrative I have taken from an early portion of Black Elk Speaks *sets the tone for the rest of the book, and thus directs our attention to the underlying transformational nature of the events usually perceived as historical. But Black Elk knew the difference, as the details he chose to recount throughout the narrative make clear. Neihardt must also have known, for he took the accounts and shaped them into a book. As testimony to his comprehension, the book survived as an underground classic during the next few decades, to resurface stronger than before during the Native renaissance that has characterized the final three decades of the twentieth century.*

It should be noted by readers that The Vision is a man's vision, and as such revolves around male symbols and sacred understandings; this is not to say that it is chauvinistic, for such terms do not apply within Native narrative or transformational ritual structures. It is of the male tradition, rather than the female tradition; both are valid, each is precious, and together they "hold up the sky."

Neihardt thought that Black Elk foresaw World War II in the third ascent. In a footnote, Neihardt commented: "At this point Black Elk remarked: 'I think we are near that place now, and I am afraid something very bad is going to happen all over the world.' He cannot read and knows nothing of world affairs."

Blue and black are interchangeable words in Lakota; it is the road of destruction and war. The red road runs from south to north, and it is the path of life, in the mortal or mundane sense. The herb of understanding is composed of four blossoms on one stem: blue, white, scarlet, and yellow. It comes from the sky, and its radiance streams upward so that no place is dark. In North America the great flower sent to earth by a Lakota holy man has taken root. Its colors are the colors of maize, of the directions, and of the four races who together make up this nation. May that sacred herb take root in our hearts.

What happened after that until the summer I was nine years old is not a story. There were winters and summers, and they were good; for the Wasichus had made their iron road along the Platte and traveled there. This had cut the bison herd in two, but those that stayed in our country with us were more than could be counted, and we wandered without trouble in our land.

Now and then the voices would come back when I was out alone, like someone calling me, but what they wanted me to do I did not know. This did not happen very often, and when it did not happen, I forgot about it; for I was growing taller and was riding horses now and could shoot prairie chickens and rabbits with my bow. The boys of my people began very young to learn the ways of men, and no one taught us; we just learned by doing what we saw, and we were warriors at a time when boys now are like girls.

It was the summer when I was nine years old, and our people were moving slowly towards the Rocky Mountains. We camped one evening in a valley beside a little creek just before it ran into the Greasy Grass, and there was a man by the name of Man Hip who liked me and asked me to eat with him in his tipi.

While I was eating, a voice came and said: "It is time; now they are calling you." The voice was so loud and clear that I believed it, and I thought I would just go where it wanted me to go. So I got right up and started. As I came out of the tipi, both my thighs began to hurt me, and suddenly it was like waking from a dream, and there wasn't any voice. So I went back into the tipi, but I didn't want to eat. Man Hip looked at me in a strange way and asked me what was wrong. I told him that my legs were hurting me.

The next morning the camp moved again, and I was riding with some boys. We stopped to get a drink from a creek, and when I got off my horse, my legs crumpled under me and I could not walk. So the boys helped me up and put me on my horse; and when we camped again that evening, I was sick. The next day the camp moved on to where the different bands of our people were coming together, and I rode in a pony drag, for I was very sick. Both my legs and both my arms were swollen badly and my face was all puffed up.

When we had camped again, I was lying in our tipi and my mother and father were sitting beside me. I could see out through the opening, and there two men were coming from the clouds, headfirst like arrows slanting down, and I knew they were the same that I had seen before. Each now carried a long spear, and from the points of these a jagged lightning flashed. They came clear down to the ground this time and stood a little way off and looked at me and said: "Hurry! Come! Your Grandfathers are calling you!"

Then they turned and left the ground like arrows slanting upward from the bow. When I got up to follow, my legs did not hurt me anymore and I was very light. I went outside the tipi, and yonder where the men with flaming spears were going, a little cloud was coming very fast. It came and stooped and took me and turned back to where it came from, flying fast. And when I looked down I could see my mother and my father yonder, and I felt sorry to be leaving them.

Then there was nothing but the air and the swiftness of the little cloud that bore me and those two men still leading up to where white clouds were piled like mountains on a wide blue plain, and in them thunder beings lived and leaped and flashed.

Now suddenly there was nothing but a world of cloud, and we three were there alone in the middle of a great white plain with snowy hills and mountains staring at us; and it was very still; but there were whispers.

Then the two men spoke together and they said: "Behold him, the being with four legs!"

I looked and saw a bay horse standing there, and he began to speak: "Behold me!" he said. "My life history you shall see." Then he wheeled about to where the sun goes down, and said: "Behold them! Their history you shall know."

I looked, and there were twelve black horses yonder all abreast with necklaces of bison hooves, and they were beautiful, but I was frightened, because their manes were lightning and there was thunder in their nostrils.

Then the bay horse wheeled to where the great white giant lives (the north) and said: "Behold!" And yonder there were twelve white horses all abreast. Their manes were flowing like a blizzard wind and from their noses came a roaring, and all about them white geese soared and circled.

Then the bay wheeled round to where the sun shines continually (the east) and bade me look, and there twelve sorrel horses, with necklaces of elk's teeth, stood abreast with eyes that glimmered like the day-break star and manes of morning light.

Then the bay wheeled once again to look upon the place where you are always facing (the south), and yonder stood twelve buckskins all abreast with horns upon their heads and manes that lived and grew like trees and grasses.

And when I had seen all these, the bay horse said: "Your Grandfathers are having a council. These shall take you; so have courage."

Then all the horses went into formation, four abreast—the blacks, the whites, the sorrels, and the buckskins—and stood behind the bay, who turned now to the west and neighed, and yonder suddenly the sky was terrible with a storm of plunging horses in all colors that shook the world with thunder, neighing back.

Now turning to the north the bay horse whinnied, and yonder all the sky roared with a mighty wind of running horses in all colors, neighing back.

And when he whinnied to the east, there, too, the sky was filled with glowing clouds of manes and tails of horses in all colors singing back. Then to the south he called, and it was crowded with many colored, happy horses, nickering.

Then the bay horse spoke to me again and said: "See how your horses all come dancing!" I looked, and there were horses, horses everywhere—a whole skyful of horses dancing round me.

"Make haste!" the bay horse said, and we walked together side by side, while the blacks, the whites, the sorrels, and the buckskins followed, marching four by four.

I looked about me once again, and suddenly the dancing horses without number changed into animals of every kind and into all the fowls that are, and these fled back to the four quarters of the world from whence the horses came, and vanished.

Then as we walked, there was a heaped up cloud ahead that changed into a tipi, and a rainbow was the open door of it; and through the door I saw six old men sitting in a row.

The two men with the spears now stood beside me, one on either hand, and the horses took their places in their quarters, looking inward, four by four. And the oldest of the Grandfathers spoke with a kind voice and said: "Come right in and do not fear." And as he spoke, all the horses of the four quarters neighed to cheer me. So I went in and stood before the six, and they looked older than men can ever be—old like hills, like stars.

The oldest spoke again: "Your Grandfathers all over the world are having a council, and they have called you here to teach you." His voice was very kind, but I shook all over with fear now, for I knew that these were not old men, but the Powers of the World. And the first was the Power of the West; the second, of the North; the third, of the East; the fourth, of the South; the fifth, of the Sky; the sixth, of the Earth. I knew this, and was afraid, until the first Grandfather spoke again: "Behold them yonder where the sun goes down, the thunder beings! You shall see, and have from them my power; and they shall take you to the high and lonely center of the earth that you may see; even to the place where the sun continually shines, they shall take you there to understand."

And as he spoke of understanding, I looked up and saw the rainbow leap with flames of many colors over me.

Now there was a wooden cup in his hand and it was full of water and in the water was the sky.

"Take this," he said. "It is the power to make life, and it is yours."

Now he had a bow in his hands. "Take this," he said. "It is the power to destroy, and it is yours."

Then he pointed to himself and said: "Look close at him who is your spirit now, for you are his body and his name is Eagle Wing Stretches."

And saying this, he got up very tall and started running toward where the sun goes down, and suddenly he was a black horse that stopped and turned and looked at me, and the horse was very poor and sick; his ribs stood out.

Then the second Grandfather, he of the North, arose with a herb of power in his hand, and said: "Take this and hurry." I took and held it toward the black horse yonder. He fattened and was happy and came prancing to his place again and was the first Grandfather sitting there.

The second Grandfather, he of the North, spoke again: "Take courage, younger brother," he said, "on earth a nation you shall make live, for yours shall be the power of the white giant's wing, the cleansing wind." Then he got up very tall and started running toward the north, and when he turned toward me, it was a white goose wheeling. I looked about me now, and the horses in the west were thunders and the horses of the

north were geese. And the second Grandfather sang two songs
that were like this:

> They are appearing, may you behold!
> They are appearing, may you behold!
> The thunder nation is appearing, behold!

> They are appearing, may you behold!
> They are appearing, may you behold!
> The white geese nation is appearing, behold!

And now it was the third Grandfather who spoke, he of
where the sun shines continually. "Take courage, younger
brother," he said, "for across the earth they shall take you!"
Then he pointed to where the daybreak star was shining, and
beneath the star two men were flying. "From them you shall
have power," he said, "from them who have awakened all the
beings of the earth with roots and legs and wings." And as he
said this, he held in his hand a peace pipe which had a spotted
eagle outstretched upon the stem; and this eagle seemed alive,
for it was poised there, fluttering, and its eyes were looking at
me. "With this pipe," the Grandfather said, "you shall walk
upon the earth, and whatever sickens there you shall make
well." Then he pointed to a man who was bright red all over,
the color of good and of plenty, and as he pointed, the red man
lay down and rolled and changed into a bison that got up and
galloped toward the sorrel horses of the east, and they too
turned to bison, fat and many.

And now the fourth Grandfather spoke, he of the place
where you are always facing (the south), whence comes the
power to grow. "Younger brother," he said, "with the powers of
the four quarters you shall walk, a relative. Behold, the living
center of a nation I shall give you, and with it many you shall
save." And I saw that he was holding in his hand a bright red

stick that was alive, and as I looked it sprouted at the top and sent forth branches, and on the branches many leaves came out and murmured and in the leaves the birds began to sing. And then for just a little while I thought I saw beneath it in the shade the circled villages of people and every living thing with roots or legs or wings, and all were happy. "It shall stand in the center of the nation's circle," said the Grandfather, "a cane to walk with and a people's heart; and by your powers you shall make it blossom."

Then when he had been still a little while to hear the birds sing, he spoke again: "Behold the earth!" So I looked down and saw it lying yonder like a hoop of peoples, and in the center bloomed the holy stick that was a tree, and where it stood there crossed two roads, a red one and a black. "From where the giant lives (the north) to where you always face (the south) the red road goes, the road of good," the Grandfather said, "and on it shall your nation walk. The black road goes from where the thunder beings live (the west) to where the sun continually shines (the east), a fearful road, a road of troubles and of war. On this also you shall walk, and from it you shall have the power to destroy a people's foes. In four ascents you shall walk the earth with power."

I think he meant that I should see four generations, counting me, and now I am seeing the third.

Then he rose very tall and started running toward the south, and was an elk; and as he stood among the buckskins yonder, they too were elks.

Now the fifth Grandfather spoke, the oldest of them all, the Spirit of the Sky. "My boy," he said, "I have sent for you and you have come. My power you shall see!" He stretched his arms and turned into a spotted eagle hovering. "Behold," he said, "all the wings of the air shall come to you, and they and the winds and the stars shall be like relatives. You shall go across the earth with my power." Then the eagle soared above my head and fluttered there; and suddenly the sky was full of friendly wings all coming toward me.

Now I knew the sixth Grandfather was about to speak, he who was the Spirit of the Earth, and I saw that he was very old, but more as men are old. His hair was long and white, his face was all in wrinkles and his eyes were deep and dim. I stared at him, for it seemed I knew him somehow; and as I stared, he slowly changed, for he was growing backwards into youth, and when he had become a boy, I knew that he was myself with all the years that would be mine at last. When he was old again, he said: "My boy, have courage, for my power shall be yours, and you shall need it, for your nation on the earth will have great troubles. Come."

He rose and tottered out through the rainbow door, and as I followed I was riding on the bay horse who had talked to me at first and led me to that place.

Then the bay horse stopped and faced the black horses of the west, and a voice said: "They have given you the cup of water to make live the greening day, and also the bow and arrow to destroy." The bay neighed, and the twelve black horses came and stood behind me, four abreast.

The bay faced the sorrels of the east, and I saw that they had morning stars upon their foreheads and they were very bright. And the voice said: "They have given you the sacred pipe and the power that is peace, and the good red day." The bay neighed, and the twelve sorrels stood behind me, four abreast.

My horse now faced the buckskins of the south, and a voice said: "They have given you the sacred stick and your nation's hoop, and the yellow day; and in the center of the hoop you shall set the stick and make it grow into a shielding tree, and bloom." The bay neighed, and the twelve buckskins came and stood behind me, four abreast.

Then I knew that there were riders on all the horses there

behind me, and a voice said: "Now you shall walk the black road with these; and as you walk, all the nations that have roots or legs or wings shall fear you."

So I started, riding toward the east down the fearful road, and behind me came the horsebacks four abreast—the blacks, the whites, the sorrels, and the buckskins—and far away above the fearful road the daybreak star was rising very dim.

I looked below me where the earth was silent in a sick green light, and saw the hills look up afraid and the grasses on the hills and all the animals; and everywhere about me were the cries of frightened birds and sounds of fleeing wings. I was the chief of all the heavens riding there, and when I looked behind me, all the twelve black horses reared and plunged and thundered and their manes and tails were whirling hail and their nostrils snorted lightning. And when I looked below again, I saw the slant hail falling and the long, sharp rain, and where we passed, the trees bowed low and all the hills were dim.

Now the earth was bright again as we rode. I could see the hills and valleys and the creeks and rivers passing under. We came above a place where three streams made a big one—a source of mighty waters—and something terrible was there. Flames were rising from the waters and in the flames a blue man lived. The dust was floating all about him in the air, the grass was short and withered, the trees were wilting, two-legged and four-legged beings lay there thin and panting, and wings too weak to fly.

Then the black horse riders shouted "Hoka hey!" and charged down upon the blue man, but were driven back. And the white troop shouted, charging, and was beaten; then the red troop and the yellow.

And when each had failed, they all cried together: "Eagle Wing Stretches, hurry!" And all the world was filled with voices of all kinds that cheered me, so I charged. I had the cup of water in one hand and in the other was the bow that turned into a spear as the bay and I swooped down, and the spear's head was sharp lightning. It stabbed the blue man's heart, and as it struck I could hear the thunder rolling and many voices that cried "Un-hee!" meaning I had killed. The flames died. The trees and grasses were not withered anymore and murmured happily together, and every living being cried in gladness with whatever voice it had. Then the four troops of horsemen charged down and struck the dead body of the blue man, counting coup; and suddenly it was only a harmless turtle.

You see, I had been riding with the storm clouds, and had come to earth as rain, and it was drought that I had killed with the power that the Six Grandfathers gave me. So we were riding on the earth now down along the river flowing full from the source of waters, and soon I saw ahead the circled village of a people in the valley. And a Voice said: "Behold a nation; it is yours. Make haste, Eagle Wing Stretches!"

I entered the village, riding, with the four horse troops behind me—the blacks, the whites, the sorrels, and the buckskins; and the place was filled with moaning and with mourning for the dead. The wind was blowing from the south like fever, and when I looked around I saw that in nearly every tipi the women and the children and the men lay dying with the dead.

So I rode around the circle of the village, looking in upon the sick and dead, and I felt like crying as I rode. But when I looked behind me, all the women and the children and the men were getting up and coming forth with happy faces.

And a Voice said: "Behold, they have given you the center of the nation's hoop to make it live."

So I rode to the center of the village, with the horse troops in their quarters round about me, and there the people gathered. And the Voice said: "Give them now the flowering stick that they may flourish, and the sacred pipe that they may know the power that is peace, and the wing of the white giant that they may have endurance and face all winds with courage."

So I took the bright red stick and at the center of the nation's hoop I thrust it in the earth. As it touched the earth it
leaped mightily in my hand and was a waga chun, the rustling
tree, very tall and full of leafy branches and of all birds singing.
And beneath it all the animals were mingling with the people
like relatives and making happy cries. The women raised their
tremolo of joy, and the men shouted all together: "Here we
shall raise our children and be as little chickens under the
mother sheo's wing."

Then I heard the white wind blowing gently through the
tree and singing there, and from the east the sacred pipe came
flying on its eagle wings, and stopped before me there beneath
the tree, spreading deep peace around it.

Then the daybreak star was rising, and a Voice said: "It
shall be a relative to them; and who shall see it, shall see much
more, for thence comes wisdom; and those who do not see it
shall be dark." And all the people raised their faces to the east,
and the star's light fell upon them, and all the dogs barked
loudly and the horses whinnied.

Then when the many little voices ceased, the great Voice
said: "Behold the circle of the nation's hoop, for it is holy, being endless, and thus all powers shall be one power in the people without end. Now they shall break camp and go forth upon
the red road, and your Grandfathers shall walk with them."
So the people broke camp and took the good road with the
white wing on their faces, and the order of their going was like
this:

First, the black horse riders with the cup of water; and the
white horse riders with the white wing and the sacred herb; and
the sorrel riders with the holy pipe; and the buckskins with the
flowering stick. And after these the little children and the
youths and maidens followed in a band.

Second, came the tribe's four chieftains, and their band
was all young men and women.

Third, the nation's four advisers leading men and women neither young nor old.

Fourth, the old men hobbling with their canes and looking to the earth.

Fifth, old women hobbling with their canes and looking to the earth.

Sixth, myself all alone upon the bay with the bow and arrows that the First Grandfather gave me. But I was not the last, for when I looked behind me there were ghosts of people like a trailing fog as far as I could see—grandfathers of grandfathers and grandmothers of grandmothers without number. And over these a great Voice—the Voice that was the South—lived, and I could feel it silent.

And as we went the Voice behind me said: "Behold a good nation walking in a sacred manner in a good land!"

Then I looked up and saw that there were four ascents ahead, and these were generations I should know. Now we were on the first ascent, and all the land was green. And as the long line climbed, all the old men and women raised their hands, palms forward, to the far sky yonder and began to croon a song together, and the sky ahead was filled with clouds of baby faces.

When we came to the end of the first ascent we camped in the sacred circle as before, and in the center stood the holy tree, and still the land about us was all green.

Then we started on the second ascent, marching as before, and still the land was green, but it was getting steeper. And as I looked ahead, the people changed into elks and bison and all four-footed beings and even into fowls, all walking in a sacred manner on the good red road together. And I myself was a spotted eagle soaring over them. But just before we stopped to camp at the end of that ascent, all the marching animals grew restless and afraid that they were not what they had been, and began sending forth voices of trouble, calling to their chiefs. And when they camped at the end of that ascent, I looked down and saw that leaves were falling from the holy tree.

And the Voice said: "Behold your nation, and remember what your Six Grandfathers gave you, for thenceforth your people walk in difficulties."

Then the people broke camp again, and saw the black road before them towards where the sun goes down, and black clouds coming yonder; and they did not want to go but could not stay. And as they walked the third ascent, all the animals and fowls that were the people ran here and there, for each one seemed to have his own little vision that he followed and his own rules; and all over the universe I could hear the winds at war like wild beasts fighting.

And when we reached the summit of the third ascent and camped, the nation's hoop was broken like a ring of smoke that spreads and scatters and the holy tree seemed dying and all its birds were gone. And when I looked ahead I saw that the fourth ascent would be terrible.

Then when the people were getting ready to begin the fourth ascent, the Voice spoke like someone weeping, and it said: "Look there upon your nation." And when I looked down, the people were all changed back to human, and they were thin, their faces sharp, for they were starving. Their ponies were only hide and bones, and the holy tree was gone.

And as I looked and wept, I saw that there stood on the north side of the starving camp a sacred man who was painted red all over his body, and he held a spear as he walked into the center of the people, and there he lay down and rolled. And when he got up, it was a fat bison standing there, and where the bison stood a sacred herb sprang up right where the tree had been in the center of the nation's hoop. The herb grew and bore four blossoms on a single stem while I was looking—a blue, a white, a scarlet, and a yellow—and the bright rays of these flashed to the heavens.

I know now what this meant, that the bison were the gift of a good spirit and were our strength, but we should lose them, and from the same good spirit we must find another strength. For the people all seemed better when the herb had grown and bloomed, and the horses raised their tails and neighed and pranced around, and I could see a light breeze going from the north among the people like a ghost; and suddenly the flowering tree was there again at the center of the nation's hoop where the four-rayed herb had blossomed.

I was still the spotted eagle floating, and I could see that I was already in the fourth ascent and the people were camping yonder at the top of the third long rise. It was dark and terrible about me, for all the winds of the world were fighting. It was like rapid gunfire and like whirling smoke, and like women and children wailing and like horses screaming all over the world.

I could see my people yonder running about, setting the smoke-flap poles and fastening down their tipis against the wind, for the storm cloud was coming on them very fast and black, and there were frightened swallows without number fleeing before the cloud.

Then a song of power came to me and I sang it there in the midst of that terrible place where I was. It went like this:

A good nation I will make live.
This the nation above has said.
They have given me the power to make over.

And when I had sung this, a Voice said: "To the four quarters you shall run for help, and nothing shall be strong before you. Behold him!"

Now I was on my bay horse again, because the horse is of the earth, and it was there my power would be used. And as I obeyed the Voice and looked, there was a horse all skin and bones yonder in the west, a faded brownish black. And a Voice there said: "Take this and make him over; and it was the four-rayed herb that I was holding in my hand. So I rode above the poor horse in a circle, and as I did this I could hear the people yonder calling for spirit power, "A-hey! a-hey! a-hey! a-hey!" Then the poor horse neighed and rolled and got up, and he was a big, shiny, black stallion with dapples all over him and his mane about him like a cloud. He was the chief of all the horses, and when he snorted, it was a flash of lightning and his eyes were like the sunset star. He dashed to the west and neighed, and the west was filled with a dust of hooves, and horses without number, shiny black, came plunging from the dust. Then he dashed toward the north and neighed, and to the east and to the south, and the dust clouds answered, giving forth their plunging horses without number—whites and sorrels and buckskins, fat, shiny, rejoicing in their fleetness and their strength. It was beautiful, but it was also terrible.

Then they all stopped short, rearing, and were standing in a great hoop about their black chief at the center, and were still. And as they stood, four virgins, more beautiful than women of the earth can be, came through the circle, dressed in scarlet, one from each of the four quarters, and stood about the great black stallion in their places; and one held the wooden cup of water, and one the white wing, and one the pipe, and one the nation's hoop. All the universe was silent, listening; and then the great black stallion raised his voice and sang. The song he sang was this:

My horses, prancing they are coming.
My horses, neighing they are coming;
Prancing, they are coming.
All over the universe they come.
They will dance; may you behold them.
(4 times)

> A horse nation, they will dance. May you behold
> them.
>
> *(4 times)*

His voice was not loud, but it went all over the universe and filled it. There was nothing that did not hear, and it was more beautiful than anything can be. It was so beautiful that nothing anywhere could keep from dancing. The virgins danced, and all the circled horses. The leaves on the trees, the grasses on the hills and in the valleys, the waters in the creeks and in the rivers and the lakes, the four-legged and the two-legged and the wings of the air—all danced together to the music of the stallion's song.

And when I looked down upon my people yonder, the cloud passed over, blessing them with friendly rain, and stood in the east with a flaming rainbow over it.

Then all the horses went singing back to their places beyond the summit of the fourth ascent, and all things sang along with them as they walked.

And a Voice said: "All over the universe they have finished a day of happiness." And looking down I saw that the whole wide circle of the day was beautiful and green, with all fruits growing and all things kind and happy.

Then a Voice said: "Behold this day, for it is yours to make. Now you shall stand upon the center of the earth to see, for there they are taking you."

I was still on my bay horse, and once more I felt the riders of the west, the north, the east, the south, behind me in formation, as before, and we were going east. I looked ahead and saw the mountains there with rocks and forests on them, and from the mountains flashed all colors upward to the heavens. Then I was standing on the highest mountain of them all, and round about beneath me was the whole hoop of the world. And while I stood there I saw more than I can tell and I understood more than I saw; for I was seeing in a sacred manner the shapes of all things in the spirit, and the shape of all shapes as they must live together like one being. And I saw that the sacred hoop of my people was one of many hoops that made one circle, wide as daylight and as starlight, and in the center grew one mighty flowering tree to shelter all the children of one mother and one father. And I saw that it was holy.

Then as I stood there, two men were coming from the east, head first like arrows flying, and between them rose the day-break star. They came and gave a herb to me and said: "With this on earth you shall undertake anything and do it." It was the day-break-star herb, the herb of understanding, and they told me to drop it on the earth. I saw it falling far, and when it struck the earth it rooted and grew and flowered, four blossoms on one stem, a blue, a white, a scarlet, and a yellow; and the rays from these streamed upward to the heavens so that all creatures saw it and in no place was there darkness.

Then the Voice said: "Your Six Grandfathers—now you shall go back to them."

I had not noticed how I was dressed until now, and I saw that I was painted red all over, and my joints were painted black, with white stripes between the joints. My bay had lightning stripes all over him, and his mane was cloud. And when I breathed, my breath was lightning.

Now two men were leading me, headfirst like arrows slanting upward—the two that brought me from the earth. And as I followed on the bay, they turned into four flocks of geese that flew in circles, one above each quarter, sending forth a sacred voice as they flew: Br-r-r-p, br-r-r-p, br-r-r-p, br-r-r-p!

Then I saw ahead the rainbow flaming above the tipi of the Six Grandfathers, built and roofed with cloud and sewed with thongs of lightning; and underneath it were all the wings of the air and under them the animals and men. All these were rejoicing, and thunder was like happy laughter.

As I rode in through the rainbow door, there were cheering voices from all over the universe, and I saw the Six Grandfathers sitting in a row, with their arms held toward me and their hands, palms out; and behind them in the cloud were faces thronging, without number, of the people yet to be.

"He has triumphed!" cried the six together, making thunder. And as I passed before them there, each gave again the gift that he had given me before—the cup of water and the bow and arrows, the power to make live and to destroy; the white wing of cleansing and the healing herb; the sacred pipe; the flowering stick. And each one spoke in turn from west to south, explaining what he gave as he had done before, and as each one spoke he melted down into the earth and rose again; and as each did this, I felt nearer to the earth.

Then the oldest of them all said: "Grandson, all over the universe you have seen. Now you shall go back with power to the place from whence you came, and it shall happen yonder that hundreds shall be sacred, hundreds shall be flames! Behold!"

I looked below and saw my people there, and all were well and happy except one, and he was lying like the dead—and that one was myself. Then the oldest Grandfather sang, and his song was like this:

There is someone lying on earth in a sacred manner.
There is someone—on earth he lies.
In a sacred manner I have made him to walk.

Now the tipi, built and roofed with cloud, began to sway back and forth as in a wind, and the flaming rainbow door was growing dimmer. I could hear voices of all kinds crying from outside: "Eagle Wing Stretches is coming forth! Behold him!"

When I went through the door, the face of the day of earth was appearing with the day-break star upon its forehead;

and the sun leaped up and looked upon me, and I was going forth alone.

And as I walked alone, I heard the sun singing as it arose, and it sang like this:

With visible face I am appearing.
In a sacred manner I appear.
For the greening earth a pleasantness I make.
The center of the nation's hoop I have made pleas-
      ant.
With visible face, behold me!
The four-leggeds and two-leggeds, I have made them
      to walk;
The wings of the air, I have made them to fly.
With visible face I appear.
My day, I have made it holy.

When the singing stopped, I was feeling lost and very lonely. Then a Voice above me said: "Look back!" It was a spotted eagle that was hovering over me and spoke. I looked, and where the flaming rainbow tipi, built and roofed with cloud, had been, I saw only the tall rock mountain at the center of the world.

I was all alone on a broad plain now with my feet upon the earth, alone but for the spotted eagle guarding me. I could see my people's village far ahead, and I walked very fast, for I was homesick now. Then I saw my own tipi, and inside I saw my mother and my father bending over a sick boy that was myself. And as I entered the tipi, some one was saying: "The boy is coming to; you had better give him some water."

Then I was sitting up; and I was sad because my mother and my father didn't seem to know I had been so far away.

ZITKALA-ŠA

The Widespread Enigma Concerning Blue-Star Woman (1921)

Identity, about which this story revolves, is the most enigmatic of matters in the chaotic period of the nineteenth and twentieth centuries—and not only in North America. Populations on the move, whether by choice, by circumstance, or by force, whether geographically, psychologically, or spiritually, give rise to a shifting sense of self and to the recognition by one's society of the fundamental fact of being. So Blue-Star Woman thinks: "I am a being." We are assured that this is a story about transformation when she mutters, "The times are changed now.... My individual name seems to mean nothing." She is to be defrauded—not because she has or hasn't a valid claim to her piece of land but because a grand trick is being played out in the lives of multitudes of hapless human beings. The trick is part of Coyote's whimsical magic, and pain and suffering are inexorably involved. We see Grandfather Coyote's hand in the appearance of two young men—another clue that something sacred is going on, for the twins and the grandmother are ancient figures in the Native sacred tradition all over the hemisphere. These men are "almost white men," sort of like

Lovely Daniel in "The Singing Spirit" was almost Cherokee, like Blue-Star Woman is almost Sioux.

Of course, the trickster among the Lakota is Spider Man, Iktome, but his magical processes and Coyote's are similar: When Iktome is around, all bets are off. In the end the trick works for Blue-Star Woman, though it brings a death. And in the end, as is forever the case in trickster stories, nothing is resolved; the enigma only deepens. One can be certain of this: When identity begins to shift, something sacred is afoot!

It was summer on the western plains. Fields of golden sunflowers facing eastward, greeted the rising sun. Blue-Star Woman, with windshorn braids of white hair over each ear, sat in the shade of her log hut before an open fire. Lonely but unmolested she dwelt here like the ground squirrel that took its abode nearby—both through the easy tolerance of the landowner. The Indian woman held a skillet over the burning embers. A large round cake, with long slashes in its center, was baking and crowding the capacity of the frying pan.

In deep abstraction Blue-Star Woman prepared her morning meal. "Who am I?" had become the obsessing riddle of her life. She was no longer a young woman, being in her fifty-third year. In the eyes of the white man's law, it was required of her to give proof of her membership in the Sioux tribe. The unwritten law of heart prompted her naturally to say, "I am a being. I am Blue-Star Woman. A piece of earth is my birthright."

It was taught for reasons now forgot that an Indian should never pronounce his or her name in answer to any inquiry. It was probably a means of protection in the days of black magic. Be this as it may, Blue-Star Woman lived in times when this teaching was disregarded. It gained her nothing, however, to pronounce her name to the government official to whom she applied for her share of tribal land. His persistent question was always, "Who were your parents?"

Blue-Star Woman was left an orphan at a tender age. She did not remember them. They were long gone to the spirit-land—and she could not understand why they should be recalled to earth on her account. It was another one of the old, old teachings of her race that the names of the dead should not be idly spoken. It had become a sacrilege to mention carelessly the name of any departed one, especially in matters of disputes over worldly possessions. The unfortunate circumstances of her early childhood, together with the lack of written records of a roving people, placed a formidable barrier between her and her heritage. The fact was events of far greater importance to the tribe than her reincarnation had passed unrecorded in books. The verbal reports of the old-time men and women of the tribe were varied—some were actually contradictory. Blue-Star Woman was unable to find even a twig of her family tree.

She sharpened one end of a long stick and with it speared the fried bread when it was browned. Heedless of the hot bread's "Tsing!" in a high treble as it was lifted from the fire, she added it to the six others which had preceded it. It had been many a moon since she had had a meal of fried bread, for she was too poor to buy at any one time all the necessary ingredients, particularly the fat in which to fry it. During the breadmaking, the smoke-blackened coffeepot boiled over. The aroma of freshly made coffee smote her nostrils and roused her from the tantalizing memories.

The day before, friendly spirits, the unseen ones, had guided her aimless footsteps to her Indian neighbor's house. No sooner had she entered than she saw on the table some grocery bundles. "Iye-que, fortunate one!" she exclaimed as she took the straight-backed chair offered her. At once the Indian hostess untied the bundles and measured out a cupful of green coffee beans and a pound of lard. She gave them to Blue-Star Woman, saying, "I want to share my good fortune. Take these home with you." Thus it was that Blue-Star Woman had come into unexpected possession of the materials which now contributed richly to her breakfast.

The generosity of her friend had often saved her from starvation. Generosity is said to be a fault of Indian people, but neither the Pilgrim Fathers nor Blue-Star Woman ever held it seriously against them. Blue-Star Woman was even grateful for this gift of food. She was fond of coffee, that black drink brought hither by those daring voyagers of long ago. The coffee habit was one of the signs of her progress in the white man's civilization, also had she emerged from the tipi into a log hut, another achievement. She had learned to read the primer and to write her name. Little Blue-Star attended school unhindered by a fond mother's fears that a foreign teacher might not spare the rod with her darling.

Blue-Star Woman was her individual name. For untold ages the Indian race had not used family names. A new-born child was given a brand-new name. Blue-Star Woman was proud to write her name for which she would not be required to substitute another's upon her marriage, as is the custom of civilized peoples.

"The times are changed now," she muttered under her breath. "My individual name seems to mean nothing." Looking out into space, she saw the nodding sunflowers, and they acquiesced with her. Their drying leaves reminded her of the near approach of autumn. Then soon, very soon, the ice would freeze along the banks of the muddy river. The day of the first ice was her birthday. She would be fifty-four winters old. How futile had been all these winters to secure her a share in tribal lands. A weary smile flickered across her face as she sat there on the ground like a bronze figure of patience and long-suffering.

The breadmaking was finished. The skillet was set aside to cool. She poured the appetizing coffee into her tin cup. With fried bread and black coffee she regaled herself. Again her mind reverted to her riddle. "The missionary preacher said he could not explain the white man's law to me. He who reads daily from the Holy Bible, which he tells me is God's book, cannot understand mere man's laws. This also puzzles me," thought she to herself. "Once a wise leader of our people, addressing a president of this country, said: 'I am a man. You are another. The Great Spirit is our witness!' This is simple and easy to understand, but the times are changed. The white man's laws are strange."

Blue-Star Woman broke off a piece of fried bread between a thumb and forefinger. She ate it hungrily, and sipped from her cup of fragrant coffee. "I do not understand the white man's law. It's like walking in the dark. In this darkness, I am growing fearful of everything."

Oblivious to the world, she had not heard the footfall of two Indian men who now stood before her.

Their short-cropped hair looked blue-black in contrast to the faded civilian clothes they wore. Their white man's shoes were rusty and unpolished. To the unconventional eyes of the old Indian woman, their celluloid collars appeared like shining marks of civilization. Blue-Star Woman looked up from the lap of mother earth without rising. "Hinnu, hinnu!" she ejaculated in undisguised surprise. "Pray, who are these would-be white men?" she inquired.

In one voice and by an assumed relationship the two Indian men addressed her. "Aunt, I shake hands with you." Again Blue-Star Woman remarked, "Oh, indeed! these near white men speak my Native tongue and shake hands according to our custom." Did she guess the truth, she would have known they were simply deluded mortals, deceiving others and themselves most of all. Boisterously laughing and making conversation, they each in turn gripped her withered hand.

Like a sudden flurry of wind, tossing loose ends of things,

they broke into her quiet morning hour and threw her groping thoughts into greater chaos. Masking their real errand with long-drawn faces, they feigned a concern for her welfare only. "We come to ask how you are living. We heard you were slowly starving to death. We heard you are one of those Indians who have been cheated out of their share in tribal lands by the government officials."

Blue-Star Woman became intensely interested.

"You see we are educated in the white man's ways," they said with protruding chests. One unconsciously thrust his thumbs into the armholes of his ill-fitting coat and strutted about in his pride. "We can help you get your land. We want to help our aunt. All old people like you ought to be helped before the younger ones. The old will die soon, and they may never get the benefit of their land unless someone like us helps them to get their rights, without further delay."

Blue-Star Woman listened attentively.

Motioning to the mats she spread upon the ground, she said: "Be seated, my nephews." She accepted the relationship assumed for the occasion. "I will give you some breakfast." Quickly she set before them a generous helping of fried bread and cups of coffee. Resuming her own meal, she continued, "You are wonderfully kind. It is true, my nephews, that I have grown old trying to secure my share of land. It may not be long till I shall pass under the sod."

The two men responded with "How, how," which meant "Go on with your story. We are all ears." Blue-Star Woman had not yet detected any particular sharpness about their ears, but by an impulse she looked up into their faces and scrutinized them. They were busily engaged in eating. Their eyes were fast upon the food on the mat in front of their crossed shins. Inwardly she made a passing observation how, like ravenous wolves, her nephews devoured their food. Coyotes in midwinter could not have been more starved. Without comment she offered them the remaining fried cakes, and between them they took it all. She offered the second helping of coffee, which they accepted without hesitancy. Filling their cups, she placed her empty coffeepot on the dead ashes.

To them she rehearsed her many hardships. It had become a habit now to tell her long story of disappointments with all its petty details. It was only another instance of good intentions gone awry. It was a paradox upon a land of prophecy that its path to future glory be stained with the blood of its aborigines. Incongruous as it is, the two nephews, with their white associates, were glad of a condition so profitable to them. Their solicitation for Blue-Star Woman was not at all altruistic. They thrived in their grafting business. They and their occupation were the by-product of an unwieldly bureaucracy over the nation's wards.

"Dear Aunt, you failed to establish the facts of your identity," they told her. Hereupon Blue-Star Woman's countenance fell. It was ever the same old words. It was the old song of the government official she loathed to hear. The next remark restored her courage. "If anyone can discover evidence, it's us! I tell you, aunt, we'll fix it all up for you." It was a great relief to the old Indian woman to be thus unburdened of her riddle, with a prospect of possessing land. "There is one thing you will have to do—that is, to pay us half of your land and money when you get them." Here was a pause, and Blue-Star Woman answered slowly, "Y-e-s," in an uncertain frame of mind.

The shrewd schemers noted her behavior. "Wouldn't you rather have a half of a crust of bread than none at all?" they asked. She was duly impressed with the force of their argument. In her heart she agreed, "A little something to eat is better than nothing!" The two men talked in regular relays. The flow of smooth words was continuous and so much like purring that all the woman's suspicions were put soundly to sleep. "Look here, aunt, you knew very well that prairie fire is met with a back-fire." Blue-Star Woman, recalling her experiences in fire fighting, quickly responded, "Yes, oh, yes."

"In just the same way, we fight crooks with crooks. We have clever white lawyers working with us. They are the back-fire." Then, as if remembering some particular incident, they both laughed aloud and said, "Yes, and sometimes they use us as the back-fire! We trade fifty-fifty."

Blue-Star Woman sat with her chin in the palm of one hand with elbow resting in the other. She rocked herself slightly forward and backward. At length she answered, "Yes, I will pay you half of my share in tribal land and money when I get them. In bygone days, brave young men of the order of the White-Horse-Riders sought out the aged, the poor, the widows and orphans to aid them, but they did their good work without pay. The White-Horse-Riders are gone. The times are changed. I am a poor old Indian woman. I need warm clothing before winter begins to blow its icicles through us. I need fire wood. I need food. As you have said, a little help is better than none."

Hereupon the two pretenders scored another success.

They rose to their feet. They had eaten up all the fried bread and drained the coffeepot. They shook hands with Blue-Star Woman and departed. In the quiet that followed their departure she sat munching her small piece of bread, which, by a lucky chance, she had taken on her plate before the hungry wolves had come. Very slowly she ate the fragment of fried bread as if to increase it by diligent mastication. A self-condemning sense of guilt disturbed her. In her dire need she had become involved with tricksters. Her nephews laughingly told her, "We use crooks, and crooks use us in the skirmish over Indian lands."

The friendly shade of the house shrank away from her and hid itself under the narrow eaves of the dirt-covered roof. She shrugged her shoulders. The sun high in the sky had witnessed the affair and now glared down upon her white head. Gathering upon her arm the mats and cooking utensils, she hobbled into her log hut.

Under the brooding wilderness silence, on the Sioux Indian Reservation, the superintendent summoned together the leading Indian men of the tribe. He read a letter which he had received from headquarters in Washington, D.C. It announced the enrollment of Blue-Star Woman on their tribal roll of members and the approval of allotting land to her.

It came as a great shock to the tribesmen. Without their knowledge and consent their property was given to a strange woman. They protested in vain. The superintendent said, "I received this letter from Washington. I have read it to you for your information. I have fulfilled my duty. I can do no more." With these fateful words he dismissed the assembly.

Heavy hearted, Chief High Flier returned to his dwelling. Smoking his long-stemmed pipe he pondered over the case of Blue-Star Woman. The Indian's guardian had got into a way of usurping autocratic power in disposing of the wards' property. It was growing intolerable. "No doubt this Indian woman is entitled to allotment, but where? Certainly not here," he thought to himself.

Laying down his pipe, he called his little granddaughter from her play. "You are my interpreter and scribe," he said. "Bring your paper and pencil." A letter was written in the child's sprawling hand, and signed by the old chieftain. It read:

> My Friend:
>
> I make letter to you. My heart is sad. Washington give my tribe's land to a woman called Blue-Star. We do not know her. We were not asked to give land, but our land is taken from us to give to another Indian. This is not right. Lots of little children of my tribe have no land. Why this strange woman get our land which belongs to our children? Go to Washing-

ton and ask if our treaties tell him to give our property away without asking us. Tell him I thought we
made good treaties on paper, but now our children
cry for food. We are too poor. We cannot give even to
our own little children. Washington is very rich.
Washington now owns our country. If he wants to
help this poor Indian woman, Blue-Star, let him give
her some of his land and his money. This is all I will
say until you answer me. I shake hands with you
with my heart. The Great Spirit hears my words.
They are true.

    Your friend,

      Chief High Flier.

      X (his mark).

The letter was addressed to a prominent American woman.
A stamp was carefully placed on the envelope.

Early the next morning, before the dew was off the grass,
the chieftain's riding pony was caught from the pasture and
brought to his log house. It was saddled and bridled by a younger man, his son with whom he made his home. The old chieftain came out, carrying in one hand his long-stemmed pipe and
tobacco pouch. His blanket was loosely girdled about his waist.
Tightly holding the saddle horn, he placed a moccasined foot
carefully into the stirrup and pulled himself up awkwardly into
the saddle, muttering to himself, "Alas, I can no more leap into
my saddle. I now must crawl about in my helplessness." He was
past eighty years of age, and no longer agile.

He set upon his ten-mile trip to the only post office for
hundreds of miles around. In his shirt pocket, he carried the letter destined, in due season, to reach the heart of American people. His pony, grown old in service, jogged along the dusty
road. Memories of other days thronged the wayside, and for the
lonely rider transformed all the country. Those days were gone

when the Indian youths were taught to be truthful—to be merciful to the poor. Those days were gone when moral cleanliness was a chief virtue, when public feasts were given in honor of the virtuous girls and young men of the tribe. Untold mischief is now possible through these broken ancient laws. The younger generation were not being properly trained in the high virtues. A slowly starving race was growing mad, and the pitifully weak sold their lands for a pot of porridge.

"He, he, he! He, he, he!" he lamented. "Small Voice Woman, my own relative, is being represented as the mother of this strange Blue-Star—the papers were made by two young Indian men who have learned the white man's ways. Why must I be forced to accept the mischief of children? My memory is clear. My reputation for veracity is well known.

Small Voice Woman lived in my house until her death. She had only one child and it was a *boy*!" He held his hand over this thumping heart, and was reminded of the letter in his pocket. "This letter—what will happen when it reaches my good friend?" he asked himself. The chieftain rubbed his dim eyes and groaned, "If only my good friend knew the folly of turning my letter into the hands of bureaucrats! In face of repeated defeat, I am daring once more to send this one letter." An inner voice said in his ear, "And this one letter will share the same fate of the other letters."

Startled by the unexpected voice, he jerked upon the bridle reins and brought the drowsy pony to a sudden halt. There was no one near. He found himself a mile from the post office, for the cluster of government buildings, where lived the superintendent, were now in plain sight. His thin frame shook with emotion. He could not go there with his letter.

He dismounted from his pony. His quavering voice chanted a bravery song as he gathered dry grasses and the dead stalks of last year's sunflowers. He built a fire, and crying aloud, for his sorrow was greater than he could bear, he cast the letter into the flames. The fire consumed it. He sent his message on the wings of fire and he believed she would get it. He yet trusted that help would come to his people before it was too late. The pony tossed his head in a readiness to go. He knew he was on the return trip and he was glad to travel.

The wind which blew so gently at dawn was now increased into a gale as the sun approached the zenith. The chieftain, on his way home, sensed a coming storm. He looked upward to the sky and around in every direction. Behind him, in the distance, he saw a cloud of dust. He saw several horsemen whipping their ponies and riding at great speed. Occasionally he heard their shouts, as if calling after someone. He slackened his pony's pace and frequently looked over his shoulder to see who the riders were advancing in hot haste upon him. He was growing curious. In a short time the riders surrounded him. On their coats shone brass buttons, and on their hats were gold cords and tassels. They were Indian police.

"Wan!" he exclaimed, finding himself the object of their chase. It was their foolish ilk who had murdered the great leader, Sitting Bull. "Pray, what is the joke? Why do young men surround an old man quietly riding home?"

"Uncle," said the spokesman, "we are hirelings, as you know. We are sent by the government superintendent to arrest you and take you back with us. The superintendent says you are one of the bad Indians, singing war songs and opposing the government all the time; this morning you were seen trying to set fire to the government agency."

"Hunhunhe!" replied the old chief, placing the palm of his hand over his mouth agape in astonishment. "All this is unbelievable!"

The policeman took hold of the pony's bridle and turned the reluctant little beast around. They led it back with them and the old chieftain set unresisting in the saddle. High Flier was taken before the superintendent, who charged him with setting fires to destroy government buildings and found him guilty. Thus Chief High Flier was sent to jail. He had already suffered much during his life. He was the voiceless man of America. And now in his old age he was cast into prison. The chagrin of it all, together with his utter helplessness to defend his own or his people's human rights, weighed heavily upon his spirit.

The foul air of the dingy cell nauseated him who loved the open. He sat wearily down upon the tattered mattress, which lay on the rough board floor. He drew his robe closely about his tall figure, holding it partially over his face, his hands covered within the folds. In profound gloom the gray-haired prisoner sat there, without a stir for long hours and knew not when the day ended and night began. He sat buried in his desperation. His eyes were closed, but he could not sleep. Bread and water in tin receptacles sat upon the floor beside him untouched. He was not hungry. Venturesome mice crept out upon the floor and scampered in the dim starlight streaming through the iron bars to the cell window. They squeaked as they dared each other to run across his moccasined feet, but the chieftain neither saw nor heard them.

A terrific struggle was waged within his being. He fought as he never fought before. Tenaciously he hung upon hope for the day of salvation—that hope hoary with age. Defying all odds against him, he refused to surrender faith in good people.

Underneath his blanket, wrapped so closely about him, stole a luminous light. Before his stricken consciousness appeared a vision. Lo, his good friend, the American woman to whom he had sent his messages by fire, now stood there a legion! A vast multitude of women, with uplifted hands, gazed upon a huge stone image. Their upturned faces were eager and very earnest. The stone figure was that of a woman upon the brink of the Great Waters, facing eastward. The myriad living hands remained uplifted till the stone woman began to show signs of life. Very majestically she turned around, and, lo, she smiled upon this great galaxy of American women. She was the Statue of Liberty! It was she, who, though representing human liberty, formerly turned her back upon the American aborigine. Her face was aglow with compassion. Her eyes swept across the outspread continent of America, the home of the red man.

At this moment her torch flamed brighter and whiter till its radiance reached into the obscure and remote places of the land. Her light of liberty penetrated Indian reservations. A loud shout of joy rose up from the Indians of the earth, everywhere!

All too soon the picture was gone. Chief High Flier awoke. He lay prostrate on the floor where during the night he had fallen. He rose and took his seat again upon the mattress. Another day was ushered into his life. In his heart lay the secret vision of hope born in the midnight of his sorrows. It enabled him to serve his jail sentence with a mute dignity which baffled those who saw him.

Finally came the day of his release. There was rejoicing over all the land. The desolate hills that harbored wailing voices nightly now were hushed and still. Only gladness filled the air. A crowd gathered around the jail to greet the chieftain. His son stood at the entranceway, while the guard unlocked the prison door. Serenely quiet, the old Indian chief stepped forth. An unseen stone in his path caused him to stumble slightly, but his son grasped him by the hand and steadied his tottering steps. He led him to a heavy lumber wagon drawn by a small pony team which he had brought to take him home. The people thronged about him—hundreds shook hands with him and went away singing Native songs of joy for the safe return to them of their absent one.

Among the happy people came Blue-Star Woman's two nephews. Each shook the chieftain's hand. One of them held out an ink pad saying, "We are glad we were able to get you out of jail. We have great influence with the Indian Bureau in Washington, D.C. When you need help, let us know. Here press your thumb in this pad." His companion took from his pocket a document prepared for the old chief's signature, and held it on the wagon wheel for the thumb mark. The chieftain was taken by surprise. He looked into his son's eyes to know the meaning of these two men. "It is our agreement," he explained to his old father. "I pledged to pay them half of your land if they got you out of jail."

The old chieftain sighed, but made no comment. Words were vain. He pressed his indelible thumb mark, his signature it was, upon the deed, and drove home with his son.

JOHN JOSEPH MATHEWS

from *Sundown* (1934)

Sundown *is a novel about an Osage, Challenge Windzer. It begins with his birth and ends after his mother's death when he is in his late twenties. In the course of his short life oil has been discovered on Osage land in eastern Oklahoma, wealth and development have eroded its pristine beauty, dissolution has gripped its people, and the boom has just about gone bust. There have been murders of Osage women, as larcenous white men from the north have wooed and married them for their oil benefits, called "headrights." Along with the changes in the Osage people and land, the larger society around them has changed as well. World War I has come and gone; Windzer trained as a fighter pilot, but because of his race he was kept in this country, assigned to pilot training at a field in Oklahoma. Like Estelle Armstrong's Jose, Windzer suffers from dual rejection: Neither Indians nor whites claim him, and while his own heart recognizes the one, his education and his father's ambitions require him to try for the other.*

Like many of the fictional works of this century, Sundown *pivots on the question of identity: Windzer is a mixed-blood, but he is not able to accept white male norms, particularly those his college peers display toward women; he is wealthy, but he has no comprehension of wealth as an aspect of status and power. He is avid about his flying, but is rejected by the military on racial grounds.*

But the wealth that comes to the Osage is false; oil riches bring spiritual poverty, and Windzer finds himself aimless, alienated, helplessly drifting through his days in an alcoholic stupor. It is the time just before the Great Depression, and Chal and his friends are caught in the grip of the frenzy that holds most of the world in its thrall. It is that time later called the Jazz Age, when Harlem writers are experiencing their renaissance and the famed Cotton Club draws wealthy white people while being closed to Black people except as entertainers; it is the time when American intellectuals live abroad and write of alienation while they drown in alcohol. Mathews, like writers such as F. Scott Fitzgerald, explores the deep significances of that transitional time, though his characters are Natives, mixed- and full-bloods, whose lands and lives teeter precariously on the brink of a disaster that looms ever closer. For the Lakota, a few hundred miles to the north, the fourth ascent is a decade or so away; perhaps for the Osage, it has already begun.

Mathews' novel has seemed all too "western" to some critics, being largely bereft of the "drums and feathers" that so many take to mean "genuine Indian." But its ambling, circling structure betrays its deeper significance. Although caught in the onslaught of Western economic expansion, Sundown moves surely in ancient channels: episodic, event-centered, the story goes on and on. In that it is deeply tied to the tradition from which it arises, and into which it merges at the final page.

The years went by fast for Chal, though he did very little except ride around in his long, powerful red roadster. He attended all the dances, and became a pretty fair pool player,

betting a dollar on the side. He drove out onto the prairie sometimes, but seldom left the new paved roads. Sometimes he
picked up some of the girls of the town and circled the Newberg building, down the street, then back, and made the circle
again many times. Or he sat long hours in the Blue Front drugstore and dallied with other young people. The fact that he
wasn't doing something still worried him, but not so much
now. He took great delight in clothes, and was very careful to
wear the right thing. He never walked anywhere and his saddle
hung spanned by cobwebs out in the barn at the ranch. During
the summer he spent many weeks at some resort in the high
mountains, playing golf, drinking, and driving his red roadster
over mountain trails.

Sometimes he went with a party of young people to one
of the mushroom oil towns, where they sat in a little shack and
bought whisky for a dollar a drink—just for the hell of it, under
the impression that they were sophisticated people from
Kihekah and were slumming.

But life was full. You could get the most expensive orchestra in the state to play for the dances, and though you sometimes had the discomfort of losing the interest of your partner
to the slick-haired orchestra leader, the corn whisky flowed and
you could always have a good time.

Nearly every day brought news of a new oil well; a new
gusher in the Salt Creek field. Nearly every week brought news
that the local bandit and his gang had robbed another bank, and
you could stand and listen in the Blue Front drugstore, while
someone who had had the honor of not only seeing the bandit
but actually talking with him held his listeners spellbound.
Sometimes the *Trumpet* would scream with black headlines that
another citizen had become an oil millionaire, and seemed almost ecstatic with the honor of telling it. There would be a
short résumé of this man's life, in which his acquisitive struggle
was stressed, and his virtues recounted. And the fortunate citi-

zen had the admiration of the other citizens and immediately almost everything he said became oracular. They boasted of him for only a short time, as he almost invariably moved away to a larger town.

During the competitive bidding at the oil lease sales, you could stand and watch the auctioneer auction off a-hundred-and-sixty-acre tracts and sometimes stand within a few feet of a nationally known oil magnate whose name screamed at you from billboards along the highway. You could stand near and watch him raise his finger to the auctioneer, a movement which meant hundreds of thousands of dollars. The post oak by the new Agency office building, under the shade of which the great would sometimes lie informally, waiting for the auction to begin, was enthusiastically called "the million dollar oak" by the citizens of the town.

After the lease sales, everyone felt pretty good. Some of the citizens worried a little, wondering if they were going to get any of the "gravy" after all, but the atmosphere was one of optimism, and they felt that glory had come. But everyone knew there was no end to it. There would be a greater glory, and many of the citizens dreamed of the time when they would be rich enough to move away; dreamed of the time when they could visit again the sleepy little towns which they had left, with a chauffeur and an expensive car.

Marie Fobus came back to town.

Chal saw her walking down the street holding the hand of a little girl whose hair had just been set in a beauty parlor. The little girl could scarcely keep up with Marie's long strides, and her short silk frock was flapping midway up her fat little thighs. Chal noticed that Marie's skirts were shorter than any of the skirts in town. He wondered how they could become any shorter.

"Hello, Chal," she shouted, dragging the little girl along.

Chal wanted to smile, he thought the little girl was so funny. They stood and talked for a while, then Chal said, "Le's go in an have a drenk." They found a table at the Blue Front and he thought he had never seen anything so ungraceful as Marie when she sat down. She backed up to the chair, put her knees together with a quick movement, and sat down with her knees together and her feet slightly apart. They smoked cigarettes and talked. Nearly everyone smoked cigarettes now, but Marie lit one right in the Blue Front, and only the faster girls in town did that.

Marie had married a Princeton man during the war, and had gone East somewhere. Chal had heard that she had been divorced. He bet she couldn't stand her husband after he got into citizen's clothes again, and that was the reason she had divorced him. He wanted to ask her if she had been down to visit the University recently, as a prelude to asking about Blo. He didn't ask the question.

She sat and bit little pieces out of a straw. "By Gawd, this town's back woodsy, how do you stand it here?" The town seemed quite civilized to Chal. Everyone knew it was the fastest growing little town in the state, but he said, "Ah—I dunno." She turned to her little daughter and said, "Darlin', go look at the dolls up there—see 'em." The little caricature of her sophistication frowned and stuck out her lower lip. Marie pushed her gently and said, "Go on, now." She watched the little girl go toward the front of the store, then she turned back to Chal, "Lissen, for Chrissake, get me a drenk." Chal smiled knowingly, but he was shocked on the inside. He didn't know why he felt shocked. Everyone carried a flask of corn whisky now, and all the girls of the town drank, but the idea of Marie Fobus of the Pi's, the strait-laced, intolerant, virginal Marie Fobus asking for a drink was a surprise to him. He got up and went to his car around the corner, took out a silver flask, looked around, then put it in his hip pocket and went down the block to a stairway. At the top of the stairs he knocked at the door.

A frowzle-headed girl stuck her head out, and her very red mouth broke into a smile. "Hello, Chal, come in. I thought maybe you was the law." Chal pulled the flask out of his pocket and handed it to her, and she called back to the other room. A girl in a faded wrapper came in and took the flask.

"What's the matter with you and the law?" asked Chal.

"Well, you know I'm straight—I ain't no cheap chicken—you know. I been sellin' stuff, see, snow, you know, to all these Osage boys for a long time, and I been square with 'em—you know that. Well, someuh these new doctors that has been comin' intuh town are commencin' to take my trade away. It was gettin' pretty bad, see, so I goes over to a certain doctor and I says to um, 'Looka here,' I says, 'Le's kinda split this thing—it's only fair,' I says. He looks at me and swells up like a toad, see, 'What d'yuh mean,' he says, and I says, 'I mean that you been takin' my trade,' I says. An' I named over at least seven Osage boys and five girls I know he tuk away from me. Well, I wis you could uh seen the bastard. He puffed up and says, 'Get outta here, you—' you know. 'Get outta here,' he says. 'I'm gonna see that you go to the pen for this. If y'ever come around here again, I'm gonna see that you go to the pen,' he says. I was madder'n hell, but I kept the ole trap shut, see, 'cause I thought maybe he might do it. I'se talkin' to Tug, y' know, the man on this beat, and he says not to worry, but you know I can't pay off—I ain't got the money, see. An' y' know, that's why I been layin' low. We keep what little we got stashed, see."

The girl in the faded dressing gown brought the flask to Chal and he gave Sadie five dollars and walked out. These kind of people were always thinkin' the worst of people, he believed. Who ever heard of a respectable person like a doctor sellin' dope. Just talk, he guessed. Running Elk said he got his dope from a doctor, too, because he was drunk most of the time anyway. Chal believed that most of the things he heard were just good stories.

They drove by Marie's home and left her little daughter with the grandmother, then drove out of town. They turned into a dirt lane, bumping over dried mud ruts, then turned out of the road among the trees. Chal opened the soda water bottle as he handed the flask to Marie.

They lit cigarettes and talked, alternately taking a drink from the bottle until it was quite empty. A warmth came over Chal and he felt that the most imperative thing at that time was to get more. He started the car and backed into the road. "Maybe we better go to the field—I know a place there," he said.

They sped out through town, along the paved highway, then over the dusty road among the derricks, and stopped on the main street of Salt Creek. Chal went into one of the frame buildings, then reappeared with a hump under his coat, climbed in behind the wheel, and they drove off across the prairie.

Chal felt that he should like to have a beautiful spot in which to drink. The warmth in him made it imperative that they find some beautiful spot along the creek. They drove along lanes but when they started to turn in they found themselves stopped by barbed wire. "Le's have a snifter now," suggested Marie. "No," said Chal, "I wantta find a certain spot." The warm feeling also made him obstinate. He remembered how he used to ride to a round hole of water with elms arching above it; elms in which the prairie breezes talked eternally. That was the place he wanted to find now. Marie thought he was stubborn and was about to tell him so when he said, "That—that sycamore, that's the place." They turned out of the road and drove down to the creek. Several black wells stood about on the prairie above the trees and from each a path of sterile brown earth led down to the creek, where oil and salt water had killed every blade of grass and exposed the glaring limestone. Some of the elms had been cut down, and the surface of the water had an iridescent scum on it.

Chal stopped the car and with his hands on the wheel looked. A feeling of unhappiness came over him and the alcohol that had warmed to inspiration, to obstinacy, to remembered beauty, now caused him to feel a deep anger; a helpless anger which became bitter, injured innocence as he looked.

"Well," said Marie, eagerly. "Whatta we waitin' on?"

He pulled the bottle from the car pocket then uncapped the soda water.

Chal drove home carefully that night. He could remember the black derricks against the red afterglow, and he could remember the glazed look in Marie's eyes. He remembered her cigarette-stained fingers and that she seemed to be constantly looking for a cigarette she had dropped. He remembered that she was careless about her skirts, but the rest of the time they spent there was a haze.

He did remember, however, coming into Kihekah and stopping in Main Street, when the red stop light flashed. He remembered how proud he had been because he had stopped, and how he had looked over at Marie for approval, but she was asleep with her head hanging over on her shoulder, and he had felt annoyance that she had not seen his skill and alertness. He didn't have any idea how long they had sat there by that oil-polluted pool of water, nor when they had started home, but he did remember that he had taken unusually large drinks out of the bottle with a vindictive feeling that he could compensate for the unhappiness which that spot, so dear to his boyhood memories, had caused him.

The next morning, for the first time in the experience of his hip-pocket flask, dances, and drinking parties, he wanted more whisky. He felt that he must have a drink. Every nerve in his body called for alcohol, and his head was bursting. For three days he stayed half intoxicated, cowed by the craving that suddenly came upon him; without courage to face the terrible mornings after. Each night he made sure that there was some whisky in a bottle under his pillow before he went to bed.

Marie called Chal on the telephone.

"Got a friend uh mine visitin' here and I want to show her a good time if I can, wonder if you couldn't help me?"

"Sure."

"Well, look. She's never seen an Indian dance, and I thought we might take her out today."

The arrangements made, Chal didn't know whether he liked his responsibility or not. He knew how the dancers felt about people coming out to stare at them, yet they did nothing to stop or discourage it. They danced because they felt it impossible to give up that last expression of themselves, and though these dances at the village were only social dances for their own amusement, they adhered closely to the ancient form. They did not charge an admittance fee and because of this the dances were not swamped, perhaps because of the theory held at that time that anything free was not worthwhile.

As the party drove out to the village, Chal was pleased with the closeness of his companions. He liked the stiff fragility of their summer frocks and the vague scents wafted to him. He could see that Jean watched him out of the corner of her eye, seeming to be constantly aware of him. He had become accustomed to this interest in girls whom he met, and he was slightly disappointed when it was not present.

He found seats on the benches behind some waddling old women and several old men. The earthen floor was hard and a little uneven, and surrounding it were benches, making of the dance floor an oval. The Roundhouse was built of pine and had poles supporting the rafters. It had taken the place of the old blackjack bough-covered open structure, but had been built for some time and was becoming gray with weathering.

They were early. Chal grew nervous sitting there with these immaculate girls. Jean's fingernails glinted in the light that came down through a crack in the roof and her white shoes were still spotless, though it seemed impossible that they should be, since the party had had to wade through thick dust. The girls sat and waited for something to happen; watching every Indian who came into the room as though they expected him to whoop suddenly or climb one of the poles and hang by his toes from a rafter. Chal felt annoyed with them and with himself. He felt annoyed with them because he knew they would not be able to understand the spirit of the dance, and he was annoyed with himself because in some vague way he felt that he was not worthy of that spirit. Yet he remembered having seen a Russian dancer sit through one whole afternoon, fascinated by the dance of his people, and ever after that he had had a very warm feeling toward that particular dancer. He knew, however, that most people came to be entertained and were ready to go after a few minutes of what they thought to be monotony; leaving the Roundhouse somewhat disappointed, but boasting thereafter, "Yeah, I've seen 'em stomp-dance." As he sat there he felt vaguely that he was betraying his people; even though he had thought them backward and uncivilized, he sometimes had the feeling which he was experiencing this afternoon.

He told his companions he wanted to see his friend Sun-on-His-Wings as an excuse to leave them for a short time. The sun was brilliant but although it was becoming hot, it had not yet sapped the vivid greenness from the grass, and the air was fresh and filled with the voices of dickcissels. The dust in the road that led up to the Roundhouse was ankle deep, and he watched with amusement some citizens from the town helping their families through the dust. He noticed a chalky-faced young man wearing pince-nez. He had his hand under the arm of his well-dressed wife, whose weight Chal immediately guessed at two hundred pounds. The man's feeble gallantry made Chal feel happier inside.

An evil white man with a white apron around him was standing at a hot-dog stand decorated with red-white-and-blue cheesecloth. The man was shouting, "Git 'em while they're hot, boys—they're ready, they're hot." Some round-faced Indian children stood around the stand drinking strawberry pop, laughing and playing. Under the open, bough-covered structures surrounding the Roundhouse, the women were decorating their men for the dance.

Chal walked about with his hands in his pockets. A large car stopped and the dust swirled around it, and Little Flower climbed out from the driver's wheel. Chal saw that the left side of her face had a great spot of misplaced rouge, and that the spot on the other side of the cheek was smaller and too high on the cheekbone. He noticed that her legs seemed too small and bowed in her short skirts. Her long, bronzed arms seemed very thin, and her fingers, long and thin, seemed too weak to hold up the cluster of diamond rings. When she saw him, she smiled and he saw that her eyes were very bright and large, like the eyes of a doe. She made her way toward him through the dust, and as he watched her approach he had the thought that a white girl would have called him to the car. He disliked people who honked their auto horns to summon you.

She gave him her thin hand. "Hello, I haven't seen you for a long time." She tottered, and her breath was fume-laden.

"No," said Chal, "I don't see anybody anymore."

"Oh, I don't either." She waved her hand unsteadily around in a semicircle. "All this makes me tired."

"That's not the reason I don't see any of the people here anymore—I'm pretty busy." He wanted to defend the village to her, and he always like to appear that he was busy. He thought of how he had often admired Nelson Newberg's ability to appear busy with a pencil behind his ear and paper sticking from his pocket, hurrying across the street.

"Well, I don't live here, you know." She said this as though she didn't want him to get the wrong impression. "Well," she smiled, her teeth very white, "I just thought I'd say hello." Chal walked with her toward the car, but when he noticed that the car was full of people, he stopped.

In the front seat was one of those doubtful nonentities from a large city. He affected what he believed to be the collegiate cut in clothes; with the cheap clothes and his swaggering, the effect was a bit bizarre. Chal could see that he felt his own importance as he sat nonchalantly in the car, and he knew instinctively that he was traveling with a toothbrush and an extra shirt at the expense of Little Flower. His pal in the rear seat was the same type. By his side was a very blond girl, who sat comfortably in the corner of the seat as though she never, never wanted to leave soft cushions again.

Chal stopped when Little Flower said something about meeting her friends. Then she said, "Birdie and the rest wanted to see the dance—are they goin' to dance?" Chal thought, "Bad enough as it is," then he lied, "No, they're just gonta give away a few presents—not much dancin', I guess." He allowed her to cross the dusty road alone, then after a short consultation, she climbed in and drove away in a cloud of dust.

The People had begun to gather. There were old men Chal had not seen for several years, women and children; those who were coming to watch the dance. Some saluted with the fingers of their hand in the palm of his, and to all of the men he said, "How, my father," and they replied, "How, my son." An old woman, almost blind, came waddling along with a cane. When she saw Chal she stopped and said, "Huhn—John ee shinkah—he is man now." She went away toward the Roundhouse mumbling, "Huhn-n-n-n-n." Chal was glad that no one of his friends had seen him talking so intimately with this old woman.

Girls came in twos and threes, giggling, as Indian girls had always giggled, he remembered. But these girls had rouged their lips ludicrously, and Chal felt that they certainly looked barbaric; girls attempting to imitate white girls always seemed barbaric to him, and he didn't like their short skirts bobbing around their bony knees and their crow-black hair bobbed "windblown" style.

He heard the tinkling of many little bells and Yellow Horse came across the road, gorgeous in his paint and his scalplock. Then from all directions came the tinkling of many bells, and the proud dancers approached the Roundhouse. As Yellow Horse came close an enthusiastic photographer maneuvered in front of him and attempted to take his picture, but Yellow Horse placed his eagle-wing fan in front of his face and passed on into the Roundhouse.

Before Chal got back to his seat the singers around the kettledrum had begun to sing and beat the rhythm—TUM, tum, tum, tum—TUM, tum, tum, tum—but before he reached his seat the old rhythm in which most of the songs were sung was begun—TUM, tum, TUM, tum, TUM, tum, TUM, tum.

Marie said, "Oh, Chal, I'm glad you're back; Jean wants to know so many things, and I can't tell her—I feel 'shamed of myself."

Chal answered most of Jean's questions: why the visiting Poncas wore the little round thing behind; was that underwear that that fat fella had on; who was that—that tall good-lookin' fella; what's he doin' that for. But she grew tired of asking questions, and soon the girls grew tired of the monotony of the thing.

The singing leader led off in a high falsetto, then as he lowered his voice the others joined. The dancers rose one by one or two at a time from their benches and danced toward the center of the room, then around the singers. When the music stopped, the dancers would jingle back to their benches, sit in rows and fan themselves with their eagle-wing fans. Sitting there with gravity and dignity. Then, after an interval, the same thing.

Chal sat watching and listening. He had almost forgotten the effect which the dancing had on him, and as usual, he had a desire to join them. He had always felt that by joining them he could express that thing which came over him at times; that something which had to be expressed, but which he couldn't possibly put into words or actions. He sat there today with that feeling almost choking him, and he knew that he would not be able to express it, and that had the effect of making him slightly surly.

He watched the tall form of Sun-on-His-Wings dancing with religious gravity in his gay trappings; his scalplock quivering as he danced; his eyes looking neither to right nor left. He watched Walks Alone rise from the bench, feel behind him and straighten his beaver skin breech strap which hung almost to his heels, then dance upright toward the singers. He watched him bend with a quick movement and look intently on the ground, first on one side and then on the other, moving his head with quick jerks. As he circled the singers he touched the ground in front of him with his quirt, as though tracing footprints. Then he saw Sun-on-His-Wings put his head down like a cock prairie chicken in the spring and imitate the nuptial dance. Then he straightened a little as he danced out to the edge of the room, where he turned and danced back toward the singers, swaying and moving his head slowly from side to side like a foraging eagle. Spirit Iron seemed to grow excited as he raised his war ax and yelped, then danced, bent far over, looking for the trail of the enemy. A visiting Indian, a Ponca, by the characteristic circular mirror, encircled by turkey tail feathers placed just above his buttocks, danced frantically in his dyed long underwear. He stamped and twisted, and jerked his head fantastically; he did the black bottom, the Charleston, and other clownish tricks until Chal looked away in disgust, but he could hear murmurs of approval from the visitors on the benches. The Ponca had been on the vaudeville stage, and he knew how to please white people. Chal knew that his People didn't like to have visiting Indians desecrate their dance, but they retained their ancient courtesy and would say nothing to the Poncas about it. However, this particular Ponca had lost his ancient courtesy and continued to come to dance with the Osages.

Old Black Bull, one of the visiting Sioux, danced like a great god, with his height, his hard, thin body, and his eyes smiling; his great Siouxan scalplock quivering with the jerks of his head. They said he was eighty years old, and Chal could see that he was dancing one of his last prayers.

Chal had a desire to laugh at poor old Spoiler-of-the-Spring as he danced around the singers with his fat belly shaking like jelly.

As he watched Sun-on-His-Wings dancing there, he thought of Running Elk and their boyhood together. Running Elk was always the one to get into trouble; the lovable troublemaker. But he was dead now. They said he was shot in the head and left lying in his car in the Big Hill country.

This thing which welled in Chal again as he watched the dancers and listened to the pulse-beats of the drum, increased his surliness with the increase in the intensity of his emotion. When Marie said, "Le's go," and began powdering her face with a large powder puff as she looked into a little mirror, he was almost angry, and he said,

"You wanted to see the dance, didn't you—well, why don't you watch it—you—le's wait a minute." He wanted to explain to Marie the importance of that which was happening before them, but he believed there was no use. These girls wouldn't understand, and they'd think he was sentimental. Then as if to temper somewhat the severity of his words to Marie, he said, "We'll go in a minute." Then he couldn't refrain from adding,

"You wouldn't go in the middle of an opera." Then he thought he ought to smile.

As he forgot the summery girls at his side with their subtle scents, as he lost himself in the dance of his people, he was not aware that Jean, grown tired of watching the dancing, was looking intently at his profile, and had decided that she liked this fellow.

After one of the songs, several figures rose and walked over to some visiting Indian, or some old man or woman sitting on the benches, and presented them with gifts. A tall dancer gave a beautiful blanket to Black Bull, and Yellow Horse put clinking silver into the hands of one of the singers. Members of the family whom the last song had honored gave some gifts to several other people.

After the next song, Spirit Iron led a beautiful bay horse into the Roundhouse and gave it to Spoiler-of-the-Spring, whose embarrassed son led it out of the room.

"This is what they call 'smokin','" Chal explained to the girls. "You see, this is the third day—the last day of the social dances—and this is the time when the singers sing songs which honor the deeds of ancestors. The people whose ancestors are honored make presents not only to the singers but to other people—'specially visitin' Indians. You see, they say they 'smoke' you a horse, or some strouding or money, 'cause their ancestral song has been sung."

"Oh, how nice—wish they'd smoke me something," said Marie, gaily.

"A jug of corn?" questioned Jean, raising the thin line of her plucked eyebrows.

Then Chal's heart sank. He was suddenly flooded with emotion that felt like needles pricking him, and he thought that he could not stay any longer. The singers were singing the song of his own ancestors. The song of the "Pawnee crying on the hill." His ancestor had killed that Pawnee, and they had made a song about it in his honor.

Chal had an almost uncontrollable urge to go down on the floor and dance as the singers sang that song. But he had never danced with his people. When he was old enough to dance he was in high school, and he hadn't wanted the people at the high school to think that he was uncivilized. Sun-on-His-Wings had always danced with their people, and Running Elk had danced with them as well, until he started drinking so much and taking dope. But Chal had never danced with them.

He saw a tall figure rise from the bench across the floor, let his blanket slip behind him to the bench, and begin to dance in the rhythm of the song, remaining where he stood. It was Fire Cloud, and a pain came to Chal's heart. Then Old Circling Hawk rose slowly, and holding his eagle-wing fan in front of him, danced, standing before his seat, but soon, as though the memories were too much for the old fellow, he moved slowly out to the middle of the floor, dancing with great gravity, his old body as straight as a pine tree. But Fire Cloud remained in the one position, dancing throughout the song before his bench.

Chal thought he must get out. He felt that his emotion might take the form of tears, and he knew that he could never live down that disgrace. He arose, saying, "Le's go," and helped the girls down the benches.

When they had descended from their seats, he hung back as the girls left the Roundhouse. Then as the singers stopped, he walked up to Old Black Bull, handed him a five-dollar note, shook hands with him, and said, "How." He liked Black Bull.

D'ARCY MCNICKLE

Train Time (1936)

If there is any symbol more suggestive of Native engulfment by white society than the Iron Horse, I can't think what it might be. For Anglo-America it meant "progress": westward expansion, the settlement of some 9 million square miles of other people's lands, "civilization," trade, prosperity, and mobility. It was the overwhelming symbol of the industrial supremacy of the United States, and on its back Americans rode into their manifest destiny. The railroad that ran from east to west sliced the continent in two. Its effect on the great buffalo herds alone was devastating, and no one knows how many other species fell to its implacable presence. Perhaps it was a Person, like Saynday, the Kiowa trickster, who, about the time the Iron Horse groped its blind way to the west, paralleling Black Elk's black road, devastated with small pox millions of Native people.

It was the railroad that sent thousands of Native children to boarding schools hundreds of miles from their homes and homelands—so removed were they that their families could not influence or deflect the implacable power of "education." McNickle suggests all of this; it is the subtext of "Train Time," a title that sums up in two simple words all the profound significances in-volved in being Indian in such times. My grandmother once told me that she and her siblings went to boarding school in Albuquerque by train from Laguna Pueblo. She said that while the Laguna and Acoma children were docile, the Navajo students were chained to the hard benches.

McNickle's title is heavy with significance: time to train the Indian children in the ways of machines that even determine time; time to train them to their proper place in a permanent underclass; time to train them to forget who they are, or that they were ever free. In McNickle's northwest, the Salish people lost as much as two-thirds of their population in boarding schools; all dead of malnu-trition, infections, and despair. This horror occurred in this century, not the last one; here, not in Germany. Geronimo was de-fending his people until the late 1920s, sixty-two or so years after Lincoln signed the Emancipation Proclamation; he was captured and, with his people, taken across the continent by train to prisons where many died.

As McNickle wrote in Indians and Other Americans, *"the schools were dedicated to the ultimate eradication of all traits of Indian culture...." By the late 1930s, when "Train Time" was published, McNickle had found his way back to himself. He in-volved himself more deeply in Native issues, history, and life. Per-haps we can take from this some hope for little Eneas Lamartine, a small and helpless voyager into an alien unknown.*

On the depot platform everybody stood waiting, listening. The train has just whistled, somebody said. They stood listening and gazing eastward, where railroad tracks and creek emerged together from a tree-choked canyon.

Twenty-five boys, five girls, Major Miles—all stood waiting and gazing eastward. Was it true that the train had whistled?

"That was no train!" a boy's voice explained.

"It was a steer bellowing."

"It was the train!"

Girls crowded backward against the station building, heads hanging, tears starting; boys pushed forward to the edge of the platform. An older boy with a voice already turning heavy stepped off the weather-shredded boardwalk and stood wide-legged in the middle of the track. He was the doubter. He had heard no train.

Major Miles boomed, "You! What's your name? Get back here! Want to get killed! All of you, stand back!"

The Major strode about, soldierlike, and waved commands. He was exasperated. He was tired. A man driving cattle through timber had it easy, he was thinking. An animal trainer had no idea of trouble. Let anyone try corraling twenty to thirty Indian kids, dragging them out of hiding places, getting them away from relatives and together in one place, then holding them, without tying them, until train time! Even now, at the last moment, when his worries were almost over, they were trying to get themselves killed!

Major Miles was a man of conscience. Whatever he did, he did earnestly. On this hot end-of-summer day he perspired and frowned and wore his soldier bearing. He removed his hat from his wet brow and thoughtfully passed his hand from the hair line backward. Words tumbled about in his mind. Somehow, he realized, he had to vivify the moment. These children were about to go out from the Reservation and get a new start. Life would change. They ought to realize it, somehow—

"Boys—and girls—" there were five girls he remembered. He had got them all lined up against the building, safely away from the edge of the platform. The air was stifling with end-of-summer heat. It was time to say something, never mind the heat. Yes, he would have to make the moment real. He stood soldierlike and thought that.

"Boys and girls—" The train whistled, dully, but unmistakably. Then it repeated more clearly. The rails came to life, something was running through them and making them sing.

Just then the Major's eye fell upon little Eneas and his sure voice faltered. He knew about little Eneas. Most of the boys and girls were mere names; he had seen them around the Agency with their parents, or had caught sight of them scurrying behind tipis and barns when he visited their homes. But little Eneas he knew. With him before his eyes, he paused.

He remembered so clearly the winter day, six months ago, when he first saw Eneas. It was the boy's grandfather, Michel Lamartine, he had gone to see. Michel had contracted to cut wood for the Agency but had not started work. The Major had gone to discover why not.

It was the coldest day of the winter, late in February, and the cabin, sheltered as it was among the pine and cottonwood of a creek bottom, was shot through by frosty drafts. There was wood all about them. Lamartine was a woodcutter besides, yet there was no wood in the house. The fire in the flat-topped cast-iron stove burned weakly. The reason was apparent. The Major had but to look at the bed where Lamartine lay, twisted and shrunken by rheumatism. Only his black eyes burned with life. He tried to wave a hand as the Major entered.

"You see how I am!" the gesture indicated. Then a nerve-strung voice faltered. "We have it bad here. My old woman, she's not much good."

Clearly she wasn't, not for wood-chopping. She sat close by the fire, trying with a good-natured grin to lift her ponderous body from a low seated rocking chair. The Major had to motion her back to her ease. She breathed with an asthmatic roar. Wood-chopping was not within her range. With only a squaw's hatchet to work with, she could scarcely have come within striking distance of a stick of wood. Two blows, if she had struck them, might have put a stop to her laboring heart.

"You see how it is," Lamartine's eyes flashed.

The Major saw clearly. Sitting there in the frosty cabin, he pondered their plight and at the same time wondered if he would get away without coming down with pneumonia. A stream of wind seemed to be hitting him in the back of the neck. Of course, there was nothing to do. One saw too many such situations. If one undertook to provide sustenance out of one's own pocket there would be no end to the demands. Government salaries were small, resources were limited. He could do no more than shake his head sadly, offer some vague hope, some small sympathy. He would have to get away at once.

Then a hand fumbled at the door; it opened. After a moment's struggle, little Eneas appeared, staggering under a full armload of pine limbs hacked into short lengths. The boy was no taller than an ax handle, his nose was running, and he had a croupy cough. He dropped the wood into the empty box near the old woman's chair, then straightened himself.

A soft chuckling came from the bed. Lamartine was full of pride. "A good boy, that. He keeps the old folks warm."

Something about the boy made the Major forget his determination to depart. Perhaps it was his wordlessness, his uncomplaining wordlessness. Or possibly it was his loyalty to the old people. Something drew his eyes to the boy and set him to thinking. Eneas was handing sticks of wood to the old woman and she was feeding them into the stove. When the firebox was full a good part of the boy's armload was gone. He would have to cut more, and more, to keep the old people warm.

The Major heard himself saying suddenly: "Sonny, show me your woodpile. Let's cut a lot of wood for the old folks."

It happened just like that, inexplicably. He went even farther. Not only did he cut enough wood to last through several days, but when he had finished he put the boy in the Agency car and drove him to town, five miles there and back. Against his own principles, he bought a week's store of groceries, and excused himself by telling the boy, as they drove homeward,

"Your grandfather won't be able to get to town for a few days yet. Tell him to come see me when he gets well."

That was the beginning of the Major's interest in Eneas. He had decided that day that he would help the boy in any way possible, because he was a boy of quality. You would be shirking your duty if you failed to recognize and to help a boy of his sort. The only question was, how to help?

When he saw the boy again, some weeks later, his mind saw the problem clearly. "Eneas," he said, "I'm going to help you. I'll see that the old folks are taken care of, so you won't have to think about them. Maybe the old man won't have rheumatism next year, anyhow. If he does, I'll find a family where he and the old lady can move in and be looked after. Don't worry about them. Just think about yourself and what I'm going to do for you. Eneas, when it comes school time, I'm going to send you away. How do you like that?" The Major smiled at his own happy idea.

There was silence. No shy smiling, no look of gratitude, only silence. Probably he had not understood.

"You understand, Eneas? Your grandparents will be taken care of. You'll go away and learn things. You'll go on a train."

The boy looked here and there and scratched at the ground with his foot. "Why do I have to go away?"

"You don't have to, Eneas. Nobody will make you. I thought you'd like to. I thought—" The Major paused, confused.

"You won't make me go away, will you?" There was fear in the voice, tears threatened.

"Why, no Eneas. If you don't want to go. I thought—"

The Major dropped the subject. He didn't see the boy again through spring and summer, but he thought of him. In fact, he couldn't forget the picture he had of him that first day. He couldn't forget either that he wanted to help him. Whether the boy understood what was good for him or not, he meant to see to it that the right thing was done. And that was why, when he made up a quota of children to be sent to the school in Oregon, the name of Eneas Lamartine was included. The Major did not discuss it with him again but he set the wheels in motion. The boy would go with the others. In time to come, he would understand. Possibly he would be grateful.

Thirty children were included in the quota, and of them all Eneas was the only one the Major had actual knowledge of, the only one in whom he was personally interested. With each of them, it was true, he had had difficulties. None had wanted to go. They said they "liked it at home," or they were "afraid" to go away, or they would "get sick" in a strange country; and the parents were no help. They, too, were frightened and uneasy. It was a tiresome, hard kind of duty, but the Major knew what was required of him and never hesitated. The difference was, that in the cases of all these others, the problem was routine. He met it, and passed over it. But in the case of Eneas, he was bothered. He wanted to make clear what this moment of going away meant. It was a breaking away from fear and doubt and ignorance. Here began the new. Mark it, remember it.

His eyes lingered on Eneas. There he stood, drooping, his nose running as on that first day, his stockings coming down, his jacket in need of buttons. But under that shabbiness, the Major knew, was real quality. There was a boy who, with the right help, would blossom and grow strong. It was important that he should not go away hurt and resentful.

The Major called back his straying thoughts and cleared his throat. The moment was important.

"Boys and girls—"

The train was pounding near. Already it had emerged from the canyon, and momentarily the headlong flying locomotive loomed blacker and larger. A white plume flew upward— *Whoo-oo, whoo-oo.*

The Major realized in sudden sharp remorse that he had

waited too long. The vital moment had come, and he had paused, looked for words, and lost it. The roar of rolling steel was upon them.

Lifting his voice in desperate haste, his eyes fastened on Eneas, he bellowed: "Boys and girls—be good—"

That was all anyone heard.

D'ARCY MCNICKLE

Snowfall (1944)

Several of the stories in this volume explore Anglo-American perceptions of Native people. Characters such as Jimmy Robinson and Charlie McDonald, Alfred Densmore, Luther Standing Bear's teachers, Miss Rowell and Miss Evans, and Major Miles explore these issues but their roles are secondary to the main action. "Snowfall" is told from the point of view of the Indian Agent Ephraim Morse—and a more Anglo-American name can hardly be imagined. Mr. Morse is an honorable man; he does his job, although he is often perplexed by the incomprehensible behavior of his charges.

Thus the interactions between the races are defined: each is incomprehensible to the other: the white man has papers, proofs, permissions, procedures, while the Native has knowing, timing, needs to meet that cannot be "according to the book."

That summer it snows—a surprising event. It snows at the wrong time, and the meaning that eludes Agent Morse, a man who does his job, accepts his bewilderment, and is possessed of honor of his own, almost becomes clear.

The setting of Henry Jim's farm is powerfully evocative of the relation of white forms to Native soul. "There was an order in it that went according to the book." All the buildings, barns, fences, gates are as they should be, in a white man's view—all except for the heart of the spread where there "was something different, another world entirely."

"Snowfall" is a story about the old ways, and the closeness of the earth and her vast intelligence to the traditional mind. The transformation that occurs has two sides: One that comes to bear on Henry Jim, and the other that touches Ephraim Morse. In the instant that a balance is struck between the two ways of being, a ritual moment occurs.

The Indian sitting in the chair was old, but not so old that he wind-tottered. He was dry fiber, with stooped shoulders. His hair, colored like the ash of a burnt-out log, hung in side braids with the ends coiled neatly in red felt. His blue serge suit, buttonless and baggy, had traveled a long way from its lower Broadway fabricator. Slit eyes that twinkled, bland smile. This was Henry Jim.

He was saying something about selling a team of horses. Something as simple as that.

The Indian agent stirred out of his preoccupation. His smile, which broke slowly on his heavy face, had a quality of friendliness, a kind of enduring tolerance. He had been barely conscious of the Indian's approach, of his noiseless gliding toward the chair at the left of the desk. Now he pushed aside the papers on his desk top and waited for the Indian to speak again.

"My team, the big bay ones." The old man's voice was thin and wavering, but not unpleasant.

"The big— You mean your team?"

"Eh. The team."

"What then? Are they sick?"

"No. Not sick. I want to sell."

The spreading smile receded. The agent's gray eyes glinted to an opening uncertainty.

"It's a good team, Henry. You got lots of horses, ponies, cow horses. Good enough. Why don't you sell some of them? Save the team."

Henry waved it aside. "Everybody got that kind of horses. Nobody will pay money for that kind."

No denying that. The man behind the desk straightened out of his relaxed position and regarded the papers before him. A trifling frown gathered his eyebrows nearer. He was forced to express his real concern.

"Let's talk about this, Henry. Here on Two Buttes Reservation"—his gesturing hand swept toward a window view of rolling hills, scrub-timbered, well-grassed, and of a broad valley sweeping northward—"you're the best rancher we have. Most years white men have to buy hay from you. They say, 'Henry, how is it you got hay to sell when ours is gone?' They respect you for it. Isn't that so? Now you want to sell your team, a fine team. I helped you pick them out. How will you get your haying done? Cow ponies are no good for that."

Henry Jim ignored the question. "I want to pay my debts."

"Pay your debts?" It sounded more and more irrational, quite unlike Henry Jim. The government man's frown furrowed deeper. "Your debts are small. Nobody is looking for you to run off. It's August already. Almost fall. Pay your debts when you sell some hay. Or if you want to borrow a little cash—"

The suggestion was waved aside.

The old man was rising to his feet, a little shakily, but with the strength of a settled spirit. He wanted no further talk. He was distracted, remote. He had not come to the office to be humored. One was always missing those signals.

The warm August afternoon pressed in and made the

room more stifling than it had been. Voices speaking beyond the office wall emphasized the silence that followed the broken thread of speech.

The agent rose with the old man, showing his uncertainty by getting his feet entangled in the spread legs of his swivel chair and almost falling. He got to the door just as Henry Jim stood ready to open it.

The Indian paused and turned part way around to face his agent. His dark eyes, looking rather watery, seemed not to focus but look at far things. Obviously he was addressing the agent, but only his words showed it. His thought was somewhere beyond.

"When the time comes, when snow flies, I will send for you. I will tell you then."

"Yes, Henry. Of course. Send for me and I will come any time."

It was a relief to have something to say. The Indian had moved through the door and out into the strong August sunlight before the agent could think of asking what the Indian meant. What was it he wanted to talk about that he couldn't mention now.

Ephraim Morse stood looking across the agency compound. An Indian superintendent had to be a busybody. That was the worst part of the job. If one of his wards came wanting to sell a team of horses to pay his debts, the superintendent was expected to look into it. "Now, now," he must say, "why do you want to do that? If you knew better, if you knew as much as I do, you wouldn't. Take my word for it."

Always the matter of seeing to it that the Indians knew what they were doing. And always, too, the sense of working against time, of time looking over your shoulder, nudging you. Someone would be waiting, not simply for a letter from Washington with instruction on procedure, but for a chance to live or to bury the dead. Always someone waiting. Time looking over your shoulder.

"We don't just grow old," Ephraim Morse would tell his wife, explaining himself and his brothers in service. "We pass through ten lifetimes. We become a walking tomb of people who died waiting for a short word from us, when we had to wait on somebody else. We bury them, then carry them with us." And his wife would nod an assent that was at once silent and remote.

The August days ran on, searing the leaves of the cottonwood trees to crispness. The reservation roads were piled deep in yellow dust, which every puff of hot wind tossed high against the horizon of mountains. Wheat harvesters rolled their heaped-up golden wagons across the stubble fields.

Then there was a morning in September—the twenty-second, Ephraim Morse noted when his secretary flipped over the page of his calendar pad—which began in sunshine, a sort of lukewarm sunshine, with a strengthening wind blowing out of the northwest. He left his office in mid-morning to inspect some repairs being made on the horse barn over at the edge of the compound. He noted then that the wind had piled wind-rows of clouds all across the sky. The sun had paled until even the spot it had occupied went quite gray. The wind turned colder.

He was down at the barn talking to his carpenter when Henry Jim's forty-year-old son, Aloysius, came across to meet him. The son was grave and halting, traits of countenance and manner that reminded one of the father. He did not call out or speak at once, just came up and halted.

"How is your father?" Morse asked, offering his hand.

The son, moccasin-footed, tipped his head upward until the straight-edge brim of his hat made a line with the topmost wave of the background mountains. He was squinting at the blowing clouds, looking for something which his eyes told him was not there.

"It is going to snow," he said in a flat voice that suggested utter lack of faith in his own words.

"Snow!" Morse exclaimed and looked to the sky in bewilderment. On the twenty-second of September? No. The wind would grow still stronger and blow the clouds away by noon. Or it would die down and there would be rain. A cold autumn rain. That was the best his weather sense could make of it.

"Maybe rain, Aloysius. But not snow."

Aloysius shifted his feet, looked from this to that, worried.

"My father said it would snow and asks you to come to see him."

Morse looked more sharply at Henry's son. He didn't know him well enough to judge his mood. Was it fear that showed in his eyes?

"Is he sick, then?"

Aloysius shrugged his heavy shoulders. The rawhide thong which passed from his hat and tied under his chin swayed its loose ends with the gesture.

"He sleeps a lot."

"Sleeps a lot?" Was that bad?

Aloysius did not expand on the statement.

"Tell me, Aloysius. What does your father want to talk about?"

To that there was no response, only a silent regard which Morse found baffling.

"And why does your father want to sell his horses? Will he quit farming?"

He might as well have saved his breath. Aloysius only shrugged.

Driving his bay-matched mares that September day, Morse wished he had stopped by his house to put on warmer clothing. The wind had a bite to it. It drew water to the eyes. If his wife knew he had gone off wearing only a summer coat—

As he neared the end of the five-mile drive and looked upward to where Henry Jim's ranch lay outspread on rising ground, he was forced to realize anew how well the old full-blood had caught the white man's idea. Not only were the fields fenced, but the barn and house lots were enclosed separately; there were gates in good repair and fastened shut. Machinery was sheltered. There was an order in it that went according to the book.

His smiling recognition was jarred suddenly. In the barn lot, looking toward the road on which he passed, was one of the mates of Henry Jim's team. He looked closely to verify his first impression. He was not mistaken. Only one horse was in sight. The animal stood with its head up, evidently searching the wind for scent of the lost mate.

The inner cabin was something different, another world entirely. One faltered, letting the eyes adjust themselves to the gloom, being uncertainly aware of people sitting in silence back against the walls.

Henry Jim lay fully clothed on top of the bed, and his eyes, slowly following the agent, seemed to be the only part of him still muscled. He looked tired. Morse sat down, trying to keep his weight off of the roundless, spread-legged chair beside the bed. It was some time before he spoke.

"When men get our age they need rest once in a while. That's what it is. Not sick, Henry. Just a rest."

It was an amiable thing to say, so Morse thought, but he could not tell whether Henry Jim found it so.

One never knew, of course, what effect one's words had. These old fellows had a kind of courtesy which would not permit them, even if they liked you, to tell you what they thought of you. They looked at you through eyes which never gave anything away.

Morse tried to explain in his own thoughts what it was that his senses prickled to there in the cabin and which marked it off from the world outside. It was not one man's past, not one race's, but mankind's, it seemed. That was the sense of it. Was it the gloomy cabin which made him think so? And those confusing, old-as-earth smells? It seemed to be, in a moment's summary, history before there was history. A fragment split off from Asia, cradle of humankind—didn't someone say so? Or was this nonsense?

He couldn't tell by looking at Henry Jim, whose staring eyes had come to rest on Morse's face.

"A few days in bed and you'll feel better. Men our age need rest." He tried to make the silence sit more easily.

And then Henry Jim spoke, with unexpected clarity.

"Now it is going to snow," he said. Just that.

Morse faltered, almost agreeing before his rational mind impeded him.

"Snow? In September, Jim?"

The old man ignored the question.

"I have to wait until it starts before I can talk to you."

The agent reared back, irritated, yet willing to be patient. He had learned that much in twenty years.

"I try to follow you, Henry. My thought tries to go along, and then it stops. What is it you want to talk about?"

It was a stupid question, but Henry did not reject it. He even smiled, and let it go at that.

In a kind of helpless gesture, Morse turned to the others to learn what they were thinking—to Aloysius, who had just come in; to Henry's old wife, toothless and sightless; to relatives of greater and lesser degree—all sitting motionless, eyes averted, merging in shadow. He would learn nothing from them.

"Snowfall won't be soon." He tried to stay casual.

"Yes. Quite soon." Henry turned his face away, as if withdrawing from the contest.

It was just at that point Morse got the intimation of finality which, until then, he had been missing. He was immediately apprehensive, and sat up straight in his chair. Now he really had to know what was going on.

"Henry, when your people see you sell horses and quit farming—what will they do? Quit?"

That, he realized, was the special interest which had carried him at a fast trot from the Agency. It was a vital point. Because, after months of preparing field reports and receiving experts out from Washington, he had won approval of a program of increased expenditure on farm equipment. An enlarged effort to make farmers out of Indians. And what now? If Henry Jim gave up, retired to a moody living in the past, would plows rot to rust all over the reservation? Was the old man renouncing the faith that was work horses and machinery and fenced-up acres?

The old Indian stirred at the question. With great effort, he rolled part way on his side and looked at Morse.

The heavy breathing began to sound like roaring wind in the deepening silence of the room. As his voice emerged, the roaring subsided.

"You think I will be here, maybe. You want me to work my horses. But I am only waiting for snowfall. Then—"

Morse's eyes opened wide. This was really alarming. There was meaning in Henry Jim's words which had to be taken into account. This talk about snow obscured the real matter.

"I have to understand, Henry, if you want me to help. I have to know. Why did you sell just one horse?"

Henry Jim turned his head away.

"I can't talk about that now. When the snow begins to fall, you come. I will explain."

The agent knew when to stop and when to smile. He knew when talking had become useless. He rose uncertainly.

Stepping through the low doorway, Morse looked skyward and saw heavy clouds, looking as if they had been compressed into a solid. The wind was slackening.

Glancing earthward again, he reasoned. It never snowed in September—well, the Agency record said it didn't.

Aloysius was waiting outside, hands in pockets.

"What do you think—" Morse's question ended vaguely.

The forty-year-old son turned and stared toward the creek-and-willow-bordered pasture. Horses were down there, cow ponies, their tails flying in the cold wind. Their heads were up, uncertainly, as if they, too, sensed an unseasonableness.

"When it snows, you come, eh? He wants to say something?"

"Say what?"

A shoulder shrug. What Morse should have expected. You could go so far, and then that shrug. In twenty years, from Sioux to Apache, and now among these mountain people, these root-diggers, the gesture had not changed.

How many times had he gone lanternless into the nebulous world of Indian pattern, grasping at the airy substance of mythical ideas, looking for himself among the shadows.

"They are not like us," he told his wife, Clarisse, that night, for what to her must have seemed like the thousandth time. "The earth is more real to them—much. They're barely separated from it—each generation is born back to it, while we get farther away all the time. We lose touch with our beginning, our senses get thick-skinned. But they are everlastingly sensitive. We call them fatalists, but perhaps their fatalism is hidden knowledge."

In dawn chilliness Morse heard his wife exclaiming, childishly surprised—"Why, Ephraim! It's snowing! I can't believe it!"

Morse thrust his head out of the bedcovers. What had he to do with snow? What had he dreamt—

His wife was up, raising higher a half-raised window shade.

"See! It's just begun. There's hardly any on the ground. It melts as fast as it lights."

233

By the time she turned from the window, wondering whether her husband would plunge outward into the day, he was on his way.

The five-mile drive was a journey into a fabulous land. It snowed sparsely and drearily, the sky hanging low and dark and wet. Prophesy lay in just such witch's weather, not in sunshine and bird song. What was the world? Was one held in hand, used, wore on one's body? Was it the power one extracted from machinery, from electrical impulse, from the brawn of a horse's leg? Or was the real stuff a thing of no dimensions, immeasurable, from which all things were predicted, and did one have to be as uncomplicated as Henry Jim to feel the flow of the inward current?

Long before he reached the end of the drive, he knew what Henry Jim had been talking about. It was even possible, he thought, looking back, that he had understood even on that August afternoon, but had been too rational to admit it.

Henry Jim lay listless abed, fully clothed in the serge suit from lower Broadway, New York City.

There were the same hushed, bunched forms in the twilight cabin. Morse's entering caused no stir. He stepped cautiously toward the bedside, found the spraddle-legged chair on which he had rested uneasily the day before.

The old fellow's eyes were closed and Morse first thought that he was asleep. He remembered what Aloysius had said. "He sleeps a lot," and wondered how long he would have to wait. Then the eyelids fluttered and Morse caught a gleam of glazed eyeball. But no stir of lips. No effort even at acknowledgment.

He surrendered then to the silence. He dared not go out in the fresh air to wait because he wanted to be there when Henry finally came awake.

His shoulders went slack and he seemed literally to plunge into the silence, as if he had plunged into a pool of dark mountain water. Once beneath the surface, only the things within his own head moved, round and round, trying to fit odds and ends together. First he tried to sort out the odors—smoked buckskin, so pungent that it overpowered almost all other smells, except strong pipe smoke. And he was sure that somewhere in the depths of the interior a pot of meat was boiling. These were only the known, the identifiable; and back of them was a hint of old earth itself, of mankind emerging from smoke-filled caves and battling the land and the beasts of the land, and arriving here in a shadowy cabin that was still part cave.

He wondered how it was that silence sat so easily with these people, while it produced such churning in him. He could not know. But he could guess that there was in them an over-powering sense of continuity, of things coming to them whole-made out of the past, against which their wills and their emotions never warred. While he, split from the past, felt the si-lence as a burden that strained muscle and nerve. He labored over each passing moment.

He was startled to find that Henry Jim had turned his head toward him and was watching him through weary eyes. Something like a smile pulled at his loose lips.

"The snow is here. Now I can tell you—"

Morse was wordless. For when the old man spoke, what was there to say, except perhaps to assert (which he did not think of doing) that he had seen faith work its way to its own inner core? It was surely faith—and yet, how did it work? What was the mechanism by which he knew?

There was still the suggestion of a smile when Henry spoke again. "I sold only one horse," he remarked, his voice gaining in strength. "I didn't need much money. A few debts. One horse was enough." There he hung for a moment, consid-ering. "This now is what I have to say. This good horse I have left. I want to take him with me. It troubles me. I know things have changed. In the old days our relatives killed a horse and put it on our grave so we could travel beyond. Now it is different. I know that—"

He fumbled with one hand at his pillow, withdrawing from underhead a soiled bit of cotton, possibly a remnant of old shirt, which in his weakness he trembled at unrolling.

"This is left—"

A crumble of bank notes lay wadded in his hand, some loose ends protruding.

The agent received the offered wad, separated the individual notes, smoothed them on the bed's edge, leaning forward from his rickety perch. The money was old, limp, in different denominations, tens, fives, ones—over fifty dollars.

"You take this money. Put me in a white man's box. Bury me in the ground. Up there where my land looks over the river. You know the place, where the river cuts a high bank. Bury me there. And I want a looking-glass there. Turn it down river."

Again a silence held intact by the old man's gesturing spectral hand.

"It was my father stood on that hill and watched the first white men our people ever knew come up the river. It was his eyes first watched them. And since then we have all grown old watching the white men come. So I want this looking-glass to face down river and it will be my eye. I will watch what comes." A long pause, then, "You can decide about the horse. . . ."

That ended his talking. Henry Jim was tired. Mortal weariness. The twilight room perfected its mood of waiting, perhaps listening. The dust-powdered window light showed feebly that snow still fell.

Morse realized that he had to speak quickly, firmly, while old Henry was still within hearing. There was no time, this once, to await on instructions. So he spoke, and was startled to hear himself saying:

"We will do what you ask. Everything. You will have the horse—"

And then he thought, "My God! Will they all kill their horses after this?"

Henry Jim looked once more, fleetingly, then hooded his eyes under relaxing lids.

When Morse went out, he saw the bay horse again. The animal stood at the fence, as before, and gazed with whited eye toward the cabin. Once, as the agent stepped near, the horse looked away and pawed at the snow-dampened earth, head lowered. Morse thought his nostrils dilated and quivered, as if the creature had whinnied. But there was no sound, unless it had been a sound beyond hearing.

He walked to the roadside fence and extended his hand. "Come, boy! Come, old fellow!"

The bay tossed its head impatiently and continued to gaze at the cabin. Morse felt his scalp prickle, not knowing what he had seen and felt.

Aloysius had followed Morse out into the open and now he came forward, with an air of hesitancy. He came to a full stop before speaking.

"I am glad," he said, in a tone of mild wondering, "you are doing this for the old man. None of us thought a government man would do it, and we were afraid when my father asked."

"That's all right, Aloysius. It wasn't much."

"It will mean a lot to him. He wanted that horse very bad. He didn't want a scrub horse."

"Sure, I know. He wanted his good horse." He had a sense of inward shuddering when he thought, in some other part of his mind, of what he was saying.

Then Morse asked, unable to hold back any longer: "How did your father know all this was going to happen—and why wouldn't he tell me before?"

Aloysius obviously had been waiting for the question, and he smiled.

"Oh, that. He was told in a dream. And he wasn't to speak of it until snow came. That was what the dream said."

"A dream? I see. I was afraid you were going to say that."

So he turned to go home, feeling dejected. Twenty years had not done so much for him. It had led him to a world's edge and there deserted him, with no signposts forward. And all the time, in his office, were people waiting, blue forms, plans prepared by experts. A yearly report of progress was due.

He wasn't even sure what he would tell his wife.

DON C. TALAYESVA

School Off the Reservation (1942)

*The original version of Don C. Talayesva's memoir, which covered
some eight thousand handwritten pages, was condensed and edited
by Dr. Leo V. Simmons of Yale University and published under the
title* Sun Chief: The Autobiography of a Hopi Indian. *Dr. Simmons comments: "The report is not free narrative, but selected and
condensed narration, interwoven with additional information ob-
tained by repeated interviewing [of Talayesva]. It is greatly abbre-
viated and often reorganized. . . ." Simmons admits that "the
materials are left more nearly in Don's own form of expression in
the account of his early life up to marriage . . . ," the period from
which this selection is drawn.*

*Old Oraibi, Talayesva's home, is the oldest continuously in-
habited community in North America. Set on a high mesa that
rises above the plain in what is now known as northern Arizona,
Oraibi is indeed a place of myth, where the gods visit at certain in-
tervals. Raised in this setting, among some of the most spiritually
traditional people on earth, it is small wonder that Talayesva filled
his memoir with spiritual and mundane interactions told as*

straightforwardly as a suburbanite might recount interactions at the grocery store and office.

Simmons makes a telling remark in this regard, writing, "Some parts of the account still appear a little strange and unreal to me, when I am away from Don and Hopiland for a while. But when I come again into close contact with him and his culture, they ring true."

Talayesva's story is an "inner cabin." It reveals in ways large and small how great is the difference between the Native and Western secular worlds. Many readers will find even this small selection from the entire work extremely alien, and that's all to the good. I have included it here because it is a major narrative work and because it throws considerable light on the "subtext" of every other narrative in this anthology, in part because Western contextualization is at a minimum and partly because it provides a well-wrought view of the "inner cabin" where traditional people live.

Talayesva's experience, which occurred when he was about seventeen, can best be characterized as an "out of body" or "near-death" experience of the kind that some modern physicians and psychologists are studying. The theory is that humans possess "nonlocal" consciousness; that the self, as it were, is not confined to the body only, but that it can and does exist independently. This modern scientific theory roughly parallels a primary assumption Native Americans, like tribal people all over the world, make, though they would not explain it in those terms. Indeed, as they take it to be as fundamental to life as possessing organs of sight, touch, and hearing, they don't theorize about or explain it. They just take it as a given and recount experiences of that nonlocal self in the same way they would tell about any other experience.

There are several terms in Talayesva's account, one he thought of as the most significant experience of his life, that need clarification as they are particular either to Hopi thought and usage or to anthropology. Two Hearts are people who have chosen a path of negativity (the most strongly prohibited characteristic, orientation, and/or behavior among almost all Native peoples). Because of their negativity they prevent the rain-people from coming, thus causing drought and famine. They disregard the stories of the elders; they steal or indulge in calumny, making others miserable; they project lizard tails, poisonous insects, and evil thoughts into other people, causing them to sicken and die. Envy, jealousy, bitterness, narcissism, and a vicious need for secret power over the life and happiness of others rule their lives, and, according to Native belief, determine their after-death existence for a very long time. They are out of harmony and out of balance; not only are they unhappy, but they spread that unhappiness throughout their community. Talayesva nearly dies because he dares the Two-Heart who killed his clan sister, and the Two-Heart retaliates brutally. His Guardian intervenes to show him that "life is important"—meaning he shouldn't so casually risk it.

Katcina, or Katchina, as it's more usually spelled, are best described as mediators of interactions between humans and supernaturals. There are several hundred Katcinas, each individual in appearance and characteristics. They are a central part of Hopi and other pueblo life today. Every tribe has a sense of these nonhuman Persons who live side by side with human beings. When Don was visited by the other world in the form of his Guide, he was awake, albeit very weak. He notes that the Guide said he should eat the food the nurse was just then bringing into the room; when the Guide exited the room, he used the door, which Don saw close behind him.

The House of the Dead to which Don's soul travels is the place where the dead live. It is close to the mortal world because every human goes there eventually—most go and do not return. Hopi literature, however, contains a number of stories, reports by those who have had near-death experiences, or who have in other ways traveled far in the Land of the Dead and returned to add to the community's store of information about it.

The dumalaitaka, *who Talayesva identifies in English as*

"Guardian Spirit" or "Guardian Angel," is a kind of being found in spiritual literature worldwide, as Don's difficulty with finding a satisfactory English translation for it attests. My great-grandmother called them Faeries, a result of her marriage to a Scotsman perhaps, or of her readings at Carlisle, or both.

The cornmeal path is just what it sounds like—a trail made with cornmeal. Corn is sacred and protective, keeping evil spirits or negative influence away from the village.

Wuwuchim, or as Simmons spells it, Wowochim, is one of the major ceremonies of the Hopi, corresponding to the Celtic ceremonial period known as Halloween since Christianization of Celtic lands. It lasts nine days. It should be said that English orthography and phonetics don't suit Native words, so spelling is always moot.

It is important that the Kwanitaka not touch Talayesva lest he die—that is, be unable to return to his body back in the bed at the hospital.

Don chooses the white suds, which signify rain clouds; Spider Woman's web, the web of all life; and his own soul, which seen from the outside strongly resembles the white, sticky, almost sudsy substance spiders extrude and from which their webs are made.

As he nears the end of his journey, Don is met by a number of clowns who identify themselves as his uncles. They are not clowns like you see at a circus, and they are not his parent's siblings. There are a number of clown societies such as the Mudheads and the Koshare, and they play an integral role in pueblo ceremonialism. Often comic, their English label "clown" reflects that role. It also echoes the tribal understanding of the clown as trickster, creative power, and supernaturally connected being in the old Anglo and Celtic worlds. They perform their comic role here, joking, "You will see an ugly person lying [in your bed]." Their identification of themselves as "uncles" is by way of reassurance; it signifies that they acknowledge the kinship obligations to him (which are reciprocal), defined as avuncular in his tradition.

A paho is a smooth piece of wood carved with the face of a

Cloud Person and adorned with down feathers. Pahos *are used to aid in interworld communication and as tokens of respect for the Rain Beings.*

One evening in November I made a great mistake. We had an ice-cream and cake party in the Department of Domestic Science. After the refreshments and while we were having a good time with the girls, Hattie came to me looking sad and said, "I have bad news from home. Our older sister, Viola, passed away about a week ago." When I asked her how this happened she said, "Viola had a baby after three days' labor but retained the afterbirth. During the night my father stepped outside and saw a woman fleeing with a cotton mask on her face like a person dressed for burial. He overtook her and told her that she must be the witch who cast a spell on our sister. At first she denied it, then begged him to keep her secret and offered him a string of beads and sexual favors as rewards, but warned him that if he reported her to the people he would live only four more years. He returned to the house and tried to shake the afterbirth out of our sister—until she died in his arms!" I hung my head in grief and anger at this news and cried, "These Two-Hearts want to kill us so they may live. That witch might as well kill us all and be done with it. I don't care if she does kill me, I am a single man and have no children." Hattie was frightened and said, "Don't say that. She may kill you. Those are careless words that may cause you to get sick." They did.

I asked the disciplinarian if I might be excused from the party because I had heard of the death of a clan sister. As I left the disciplinarian said, "Don, don't make yourself too sad." "I will not," I replied, "we all have to die." I had caught a cold and could not sleep. I tried to work next day but had to give up and go to bed, feeling first hot and then cold. Our assistant disciplinarian arranged for me to enter the hospital.

They took me upstairs, put me to bed, felt my pulse, examined my chest, and took my temperature. My head ached and I got worse from hour to hour. At the end of a week they moved me to the second floor near the office of the head nurse where I stayed for a month. In late December they put me on a ward with very sick boys who were not expected to live, said that I had pneumonia, and placed my name on the danger list. The head nurse said to the doctor, "Don is very sick; nothing helps him. If you agree, we will give him some whisky in orange juice." I did not want to take liquor, but with my life in despair they propped me up in bed, held a cup to my lips, and said, "Don, you are getting cold; this will warm you." It did. I got drunk, acted crazy, cursed freely, and said shameful things to the nurses. When I awoke in the morning Ollie Queen was watching over me. She was a pretty Hupa Indian from California whom I had courted several weeks.

I grew steadily worse and could barely speak. Boys and girls came to cheer me up. The pain in my chest was dreadful. I spat blood and could take no food, except a little milk through a glass tube. I refused to eat and told the nurses to leave me alone, for I wanted to die and get out of pain. They cried and begged me to live, praising my name highly. But my feet were already getting cold.

I began to think of the Two-Hearts and to review all that I had heard about them. I knew that they were very unfortunate but powerful people, members of every race and nation, organized into a worldwide society in which they spoke a common language, and that they were able to postpone their own death by taking the lives of their relatives. I understood that Hopi Two-Hearts were leaders of this terrible society, that they held their underworld convention at Red Cliff Mesa northeast of Oraibi, and that Two-Hearts in Oraibi were probably the worst of the lot. I realized that they were mean, fussy, easily offended, and forever up to mischief. I knew I had been careless, had spoken rashly, and had probably offended some of them.

On Christmas Eve, Lily Frazer, an Indian girl of some other tribe, stayed away from the entertainment to watch over me. She was not my sweetheart but my best friend—a sort of big sister—who seemed to look out for me. We had exchanged gifts and done other favors for each other. She spoke tender words and begged me to get well. I was very restless, and at about nine o'clock in the evening I looked at the door transom and saw movements. Four Hopi boys peered through the glass and made funny faces at me. A fifth face appeared, looked at me strangely, and drove the others away. The four faces were those of my schoolmates and the fifth was that of Frank Siemptewa, the husband of Susie and the Chief's lieutenant at Moenkopi. I felt angry but helpless.

Then I saw a tall human being standing by my bed in Katcina costume. He was well dressed in a dancing kilt and a sash, was barefoot, and wore long black hair hanging down his back. He had a soft prayer feather *(nakwakwosi)* in his hair and carried a blue one in his left hand—blue being the color which signifies the west and the home of the dead. He wore beads and looked wonderful as he watched me. When the nurses brought food, he said, "My son, you had better eat. Your time is up. You shall travel to the place where the dead live and see what it is like." I saw the door swing slowly back and forth on its hinges and stop just a little open. A cold numbness crept up my body, my eyes closed, and I knew I was dying.

The strange human being said, "Now, my boy, you are to learn a lesson. I have been guarding you all your life, but you have been careless. You shall travel to the House of the Dead and learn that life is important. The path is already made for you. You had better hurry, and perhaps you will get back before

245

they bury your body. I am your Guardian Spirit *(dumalaitaka)*. I will wait here and watch over your body, but I shall also protect you on your journey."

The pain disappeared and I felt well and strong. I arose from my bed and started to walk, when something lifted me and pushed me along through the air, causing me to move through the door, down the hall, and out upon the campus in broad daylight. I was swept along northeastward by a gust of wind, like flying, and soon reached the San Bernardino Mountains. There I climbed a cornmeal path about halfway up a mountain and came upon a hole like a tunnel, dimly lighted. I heard a voice on the right saying, "Don't be afraid, walk right in." Stepping in through a fog and past the little lights, I moved along swiftly, finally came out upon a flat mesa, and discovered that I was walking near the old water holes out on the ledge at Oraibi! Very much surprised, I thought, "I will go home and get some good Hopi food."

As I entered the door, I saw my mother sitting on the floor combing my father's hair. They just stared at the door for a moment and then turned back to their interests. They didn't say a word, causing me to wonder sadly. I walked about the room for a minute and then sat down on a sheep pelt by the stove to think. I said to myself, "Well, perhaps my grandfather will come and give me food." After about an hour of silence, my grandfather did come in, stared at me for a moment, and said nothing, but he sat down opposite me and dropped his head as though worried. Then I thought to myself, "They don't care for me. I had better go and leave them alone." When I arose to leave they didn't even look up or say goodbye.

I walked out by the dry basin near the Oraibi Rock. There was a little stone wall on the rim of the dam. A large lizard ran along the ground and into the wall. As I drew near I saw peeping out from the rocks an ugly, naked woman with drawn face and dry lips. She looked tired, half-starved, and very thirsty. It was my old grandmother, Bakabi, my mother's mother's sister. Since she was still living, I didn't know how her spirit could be on its way to Skeleton House, but I think my Guardian Angel placed her there to teach me a lesson and to show me that she was a Two-Heart. She said, "My grandson, will you please give me a drink?" "No, I have no water," I replied. "Well, please spit in my mouth to quench my thirst?" she pleaded. I said, "No, I have nothing for you. Are you the one I saw as a lizard?" "Yes, my father is a lizard and I have two hearts." "Then I will have nothing to do with you, for you killed our sister!" I said. "I am one of those who are killing your people," she answered, "but I am not the one who killed you. From here to the House of the Dead you will see people like me who can take only one step a year over a path of sorrow. Please let me go along with you. You have only one heart and will arrive safely." "Never mind," I said, and hurried along, for I had no time to monkey with a witch.

I moved along quickly, touching the ground only in spots until I came to the west point of the mesa. Along this way I saw many faces of Two-Hearts who called out to me for food and drink, but I had no time for them. When I reached the foot of Mount Beautiful, the Judgment Seat, I looked up and saw nice regular steps about twelve feet wide and twelve feet high, of a red color, and reaching like a mighty stairway to the highest point. I started to climb but seemed to float up on air, just touching my feet lightly on the top step. There a bell rang from the west side so clearly that I heard echoes out among the mesa walls.

As the ringing grew louder, I looked and saw a man climbing up the mountain from the west, dressed in a white buckskin, wearing a horn, and holding a spear and a bell. It was a Kwanitaka, a member of the Kwan or Warrior society, who watches the kivas during prayers and guards the village to keep out strangers and let in the dead during the Wowochim ceremonies. He came up to me but did not shake hands, because he was now a spirit god and doing police duty directing good people over the smooth highway and bad people over the rough road to the House of the Dead. He said, "My boy, you are just in time, hurry! Look to the west and you will see two roads. You take the broad one, the narrow one is crooked and full of rocks, thorns, and thistles; those who take it have a hard journey. I have prepared this broad road for you. Now hurry and you will find someone to guide you."

I looked to the left and saw a wide road sprinkled with cornmeal and pollen. On the right was a narrow path about a foot wide and very rough. Strewn along the side were Hopi clothes that had been dropped by Two-Heart women who had received them from men with whom they had slept. I saw naked, suffering people struggling along the path with heavy burdens and other handicaps such as thorny cactus plants fastened to their bodies in tender places. Snakes raised their heads along the edge of the path, sticking out their tongues in a threatening manner. When they saw me looking at them they dropped their heads, but I knew they could bite anyone that they did not like.

I chose the broad road to the left and went along swiftly, almost flying, until I came to a large mesa, which I shot up like an arrow and landed on top. There I saw on my left summer birds singing and flowers in full bloom. Moving rapidly, I passed along the edge of Cole Canyon with its steep white walls which I had seen before on my way to Moenkopi. In the distance were twelve queer-looking striped animals chasing one another. As I drew nearer I saw that they were clowns *(tcuka)* who had painted their bodies with black and white stripes and were joking and teasing one another. The leader—who was of the Eagle Clan, which is linked to my Sun Clan—said, "My nephew, we have been expecting you. It is late and you must hurry. We think you will return, so we will wait here for you. Your Guardian Spirit is protecting you, but you must hurry back to your body. You may live a long time yet if you get back."

Somewhat frightened, I sped along to the left, reached the top of a steep mesa, and sort of floated down. Before me were the two trails passing westward through the gap of the mountains. On the right was the rough narrow path, with the cactus and the coiled snakes, and filled with miserable Two-Hearts making very slow and painful progress. On the left was the fine, smooth highway with no person in sight, since everyone had sped along so swiftly. I took it, passed many ruins and deserted houses, reached the mountain, entered a narrow valley, and crossed through a gap to the other side. Soon I came to a great canyon where my journey seemed to end, and I stood there on the rim wondering what to do. Peering deep into the canyon, I saw something shiny winding its way like a silver thread on the bottom, and I thought that it must be the Little Colorado River. On the walls across the canyon were the houses of our ancestors with smoke rising from the chimneys and people sitting out on the roofs.

Within a short time I heard a bell on the west side at the bottom of the canyon and another one somewhat behind me. The same Kwanitaka who had directed me on Mount Beautiful came rushing up the cliff carrying a blanket and dressed in a cloak and buckskin moccasins as white as snow. Another Kwanitaka came rapidly from the rear, ringing his bell. The first one said, "We have been expecting you all morning. This partner and I have raced here for you. I won and you are mine. You have been careless and don't believe in the Skeleton House where your people go when they die. You think that people, dogs, burros, and other animals just die and that's all there is to it. Come with us. We shall teach you a lesson on life." I followed the first Kwanitaka to the southwest and was trailed by the second who kept off evil spirits. We came to a house where we saw a Kwanitaka in red buckskin moccasins making red yucca suds in a big earthen pot. Nearby was another Kwanitaka from the west in white moccasins making white suds. Each one stirred the suds with a stick, causing a vapor to rise like a cloud. Then one of them said, "Now we are ready, take your choice. From which pot will you be washed?" I chose the white suds. "All right, you are lucky," said the Kwanitaka. "It means that you may journey back along the Hopi trail and return to life." I knelt down so that he could wash my hair and rinse it with fresh water. Finally he said, "Get up and come along. We must hurry because the time is going fast."

The Kwanitakas led me southwest toward the smoke rising in the distance. As we drew near I saw a great crowd of people watching a fire which came out of the ground. On the very edge of the flaming pit stood four naked people, each of them in front of another individual who wore clothing. On the north and south sides stood a naked man in front of a clothed woman, on the east and west sides a naked woman in front of a clothed man. I could see these people as plain as day, even their private parts, but I did not know a single one of them. They had been traveling for a long, long time at the rate of one step a year, and had just reached this place. I noticed on the ground paths leading from four directions to the hole. Nearby I saw another Kwanitaka tending the fire in a deeply tunneled pit like that in which sweet corn is baked.

"Look closely," said a Kwanitaka. "Those in front are Two-Hearts. They killed the people standing behind them and now it is their turn to suffer. The crowds of people have come from the House of the Dead to see the Two-Hearts get their punishment. Look!" Then he called out, "Ready, push!" The woman on the north pushed her Two-Heart into the pit, and I could see the flames lap him up, sending out rolls of black smoke. Then the man on the west pushed over his naked woman, and the woman on the south shoved in her man, causing great volumes of smoke to rise out of the pit. Finally the man on the east pushed in his girl and the work was done. No Two-Heart said a word; it seemed they had no feelings. The Kwanitaka said to the people, "Now go back where you belong."

"Now, my boy," said the Kwanitaka to me, "come and look into the pit." I stepped up close to the rim and saw an empty hole with a network of two-inch cracks broken into the walls through which flames of fire were leaping. In the center at the bottom were four black beetles crawling about, two carrying the other two on their backs. The Kwanitaka asked me, "What do you see?" "Beetles," I replied. "That's the end of these Two-Hearts," said he, "and the fate of all their kind. They will stay there as beetles forever, except to make occasional visits to Oraibi and move about the village doing mischief on hazy days."

The Kwanitakas then took me back over the course that we had traveled until we came to the steep ledge where the road had ended. I had stood there before, looking across the canyon to the opposite wall where the people sat on their housetops. Now the canyon was full of smoke, and when I peered down I saw a gruesome creature in the shape of a man climbing the cliff. He was taking long strides with his shining black legs and big feet; an old tattered rag of a blanket was flying from his shoulder as he approached swiftly with a club in his hand. It was big, black, bloody-headed Masau'u, the god of Death, coming to catch me. One of the Kwanitakas pushed me and cried, "Flee for your life and don't look back, for if Masau'u catches you, he will make you a prisoner in the House of the Dead!" I turned and ran eastward, while they pushed me along with their wands or spears so that I rose about six inches from the ground and flew faster than I had ever traveled before.

When I reached Cole Canyon the clowns were waiting for me, standing in a straight line facing west with their arms about each other, as children do in playing London Bridge. As I approached them at full speed, they cried, "Jump, Masau'u is gaining!" I jumped and landed on the chest of the leader, knocking him down. They all laughed and yelled, seeming not to mind, for clowns are always happy. They said, "You just reached here in time, now you belong to us, turn around and look!" I looked west and saw Masau'u going back, looking over his shoulder as he ran. Then the leader of the clowns said, "Now, my nephew, you have learned your lesson. Be careful, wise, and good, and treat everybody fairly. If you do, they will respect you and help you out of trouble. Your Guardian Spirit has punished you so that you may see and understand. Lots of people love you. We are your uncles and will see that no harm comes to you. You have a long time to live yet. Go back to the hospital and to your bed. You will see an ugly person lying there, but don't be afraid. Put your arms around his neck and warm yourself, and you'll soon come to life. But hurry, before the people put your body in a coffin and nail down the lid, for then it will be too late."

I turned and ran quickly, circling back to the mountains through the tunnel and over the foothills to the hospital. I entered quickly and saw my Guardian Spirit and a nurse at the bedside. He greeted me kindly and said, "Well, you are lucky, and just in time. Slip quickly under the cover at the foot, move up alongside your body, put your arms around its neck, and be still." My body was cold and little more than bones, but I obeyed the command and lay there clinging to its neck. Soon I became warm, opened my eyes, and looked up to the ceiling and at the door transom. Nurses were about the bed, and a head nurse was holding my hand. I heard her say, "The pulse beats."

I thought I heard bees buzzing, but it was the music of a band, for it was Christmas morning and students were marching from building to building singing carols. I said, "Father, mother." A nurse said, "Here we are." The head nurse said, "Sonny, you passed away last night, but did not cool off quite like a dead person. Your heart kept on beating slowly and your pulse moved a little, so we did not bury you. Now we will get the credit for saving your life." All the nurses shook hands as if I had been away for a long time, and said, "We worked on you because your parents did not know that you were sick and we wanted you to be able to return to them. We love you more than the other boys and girls because you are kind-hearted and act like a brother."

Ollie Queen, my best girl, took hold of my hand and with tears in her eyes said, "Well, you have had a hard time, but you have come back to life. Now I shall keep you always." The head nurse said, "We ordered your coffin and perhaps it is now on its way, but you won't need it. Look what Santa Claus brought you." At the foot of the bed were lying gifts of candy and fruit, a uniform suit, and a bouquet of flowers. I found that my face had been washed and my hair combed in readiness for the coffin, and that the new suit was to have been my burial shroud. I felt grateful but took pity on myself and cried, saying in my heart, "I have learned a lesson and from now on I shall be careful to do what is right." When the nurses had given me a good massage to warm and limber up my body, I begged for food and received a little milk and toast. I grew dizzy and pleaded for more food even in small quantities, but the nurses patted me on my shoulder and told me to wait. At noon they gave me a good square meal, which made me feel perfectly well.

After lunch my Guardian Angel appeared to me and said in a soft voice: "Well, my boy, you were careless, but you have learned a lesson. Now if you don't obey me I shall punish you again, but for only four trials—then let you die. I love you, and that is why I watch over you. Eat and regain your strength. Someday you will be an important man in the ceremonies. Then make a *paho* for me before all others, for I am your Guardian Spirit that directs and protects you. Many people never see their Guide, but I have shown myself to you to teach you this lesson. Now I shall leave you. Be good, be wise, think before you act, and you will live a long time. But I shall hold you lightly, as between two fingers, and if you disobey me I will drop you. Goodbye and good luck." He made one step and disappeared.

Then I saw a soft eagle prayer feather rise up from the floor, float through the door into the hall, and vanish. I spoke out loud, "Now my Guide is gone and I shall not see him again." "What guide?" asked the nurse sitting by the bedside. "The Guide who protects me and brought me back to life," I answered. "You act crazy," she replied. "We protected you and brought you back to life." I didn't argue about it but just asked for more food.

That night Ollie Queen sat in a rocker by the bed and watched. She said she was afraid I might die again, and waked me ever so often to see if I were all right. Next morning I felt better. Chief Tewaquaptewa visited me in the hospital, and when I told him about my death journey he said it was true, for those were the same things that the old people said they saw when they visited the House of the Dead.

In May 1909, Ira and I were sent with others to Hazel Ranch, where we worked pitching hay for board and $2 a day. On the second day our superintendent came and told us to go back to Sherman and prepare to return to Oraibi. In the evening of the third day our boss wrote our checks, hitched his team to the buckboard, and took us back to school. We had a bath and packed our things to start for Oraibi.

Early next morning . . . we boys walked to Arlington station, while the girls came in wagons. I went into the packing house and bought a gunnysack full of oranges for ten cents.

When the train came we got on board with all our possessions. There was a crowd of us, enough to fill twelve or fifteen wagons. My girl, Mettie, got in a seat with Philip from Second Mesa. I sat in my seat alone and ate oranges. Later, when I went to the toilet and returned, I found Irene of the Masau'u Clan in my seat. She was the granddaughter of old Chief Lolulomai and a pretty girl. I had paid no attention to her in school. But I knew, of course, that Sun Clan boys often married Fire Clan women. Ira was already going with a Fire Clan girl. I sat down beside her and treated her to some oranges from my gunnysack. While we were eating I joked with her a little and asked her if she would think of becoming my wife some time. She laughed and said, "Well, if Mettie doesn't get you I may, but you will have to drop her first." I liked Mettie far better.

As we got off the train in Winslow we found our relatives with their wagons to meet us. A man who looked like a Navaho and was dressed "sporty" came along asking for Chuka. Coming up to me, he said, "I am Frank, the new husband of your sister Gladys. I have come to take you to Shipaulovi." I hated to go with him because I had planned to travel in the wagon with Mettie.

After lunch I asked, "Well, brother-in-law, when are we leaving?" "Tomorrow," he answered. "I will have a white man in the morning to take to Hopiland."

· · ·

After supper some of us walked back to town, went through the stores that were still open, and then went to a movie. When we came out I told them that I was going to the Oraibi camp, and followed along behind a bunch of girls who were returning from the show. At the camp the men had a big bonfire and were dancing their Katcina dances. I had been out of this for three years and did not know the tunes. We stayed up until after midnight.

· · ·

After breakfast we hitched up and drove to the depot to meet our white passenger, Mr. Kirkland, who was a carpenter on his way to Hopiland. I did most of the talking with him because I could speak better English. We loaded our wagon and started along the old trail. Frank had a good trotting team, and by noon we reached the foothills of the mesa south of the Hopi Buttes, where we stopped for lunch. After eating we started again and drove up on the shelf of the mesa, and crossed on the east side near the spring, where we camped for the night.

After supper I talked with the white man about my schooling and how we played football and beat most of the schools in southern California. I talked until he seemed tired. Then we lay down and Frank began teaching Ira and me the Long Hair Katcina song.

As I lay on my blanket I thought about my school days and all that I had learned. I could talk like a gentleman, read, write, and cipher. I could name all the states in the Union with their capitals, repeat the names of all the books in the Bible, quote a hundred verses of Scripture, sing more than two dozen Christian hymns and patriotic songs, debate, shout football yells, swing my partners in square dances, bake bread, sew well enough to make a pair of trousers, and tell "dirty" Dutchman stories by the hour. It was important that I had learned how to get along with white men and earn money by helping them. But my death experience had taught me that I had a Hopi Spirit Guide whom I must follow if I wished to live. I wanted to become a real Hopi again, to sing the good old Katcina songs, and to feel free to make love without fear of sin or a rawhide. I wondered where Mettie and the Oraibi party were camping that night and made up my mind to see more of her among our own people.

N. SCOTT MOMADAY

Feast Day (1968)

The following sequence from House Made of Dawn *is a portion of the novel's first section, "The Longhair." It is set at Walatowa, a pueblo in the northern New Mexican mountains. It is July 25 in the late 1940s, at the end of World War II. The protagonist, Abel, served in Germany—infantry. The story of Santiago, or San Diego (St. James), told by Father Olguin is part of a shared mythology: It comes from the conquistadores, who yelled "Santiago!" as they marched into battle, but it is also the story of corn, the fundamental sacred vegetable of the Native world. As corn is usually given the people by female supernatural power, we are alerted that this is a patriarchal story from the start.*

Abel is one of the Indians Colonel Pratt sought sincerely to create, and the dreadful pain and alienation he endures is the result. Jose, Eneas, Don—all those Indian men who were trained to serve in American armies; Abel is Everyman, First Man, a being engulfed in forces he did not shape and cannot control. He tries the latter, going after the albino who is called "the white man," over and over in the narrative. The albino is white-skinned, and he is also a Two-Hearts. He is not an Anglo like Angela St. John, who is visiting the famous baths, or a Mexican-American like Father Olguin, who is assigned to Walatowa as his parish. He is a member of the Walatowa, but his heart is bad.

"A man kills such an enemy if he can," Abel believes, but he has the wrong idea. In the Pueblo world, from which he is entirely disaffected since his army stint, there are proper ways to deal with those who, like the albino, have bad hearts. But Abel is isolated within himself; a product of history, tradition, education, and dis-affection, fatherless and motherless, he drifts. His "crippled" grand-father Francisco, who has "long known evil," has waited alone for his grandson's return, but it goes badly. The soldier is home only a few days before the albino assaults him, leading him into exile again, victim of his alienation, his rage, and the Anglo-American justice system.

The episodic structure of these excerpts characterize the novel as a whole—a feature that identifies House Made of Dawn as es-sentially Native in structure and significance. A notable feature Momaday employs that is direct from the Native Narrative Tradi-tion is the shifting of point of view. Thus the narrative moves from Father Olguin's point of view to Angela St. John's, to Abel's, to Francisco's, pointing to the transitory nature of both perception and identity. Francisco, unlike his grandson, can cope with an ever-changing sense of self, as traditional people usually can, but for Abel, the shifting of identity evokes only a profound loss of self.

It is Momaday's gift to write prose in which every word is sig-nificant, every event is connected to every other, and every image is holographic. He is particularly skilled at evoking a sense of place—smells, sights, tactile sensations, and inner responses to them.

Piki is a kind of corn bread, sort of very thin Indian crepes; the paste he mentions is thick red chili, roasted and ground with just enough water to make a wonderful, very hot spread for the delicious outdoor oven bread of the Pueblos, called sotobalau; posole is a com-bination of hominy, pork, and red chili made into a savory, hearty stew. The Middle is the central rectangular space in the center of the

*pueblo "condos"—they are very ancient, but condos nonetheless—
where the Dances take place.*

*The feast of Santiago with its rooster pull is celebrated all
over rural New Mexico and is enjoyed in Mexican-American villages on San Juan's Day, June 24.*

July 25

This, according to Father Olguin:

Santiago rode southward into Mexico. Although
his horse was sleek and well bred, he himself was
dressed in the guise of a peon. When he had journeyed a long way, he stopped to rest at the house of
an old man and his wife. They were poor and miserable people, but they were kind and gracious, too,
and they bade Santiago welcome. They gave him cold
water to slake his thirst and cheerful words to comfort him. There was nothing in the house to eat, but
a single, aged rooster strutted back and forth in the
yard. The rooster was their only possession of value,
but the old man and woman killed and cooked it for
their guest. That night they gave him their bed while
they slept on the cold ground. When morning came,
Santiago told them who he was. He gave them his
blessing and continued on his way.

He rode on for many days, and at last he came
to the royal city. That day the king proclaimed that
there should be a great celebration and many games,
dangerous contests of skill and strength. Santiago entered the games. He was derided at first, for everyone
supposed him to be a peon and a fool. But he was vic-
torious, and as a prize he was allowed to choose and

marry one of the king's daughters. He chose a girl with almond-shaped eyes and long black hair, and he made ready to return with her to the north. The king was filled with resentment to think that a peon should carry his daughter away, and he conceived a plan to kill the saint. Publicly he ordered a company of soldiers to escort the travelers safely on their journey home. But under cover he directed that Santiago should be put to death as soon as the train was away from the city gates.

Now by a miracle Santiago brought forth from his mouth the rooster, whole and alive, which the old man and woman had given him to eat. The rooster warned him at once of what the soldiers meant to do and gave him the spur from its right leg. When the soldiers turned upon him, Santiago slew them with a magic sword.

At the end of the journey Santiago had no longer any need of his horse, and the horse spoke to him and said: "Now you must sacrifice me for the good of the people." Accordingly, Santiago stabbed the horse to death, and from its blood there issued a great herd of horses, enough for all the Pueblo people. After that, the rooster spoke to Santiago and said: "Now you must sacrifice me for the good of the people." And accordingly Santiago tore the bird apart with his bare hands and scattered the remains all about on the ground. The blood and feathers of the bird became cultivated plants and domestic animals, enough for all the Pueblo people.

The late afternoon of the feast of Santiago was still and hot, and there were no clouds in the sky. The river was low, and the grape leaves had begun to curl in the fire of the sun. The pale yellow grass on the river plain was tall, for the cattle and sheep had been taken to graze in the high meadows, and alkali lay like frost in the cracked beds of the irrigation ditches. It was a pale midsummer day, two or three hours before sundown.

Father Olguin went with Angela St. John out of the rectory. They walked slowly, talking together, along the street which ran uphill toward the Middle. There were houses along the north side of the street, patches of grapes and corn and melons on the south. There had been no rain in the valley for a long time, and the dust was deep in the street. By one of the houses a thin old man tended his long hair, careless of their passing. He was bent forward, and his hair reached nearly to the ground. His head was cocked, so that the hair hung all together on one side of his face and in front of the shoulder. He brushed slowly the inside of it, downward from the ear, with a bunch of quills. His hands worked easily, intimately, with the coarse, shining hair, in which there was no appearance of softness, except that light moved upon it as on a pouring of oil.

They saw faces in the dark windows and doorways of the houses, half in hiding, watching with wide, solemn eyes. The priest paused among them, and Angela drew away from him a little. She was among the houses of the town, and there was an excitement all around, a ceaseless murmur under the sound of the drum, lost in back of the walls, apart from the dead silent light of the afternoon. When she had got too far ahead, she waited beside a windmill and a trough, around which there was a muddy black ring filled with the tracks of animals. In the end of July the town smelled of animals, and smoke, and sawed lumber, and the sweet, moist smell of bread that has been cut open and left to stand.

When they came to the Middle, there was a lot of sound going on. The people of the town had begun to gather along the walls of the houses, and a group of small boys ran about, tumbling on the ground and shouting. The Middle was an ancient place, nearly a hundred yards long by forty wide. The smooth, packed earth was not level, as it appeared at first to be, but rolling and concave, rising slightly to the walls around it so that there were no edges or angles in the dry clay of the ground and the houses; there were only the soft contours and depressions of things worn down and away in time. From within, the space appeared to be enclosed, but there were narrow passages at the four corners and a wide opening midway along the south side, where once there had been a house; there was now a low, uneven ruin of earthen bricks, nearly indistinguishable from the floor and the back wall of the recess. There Angela and the priest entered and turned, waiting, conscious of themselves, to be absorbed in the sound and motion of the town.

The oldest houses, those at the west end and on the north side, were tiered, two and three stories high, and clusters of men and women stood about on the roofs. The drummer was there, on a rooftop, still beating on the drum, slowly, exactly in time, with only a quick, nearly imperceptible motion of the hand, standing perfectly still and even-eyed, old and imperturbable. Just there, in sight of him, the deep vibration of the drum seemed to Angela scarcely louder, deeper, than it had an hour before and a half mile away, when she was in a room of the rectory, momentarily alone with it and borne upon it. And it should not have seemed less had she been beyond the river and among the hills; the drum held sway in the valley, like the breaking of thunder far away, echoing on and on in a region out of time. One has only to take it for granted, she thought, like a storm coming up, and the certain, rare downfall of rain. She pulled away from it and caught sight of window frames, blue and white, earthen ovens like the hives of bees, vigas, dogs, and flies. Equidistant from all the walls of the Middle there was a fresh hole in the ground, about eight inches in diameter, and a small mound of sandy earth.

In a little while the riders came into the west end in

groups of three and four, on their best animals. There were seven or eight men and as many boys. They crossed the width of the Middle and doubled back in single file along the wall. Abel rode one of his grandfather's roan black-maned mares and sat too rigid in the saddle, too careful of the gentle mare. For the first time since coming home he had done away with his uniform. He had put on his old clothes: Levi's and a wide black belt, a gray work shirt, and a straw hat with a low crown and a wide, rolled brim. His sleeves were rolled high, and his arms and hands were newly sunburned. The appearance of one of the men was striking. He was large, lithe, and white-skinned; he wore little round colored glasses and rode a fine black horse of good blood. The black horse was high-spirited, and the white man held its head high on the reins and kept the stirrups free of it. He was the last in line, and when he had taken his place with the others in the shade of the wall, an official of the town brought a large white rooster from one of the houses. He placed it in the hole and moved the dirt in upon it until it was buried to the neck. Its white head jerked from side to side, so that its comb and wattles shook and its hackles were spread out on the sand. The townspeople laughed to see it so, buried and fearful, its round, unblinking eyes yellow and bright in the dying day. The official moved away, and the first horse and rider bolted from the shade. Then, one at a time, the others rode down upon the rooster and reached for it, holding to the horns of their saddles and leaning sharply down against the shoulders of their mounts. Most of the animals were untrained, and they drew up when their riders leaned. One and then another of the boys fell to the ground, and the townspeople jeered in delight. When it came Abel's turn, he made a poor showing, full of caution and gesture. Angela despised him a little; she would remember that, but for the moment her attention was spread over the whole fantastic scene, and she felt herself going limp. With the rush of the first horse and rider all her senses were struck at once. The sun, low and growing orange, burned on her face and arms. She closed her eyes, but it was there still, the brilliant disorder of motion: the dark and darker gold of the earth and earthen walls and the deep incisions of shade and the vague, violent procession of centaurs. So unintelligible the sharp sound of voices and hooves, the odor of animals and sweat, so empty of meaning it all was, and yet so full of appearance. When he passed in front of her at a walk, on his way back, she was ready again to deceive. She smiled at him and looked away.

The white man was large and thickset, powerful and deliberate in his movements. The black horse started fast and ran easily, even as the white man leaned down from it. He got hold of the rooster and took it from the ground. Then he was upright in the saddle, suddenly, without once having shifted the center of his weight from the spine of the running horse. He reined in hard, so that the animal tucked in its haunches and its hooves plowed in the ground. Angela thrilled to see it handled so, as if the white man were its will and all its shivering force were drawn to his bow. A perfect commotion, full of symmetry and sound. And yet there was something out of place, some flaw in proportion or design, some unnatural thing. She keened to it, whatever it was, and an old fascination returned upon her. The black horse whirled. The white man looked down the Middle toward the other riders and held the rooster up and away in his left hand while its great wings beat the air. He started back on the dancing horse, slowly, along the south wall, and the townspeople gave him room. Then he faced her, and Angela saw that under his hat the pale yellow hair was thin and cut close to the scalp; the tight skin of the head was visible and pale and pink. The face was huge and mottled white and pink, and the thick, open lips were blue and violet. The flesh of the jowls was loose, and it rode on the bone of the jaws. There were no brows, and the small, round black glasses lay like pennies close together and flat against the enormous face. The albino was directly above her for one instant, huge and hideous at the extremity of the terrified bird. It was then her eyes were drawn to the heavy, bloodless hand at the throat of the bird. It was like marble or chert, equal in the composure of stone to the awful frenzy of the bird, and the bright red wattles of the bird lay still among the long blue nails, and the comb on the swollen heel of the hand. And then he was past. He rode in among the riders, and they, too, parted for him, watching to see whom he would choose, respectful, wary, and on edge. After a long time of playing the game, he rode beside Abel, turned suddenly upon him, and began to flail him with the rooster. Their horses wheeled, and the others drew off. Again and again the white man struck him, heavily, brutally, upon the chest and shoulders and head, and Abel threw up his hands, but the great bird fell upon them and beat them down. Abel was not used to the game, and the white man was too strong and quick for him. The roan mare lunged, but it was hemmed in against the wall; the black horse lay close against it, keeping it off balance, coiled and wild in its eyes. The white man leaned and struck, back and forth, with only the mute malice of the act itself, careless, undetermined, almost composed in some final, preeminent sense. Then the bird was dead, and still he swung it down and across, and the neck of the bird was broken and the flesh torn open and the blood splashed everywhere about. The mare hopped and squatted and reared, and Abel hung on. The black horse stood its ground, cutting off every line of retreat, pressing upon the terrified mare. It was all a dream, a tumultuous shadow, and before it the fading red glare of the sun shone on bits of silver and panes of glass and softer on the glowing, absorbent walls of the town. The feathers and flesh and entrails of the bird were scattered about on the ground, and the dogs crept near and crouched, and it was finished. Here and there the townswomen threw water to finish it in sacrifice.

It is somehow in keeping, she thought afterward, this

strange exhaustion of her whole being. She was bone weary, and her feet slipped down in the sand of the street, and it was nearly beyond her to walk. Like this, her body had been left to recover without her when once and for the first time, having wept, she had lain with a man; and it had been the same sacrificial hour of the day. She had been too tired for guilt and gladness, and she lay for a long time on the edge of sleep, empty of the least desire, in the warm current of her blood. Like this, though she could not then have known—the sheer black land above the orchards and the walls, the scarlet sky, and the three-quarter moon.

· · ·

As always in summer, the moment at which evening had come upon the town was absolute and imperceptible. And out of the town, among the hills and fields, the shadows had grown together and taken hold of the dusk until the valley itself was a soft gray shadow. Even so, there was a great range of colors within it, more various even than the sky, which now had begun to blush and fade. And the tinted rocks and soils grew supple and soft, and the shine went off the leaves.

Whispers rose up among the rows of corn, and the old man rested for a moment, bent still with his hands to the hoe. For nearly an hour now he had not been able to see well into the furrows, and he had reckoned their depth by the feel of the blade against the earth and made them true by the touch of the fronds and tassels on his neck and arms. The sweat dried up on his neck and the mud dried at his feet, and still he rested, holding off for another moment the pain of straightening his fingers and his back. At last he raised up against the stiffness in his spine, gathering the crippled leg under him. He breathed out sharply with the effort, and at the same time unlocked his hands and let the handle of the hoe fall into the crook of his arm. There was a lot of work left to do; he must yet bend again

to the fetlocks of the mares, and his fingers must slip the hob-
bles from the hooves; must yet lay hold of the wagon tongue
and the buckles and stays of the harness, twice, even; must then
carry water to the trough and cleave the portions from the bale.
But he didn't think of that; he thought instead of coffee and
bread and the dark interior of his room.

But *were* they whispers? Something there struck beneath
the level of his weariness, struck and took hold in his hearing
like the cry of a small creature—a field mouse or a young rabbit.
Evening gives motion to the air, and the long blades of corn ca-
reen and collide, and there is always at dusk the rustling of
leaves that settle into night. But was it that? All day his mind
had wandered over the past, habitually, beyond control and even
the least notion of control, but his thoughts had been by some
slight strand of attention anchored to his work. The steady repetition of his backward steps—the flash of the hoe and the sure
advance of the brown water after it—had been a small reality
from which his mind must venture and return. But now, at the
end of long exertion, his aged body let go of the mind, and he
was suddenly conscious of some alien presence close at hand.
And he knew as suddenly, too, that it had been there for a long
time, not approaching, but impending for minutes, and even
hours, upon the air and the growth and the land around. He
held his breath and listened. His ears rang with weariness; beyond that there was nothing save the soft sound of water and
wind and, somewhere among the farthest rows, the momentary
scuttle of a quail; then the low whistle and blowing of the
mares in the adjacent field, reminding him of the time. But
there was something else; something apart from these, not quite
absorbed into the ordinary silence: an excitement of breathing
in the instant just past, all ways immediate, irrevocable even
now that it had ceased to be. He peered into the dark rows of
corn from which no sound had come, in which no presence
was. There was only the deep black wall of stalks and leaves, vi-

brating slowly upon his tired vision like water. He was too old to be afraid. His acknowledgment of the unknown was nothing more than a dull, intrinsic sadness, a vague desire to weep, for evil had long since found him out and knew who he was. He set a blessing upon the corn and took up his hoe. He shuffled out between the rows, toward the dim light at the edge of the cornfield.

And where he had stood the water backed up in the furrow and spilled over the edge. It spread out upon the ground and filled the double row of crescents where the heels of his shoes had pressed into the earth. Here and there were the black welts of mud which he had shaken loose from the blade of the hoe. And there the breathing resumed, rapid and uneven with excitement. Above the open mouth, the nearly sightless eyes followed the old man out of the cornfield, and the barren lids fluttered helplessly behind the colored glass.

· · ·

The feasting had begun, and there was a lull on the town. The crippled old man in leggins and white ceremonial trousers shuffled out into the late afternoon. He dried his eyes on his sleeve and whimpered one last time in his throat. He was grown too old, he thought. He could not understand what had happened. But even his sorrow was feeble now; it had withered, like his leg, over the years, and only once in a while, when something unusual happened to remind him of it, did it take on the edge and point of pain. So it was that as he made his way along toward the Middle and smelled the food and fires of the feast, he wondered what his sorrow was and could not remember. Still the wagons came, and he heard in the distance the occasional laughter which brought them in. It had the sound of weariness now, and it rose up less frequently. It would soon be time for the Pecos bull to appear, and the smaller children made ready to attend. Out of the doorways he passed came the queer, halting talk of old fellowship, Tanoan and Athapascan, broken English and Spanish. He smelled the odor of boiled coffee, and it was good. He cared less for the sweet smell of piki and the moist, broken loaves of sotobalau, the hot spicy odors of paste and posole; for old men do not hunger much. Better for their novelty were the low open fires of the wagon camps, the sweet fat which dripped and sizzled on the embers; the burned, roasted mutton, and the fried bread. And more delicious than these was the laden air that carried the smoke and drew it out in long thin lines above the roofs, swelling in advance of the rain. The immense embankment of the storm had blackened out the whole horizon to the north. The compressed density of its core, like a great black snake writhing, drew out of the mouth of the canyon, recoiled upon the warm expanse of the valley, and resumed the slow, sure approach upon the intervening gullies and hills and fields above the town. And the old man had an ethnic, planter's love of harvests and of rain. And just there on the obsidian sky, extending out and across the eastern slope of the plain, was a sheer and perfect arc of brilliant colors.

It made him glad to be in the midst of talk and celebration, to savor the rich relief of the coming rain upon the rows of beans and chilies and corn, to see the return of weather, of trade and reunion upon the town. He tossed his head in greeting to the shy Navajo children who hid among the camps and peered, afraid of his age and affliction. For they, too, were a harvest, in some intractable sense the regeneration of his own bone and blood. The Diné, of all people, knew how to be beautiful. Here and there in the late golden light which bled upon the walls, he saw the bright blankets and the gleaming silverwork of their wealth: the shining weight of their buckles and belts, bracelets and bow guards, squash blossoms and pale blue stones. Had he anything at all of value, he would have liked to barter for such a stone, a great oval spider web, like a robin's egg, to wear upon his hand. And he would have been shrewd and indifferent; he would certainly have had the better of it. Such a stone was medicine, they said; it could preserve the sight. It could restore an old man's vision. They sang about it, he supposed, and no wonder, no wonder.

He turned in to the Middle and the holy place. The shrine for Porcingula, Our Lady of the Angels, had been raised at the center of the north side and adjacent to the kiva. It was a small green enclosure, a framework of wood and wire, covered with boughs of cedar and pine. He bowed before it, though as yet there was nothing but the bare altar and the benches inside. Tomorrow it would be made beautiful with candles and cloth and holy with incense. He would see to it, for he was the sacristan, after all. Two young boys would stand with rifles at the open side, and he would remind them of their trust. And after Mass the lovely Lady would be borne in procession from the church, and the little horse would come to greet her in the aisle, would precede her out into the Campo Santo and dance beside her in the streets; and the bull would lope all around and wheel and hook the air with its wooden horns, and the black-faced children, who were the invaders, and the clowns would follow, laughing and taunting with curses, upon its heels. The Lady would stand all day in her shrine, and the governor and his officials would sit in attendance at her feet, and one by one the dancers of the squash and turquoise clans would appear on top of the kiva, coming out upon the sky in their rich ceremonial dress, descend the high ladder to the earth, and kneel before her.

He took hold of the smooth poles and raised himself slowly up the rungs of the ladder, careful to place the crooked leg just so, where, if his weight should shift on it, the bone itself would suffice like a cane to hold him up. But it was a nearly empty precaution, not against his strength so much but against some element of doubt and fear that had lately come upon him like the shadow of his old age. His arms and hands were strong, and his shoulders bunched at the back of his neck and made a deep groove of his spine. He crept closer to the high vertical wall of the kiva, pressing the whole surface of his body against the slanting poles and rungs of the ladder, so that even the weight of his chest and shoulders amounted to nothing almost and there was no center to it; at last he laid his cheek on the final rung and saw the gray warp of the wood where the sun had dried and split it open and the red metal winding which spliced it to the poles and cut into it and stained it with rust. Then, without looking, could he reach upward and take hold of the wall itself. He drew himself over the top and stood for a moment to catch his breath. The rain had overtaken the hills above the town and the sky grew dark overhead. He felt the whirlwinds which ran upon the roofs and heard the distant bleating and lowing of the livestock, milling about on the weather's edge. And under him the great rafters of the kiva vibrated with the sound of thunder and drums. He looked south and west in the direction of the sunlit fields; they lay out like patchwork in the pool of light; and beyond, the black line of the mesa was edged with light. He let himself down into the great earthen darkness of the room.

When he emerged with the other holy men out of the kiva, it was dusk and the rain had begun to fall in the streets, unevenly at first, spotting and pitting the dust with dark, round stains; then it grew fine and steady, and the hard earth of the Middle began to shine. The people had come out of doors, and they stood about, waiting in the rain. He drew his blanket around him and went with the others to the house from which the little horse was now made ready to come. When they got to the doorway, he opened the screen and the horse began to dance. The collar of tin shells began to tremble with sound, and at the same time the drummer began the incessant roll and rattle of the sticks upon the drum. The little horse emerged into the dim light and the rain, and the drummer and the old men followed. The horse was an ancient likeness, like the black Arabian of the Moors, its head too small and finely wrought and the arch of its throat too severe. But it was a beautiful, sensitive thing, and the dancer gave it life. The spotted hide was taut and smooth on the frame, and the framework rode hard and low on the dancer's waist. It was he who gave it motion and mystery. He was dressed all in black, and under the bright kilt which hung from the shoulders and haunches of the little horse his black boots minced upon the earth, moving too little and too fast to follow. And his body and the body of the little horse were set in high, nervous agitation, like a leaf in the stiff wind. But all the strange and violent tremor ceased at his head, and he seemed to be standing there, perfectly still and apart, mindless and invisible behind the veil. And the black hat and the black mask of the flowing veil, which lay in the wind and rain upon the bones of the face, made a dark and motionless silhouette upon the dusk, and the blur of motion under it gave it sheer relief.

The medicine men presided over the little horse with prayers and plumes, pollen and meal. And elsewhere in the streets, approaching on a wave of sound, the bull came running. The clowns were close upon it, and it veered and drew up short and crouched, only to wheel among them and run on. And the black-faced clowns gave chase, shouting their obscene taunts, and the small invaders, absurd in the parody of fear, grabbed at their gored flesh and lay strewn about in the path of the beast. And the bull was a sad and unlikely thing, a crude and makeshift totem of revelry and delight. There was no holiness to it, none of the centaur's sacred mien and motion, but only the look of evil. It was a large skeleton of wood, drawn over loosely with black cloth upon which were painted numerous white rings like brands. Its horns were a length of wood fixed horizontally upon the sheepskin head; its eyes were black metal buttons and its tongue a bit of faded red cloth. But it was a hard thing to be the bull, for there was a primitive agony to it, and it was a kind of victim, an object of ridicule and hatred; and harder now that the men of the town had relaxed their hold upon the ancient ways, had grown soft and dubious. Or they had merely grown old. The old man heard the clamor of the clowns. He knew without looking around that the bull had come into the Middle, and it was at his back and he could see it perfectly in his mind. He thought of Mariano and of running. The rain and the cold reminded him of a time long ago when the flurries of snow rose up in the dawn and his legs were hale and he ran whole and perfectly toward the town. And once he, too, had been the bull— twice or three times, perhaps. He could not remember how many, but he could remember that it was done honorably and well. He had bent far forward and crouched with the likeness of the bull on his back, the way he must, and even so, in the angle and pain of that posture, he could have run away forever from the clowns. But he must not think of that now. The solemn little horse vibrated before him; the veiled rider held its fine head high and its croup level, never once relaxing the constant, nearly furi- ous imposition of life upon it; the black mane and tail lay out in commotion with the rain. The little horse moved here and there among the elders of the town to be received and anointed. The cacique spoke to it and sprinkled meal upon it. And the towns- people and the visitors to the town huddled in the rain and looked on. The bull went running in the streets, and the clowns and the antelope followed.

.   .   .

The rain diminished, and with nightfall the aftermath of the storm moved slowly out upon the plain. The last of the wagons had gone away from the junction, and only three or four young Navajos remained at Paco's. One of them had passed out and lay in his vomit on the floor of the room. The others were silent now, and sullen. They hung upon the bar and wheezed, helpless even to take up the dregs of the wine that remained. The precious ring of sweet red wine lay at the bottom of a green quart bottle, and the dark convexity of the glass rose and shone out of it like the fire of an emerald. The green bottle lay out in the yellow glow of the lamp, just there on the counter and within their reach. They regarded it with helpless wonder. Abel and the white man paid no attention to them. The two spoke low to each other, carefully, as if the meaning of what they said was strange and infallible. Now and then the white man laughed, and each time it carried too high on the scale and ended in a strange, inhuman cry—as of pain. It was an old woman's laugh, thin and weak as water. It issued only from the tongue and teeth of the great evil mouth, and it fell away from the blue lips and there was nothing left of it. But the mouth hung open afterward and made no sound, and the great body quaked and the white hands jerked and trembled helplessly. The Navajos became aware of him. And throughout Abel smiled; he nodded and grew silent at length; and the smile was thin and instinctive, a hard, transparent mask upon his mouth and eyes. He waited, and the wine rose up in his blood.

And then they were ready, the two of them. They went out into the darkness and the rain. They crossed the highway and walked out among the dunes. The lights of the junction shone dim in the distance and wavered like candle flames in back of the swirling mist. When they were midway between the river and the road, they stopped. They were near a telegraph pole; it leaned upon the black sky and shone like coal. All around was silence, save for the sound of the rain and the moan of the wind in the wires. Abel waited. The white man raised his arms, as if to embrace him, and came forward. But Abel had already taken hold of the knife, and he drew it. He leaned inside the white man's arms and drove the blade up under the bones of the breast and across. The white man's hands lay on Abel's shoulders, and for a moment the white man stood very still. There was no expression on his face, neither rage nor pain, only the same translucent pallor and the vague distortion of sorrow and wonder at the mouth and invisible under the black glass. He seemed to look not at Abel but beyond, off into the darkness and the rain, the black infinity of sound and silence. Then he closed his hands upon Abel and drew him close. Abel heard the strange excitement of the white man's breath, and the quick, uneven blowing at his ear, and felt the blue shivering lips upon him, felt even the scales of the lips and the hot slippery point of the tongue, writhing. He was sick with terror and revulsion, and he tried to fling himself away, but the white man held him close. The white immensity of flesh lay over and smothered him. He withdrew the knife and thrust again, lower, deep into the groin. The whole strength of his arm and back lay into the slant of the blade across the bowels, and the flesh split open and the steaming gore fell out upon his hand. The white hands still lay upon him as if in benediction, and the awful gaze of the head, still fixed upon something beyond and behind him. Then the head inclined a little, as if to whisper something of the darkness and the rain, and the pale flesh of the face twitched, and the great blue mouth still gaped open and made no sound. The white hands laid hold of Abel and drew him close, and the terrible strength of the hands was brought to bear only in proportion as Abel resisted them. In his terror he knew only to wield the knife. He turned it upon the massive white arms and at last the white man's hands fell away from him, and he reeled backward and away, whimpering now, exhausted. Abel threw down the knife and the rain fell upon it and made it clean. When he looked up, the white man still was standing there, still intent upon some vision in the near distance, waiting. He seemed just then to wither and grow old. In the instant before he fell, his great white body grew erect and seemed to cast off its age and weight; it grew supple and sank slowly to the ground, as if the bones were dissolving within it. And Abel was no longer terrified, but strangely cautious and intent, full of wonder and regard. He could not think; there was nothing left inside him but a cold, instinctive will to wonder and regard. He approached and knelt down in the rain to watch death come upon the white man's face. He removed the little black glasses from the white man's face and laid them aside, carefully. At last the eyes of the white man's face curdled and were impervious to the rain. One of the arms lay out from the body; it was there, in the pale angle of the white man's death, that Abel knelt. The sleeve had been cut away, and the whole length of the arm and the open palm of the hand were exposed. The white, hairless arm shone like the underside of a fish, and the dark nails of the hand seemed a string of great black beads. He knelt over the white man for a long time in the rain, looking down.

August 2

There was the sound of the censer and the drum. The procession of men and women wound out of the church and through the streets. The statue rode high upon the train and shone in the sun. The little horse danced on the way, and the bull went running and turning around. And the sun was high and the valley shone and the fields were bright and clean after the rain.

In a while the dancers filed out of the kiva. In two long lines they danced, and the gourds and evergreen boughs in their hands dipped and swayed to the sound of the singing and the drums. Their feet fell upon the earth in perfect time, and their eyes were solemn and looked straight ahead. And the single deep voice of the singers lay upon the dance, lay even upon the valley and the earth, whole and inscrutable, everlasting.

"Abelito." The old man Francisco rode out in the wagon to the fields. The lines lay low upon the flanks of the mares, but the mares knew the way and they went on their own to the river and the fields. The river was high, and they drew the wagon into it and drank. Without thinking, knowing only by instinct where he was, the old man looked for the reed. It was there still, but the rise of the river had reached it and made it spring; it leaned out over the water, and the little noose hung from it like a spider thread.

And later, when he had got down from the wagon and hobbled the mares, he carried his hoe into the rows of corn. The corn was high, and the long blades glistened in the sun. The harvest was all around him and the tassels were dark and damp with the rain and the great green ears were heavy and full of fragrance. He could hear the distant sound of the drums and the deep, welling voice of the singers. He tried not to think of the dance, but it was there, going on in his brain. He could see the dancers perfectly in the mind's eye, could see even how they bowed and turned, where they were in relation to the walls and the doors and the slope of the earth. He had an old and infallible sense of what they were doing and had to do. Never before had he been away from the dance. "Abelito," he said again, and he began to hoe the rows. The long afternoon went on around him, and he was alone in the fields. He knew only that he was alone again.

RONALD ROGERS

The Angry Truck (1969)

Rogers writes a story firmly fixed in Native consciousness of the modern kind. Like his predecessors Johnson, Mourning Dove, Oskison, Mathews, and McNickle, Rogers makes it clear: Indians are people, not curios; we inhabit the same world as other Americans but with a significant difference. For while we are American, we are also Natives, separate peoples with traditions reaching back on this continent over millennia. Angry trucks, college dorms, a Native voice arising out of imposed silence, how America appears to Native eyes, the strength of the tradition—the themes remain what they were throughout the first two-thirds of the century, but the metaphors, the images, and the settings change with a changing America. It's 1968: rock 'n' roll, the Vietnam War, flower children, a new wave of Anglo-American seekers trekking out to Indian Country thinking themselves to be the first. . . .

Echoing Rousseau, but with a twist, in "The Angry Truck," Rogers writes, "Try to describe blank paper. You can't. There's nothing there. It's all white and dead, dead, dead." Like the whales, like the writer, like the ever-present institution. And then the blessing: It rains.

1

My roommate passes while I sit, reams of white paper fanned out around me. A window interrupts the wall to my left. The morning sunlight is very new and the glass panes and their wood borders chop it into squares. I try not to look at it. Mostly I'm leafing through stacks of old poems.

The papers hiss lightly now and then as I lift them and set them aside.

My roommate lumbers back to me, looms above my chair. He's big and thick, a friendly house with hair sprouting crazy on his head. He makes me nervous. His nose pokes over my shoulder. "What are you looking for?" he asks.

"I'm not sure," I say. "Mind's just blank, that's all. Can't write. Excuse me a minute, will you?"

"Certainly," he says.

2

Underneath a yellow paper I see that a long time ago I wrote something about racial things. Quiet stuff, because I was trying to be honest and let the reader know (in a nice way) that I wasn't too enthusiastic about the whole thing. A poem about a race riot. I read it twice. When I finish the piece a second time my shoe scrapes on the floor. I throw it aside, hear it whisper across, nearly dig into the wooden table before me.

A poem to Leroi Jones. A window, I see. A room making walls all around me.

The race poem is like a weight in my mind. I have to force myself to see things.

I skate my chair back and stand.

3

I begin to walk around the room. The room is small, strangled with furniture. Supposed to be homey. Institution homey. Orphanage homey, maybe, I don't know. I know about orphanages . . .

I feel hostility welling up. It sharpens things a little, but nothing comes on paper.

Writing. God. I want to stop this game. It's a stupid game and I don't want to play anymore.

I look at my shoes. Knock, the heels go on the linoleum. Knick, they go. Knock. Knick, knock. Knick, knock. I think of torpedoes. Black torpedoes. Whales. Black whales with shredded gray faces skimming across the floor.

The walking stops. I lean against the wall, look toward the window, but I stand where I am. I don't want to go over there.

The window and what's outside would just confuse me.

4

I stand for awhile, five minutes or so. I'm looking at the radiator, but I'm not looking at the radiator. I'm thinking about the whales.

My roommate appears again, makes a mountain over my left shoulder. "Anything yet?" he asks.

"No," I answer. "Beat it, will you?"

"Certainly," he says. He's angry. He leaves. He actually leaves.

The door goes thump behind him.

5

I go back to the cluttered table, rummage for blank paper as I whiz a pencil out of my pocket.

The whales, I think. The whales, now, what do they do? Nothing. They all swim around and do nothing.

Well, I think, at least it's a lead. At least it's something to go on.

I'm looking at the radiator, but it's not all together. It's in sections—thin sections, upright, and they glint. The light blows up where it hits them in spots.

Not like torpedoes. Torpedoes are productive.

The whales do nothing. They swim around and eat kelp, don't they? And microscopic animals. Tons of microscopic animals. I shake my head. And some of them are black and they swim all around . . .

Whales, I think. Oh, Christ!

WHOP! goes the radiator. PIP-KLANK-WHOP!

I throw the pencil and it clatters and whistles across the floor, ducks in under the couch. Cripes, I think. I smash up the blank paper, crunch it into a ball and sling it to my right at the wastebasket.

Missed. The paper ball bounces happily and stops against the wall.

I still haven't written anything.

6

Must write on paper. With the typewriter maybe. Thinking, staring hard into the radiator. I burrow around in the poetry awhile, but it's useless.

And even the floor is dust and speckled linoleum. Lines crossing lines at right angles, perfect and tight. The straightest lines in the world, crossing over into squares.

7

Looking at the typewriter, I see keys. That's not so thrilling. Gray keys with white lettering. I lean closer. Between the keys, dust. Tiny spatterings of dust.

I pick up a piece of paper and it rasps on my thumb. I slip the edge behind the roll bar. The roll bar is rubber. Tik, the paper goes. Fast, I spin the knobs and they go ratatat-tat as the black bar chews up my paper, spits it out on the side nearest me.

Done. I sigh and gaze at the blank paper. Try to describe blank paper. You can't. There's nothing here. It's all white and dead, dead, dead.

Outside on the street a truck grumbles by. That's all. It sounds angry.

8

POEM

Once I saw a dog run over,
But I never saw an angry truck.
                    —*Ronald Rogers*

9

Glik, the door goes. Kwump. My roommate smothers me with his shadow. He stands very still for a second. Reading. I know he's reading.

He laughs.

"Knock it off," I say.

"Still fishing?" He's mad and I hear it. "Catching anything?"

"Whales." I hold the rest back.

"Angry trucks?"

"Knock it off, you bastard. Go away."

10

Stand up and walk again. I don't look at my shoes. I look at the walls, but I hear the shoes. Knock, knick. My mind is tired. Forehead oily and hot. I trace the ridges of it under the skin.

Try to sigh and I blow like bored pig.

I stand around. Outside, the world babbles. Why, I think, and my side itches. I itch all over. Burning and clawing all over me.

The air rolls, lurches like soup. It's the heat, I think. It's the stinking heat. Nobody could breathe in here.

11

I walk to the window but try not to look outside.

I reach up over the smell of dusty glass, test the metal lock and find it free. Wedge a palm against a windowpane, tighten my chest and give it a shove up.

Shhhhhhhhaaaaaaaa, it goes. Like a deep breath. Like a sigh, washing me over and cooling me down to the marrow. I go to the next window. Glass is dust. Wedge in a palm and skate it open.

Shhhhhaaaaaa, it goes. Sliding, skidding, wood to wood. Scratching the itch.

Now, then. The wind rumples papers behind me. It's raising hell and I can hear it even if I don't care to look. Papers rattle and sail all over.

I press my head against the window jamb. I look out at the dusk a moment, at the sun trading cooler shadows with the night. I hear that chattering tornado behind me, and then my roommate grumble. After a moment, I smile.

GREY COHOE

The Promised Visit (1969)

Innocent of overt political or historical content, "The Promised Visit" betrays the legacy of colonization and its attendant ills in the mixed values and views the protagonist holds toward his Navajo world. But while thinking himself above "uneducated superstitions," the narrator reveals his profound connection to the tradition, and in the episodic structure of the story invites readers to share it.

Susan Billy is one of the elusive figures that populate Native literature. In Cohoe's story she is Navajo, and this being so evinces Navajo ways in her mysterious appearance and disappearance. But many tribes tell similar stories; among the Indians of Oklahoma brushes with the mysterious Deer Woman and her cousins the shadowy Yunwitsansdi still occur and are recounted, while everywhere in Indian Country human interaction with the spirits and supernaturals occurs.

The story recounts a return to tradition. Although his consciousness is mixed with Western ways, Western beliefs, and Western accouterments like the truck and the football sweater, the narrator realizes who he is, where he comes from, and the nature

*of a different reality. In the late twentieth century the mixture is
a fact of Native life: some modern ideas, beliefs, and possessions,
some Native. But the life of the Native people is Native for all that,
as "The Promised Visit" testifies.*

It had been a long day at Window Rock, Arizona. I'd shoved
myself up at dawn and started from Shiprock early that morning. Today was a special day for me to appear for my tribal
scholarship interview. I had applied for it in the spring so I
could go on to school after my graduation from high school.
My brother-in-law, Martin, was considerate enough to lend me
his pickup truck. I would still have been there promptly for my
appointment, no matter if I'd needed to walk, hitchhike, or
crawl the hundred and twenty miles.

After all the waiting, I finally learned that I didn't need
their scholarship to attend the school of my choice. I didn't
need anything from them. They knew this all the time and
didn't write to inform me. I was so sore about the unnecessary
trip that I didn't bother to eat my lunch or supper. All I got
was waste of time, money, and strength which I would've put to
good use on the farm. Well, at least they wouldn't bother me,
complaining about their money.

Gradually the warmth at the side of my face cooled off as
the sunlight was broken up by long shadows across the plain,
then bled over the fuzzy mountainous horizon. The same as
yesterday—the usual sunny sky, the same quiet atmosphere, and
the daily herding toils handled by the desert people—the daylight disappeared, ending another beautiful day. I didn't bother
to glance a moment at the departing sun to give farewell or offer my traditional prayer for the kind sun, thanking him for his
warmth and life. I constantly stared over the blue hood of the
pickup onto the highway up ahead.

The old zigzagging road lined the shadowed flat region,

cooling from a day's heat. It was not until now that the evening wind began to form the woollike clouds, building a dark overcast stretching across my destination. At first, it was obviously summer rain clouds, and even a child could recognize the rolling grayish mass. The white lane markers rhythmically speared under me as I raced toward home.

I rolled down the window about an inch to smell the first rain that I would inhale this summer. The harsh air rushed in, cold and wild. Its crazy current tangled and teased my hair. The aroma of the flying wet dirt tensed my warm nose, a smell of rain. Immediately the chill awakened my reflexes. I balanced my body into a proper driving position according to a statement in the driver's manual. I prepared to confront the slippery pavement.

In spite of the long hard day, sitting and wrestling the stiff steering wheel, I was beaten. My muscles were too weak to fight the powerful wind, if a big thunderstorm should come upon me. I lazily moved one of my bare arms to roll up the window. I didn't like the roaring of the air leak. The chill of it made me tremble. I felt no fear of a gentle summer rain, but the dangerous hazards under a vigorous downpour frightened me.

I narrowed my eyes into the mirror to look back along the highway, hoping that someone else would be traveling along, too. Unfortunately, no one showed up. I'd have to go all alone on this road with the next nearest gas station about ninety-eight miles. It was unusual, during such a vacationing summer, to find not a single tourist going on this route. Maybe, I thought, if I wait a few minutes someone will show up, then I'll follow.

I lazily lifted my foot off the gas peddle and slowly stepped on the brakes. When I came to a stop, I gave a long stretch to relieve my stiffness. Then, I yawned. I waited in hopes until the cool evening darkness filled the valley. I stood by the open car door and thought of how mysterious the storm looked. The more I waited the more time I was wasting. Before long, after giving up waiting, I was on the road again. I sang some Navajo songs, whispered, and fitted my sweater around my shoulder. I did anything to accompany myself.

By now I could sight the lightnings spearing into the horizon, glowing against the dark overcast. I could almost see the whole valley in one flash. The black clouds came closer and angrier as I approached their overcast. Being used to the old reservation road, narrow and rough, and well adjusted to the pickup, I drove ahead to meet the first raindrops.

I thought of a joke and wanted to burst out in laughter, but only a smile came. I used to laugh when I teased my folks about my death. They would scold me and would arouse my superstitions about it. Speaking of your death is taboo. Now, when I wondered whether I'd ever make it to the other side of the storm, it didn't sound funny.

Many people had died along this same highway, never telling us what caused their accidents. Most of these tragedies occurred in bad weather, especially in thunderstorms. Several months ago the highway department stuck small white crosses along the road at each place where an accident victim was killed. This was to keep a driver alert and aware. The crosses became so numerous that it caused more confusion and more accidents. When a person sees a cross he becomes nervous.

Everytime we drove through the cross-lined highway, I would think of a parade. The invisible spectators sitting on their crosses would watch us go along. Many people believe that these ghosts bring bad luck. Of course, we Navajos get cursed by such witchcraft.

The dark clouds formed themselves into a huge ugly mass. It reminded me of the myths the people feared in such angry clouds. The suspicious appearance scared me, making my joints and very soul tremble.

My mother once mentioned a monster that lived in the

thunderclouds. Was it only one of my bedtime stories, or was it the killer of all the cross-marked victims?

The fierce monster dresses in armor of the hues in a rainbow. Only his mysterious face is uncovered, but no one knows his appearance under his irony dress. Some people believe that he is the insane son of our rain god. A few aged Navajos who have seen him tell us he is the man who first explored across our country in our great-great-grandfather's days. He still leads his armed band of Spaniards.

He swings his swift sword, slashing and striking the earth, creating a snappy, rolling noise. He enjoys lightning and thunder, which relieve his tensions. Once in a great while a big storm will indicate his anger. He slices trees, ignites mountains, breaks up hogans, or stabs people who come in his way. Many people have died by his sword. Usually tailing the rain clouds, two rainbows appear, indicating where he has traveled.

Of course there are other superstitions composed around these angry clouds. The people along this valley believe that there is a Wind Being living in a storm. This monster blows over anybody who moves or fights against his powerful blows.

Another story was told to me by my grandmother. It was told to her by her late son before he passed away in a hospital. He saw a ghost standing in his way on the highway and he drove through the rain-sogged image. Her son ran off the road after being knocked unconscious by the shock.

"Baloney! I shouldn't believe those nonsenses," I scolded myself. "I don't want to be one of those Navajos who is easily aroused by superstitions."

Carefully I drove around a big slanting curve. It was at a place where my late cousin was killed in a wreck. The cool, refreshing air was so enjoyable that it prevented the memory of the horrible incident. I anxiously went along, thinking about the day's events and waiting to meet one of the monsters.

My stomach began to tighten up with a groaning sound. It

made me weak. I imagined my sister's cooking at home. We'd butchered a sheep yesterday for meat supply. My sister had probably barbequed some mutton and made some fried bread. I swallowed down my empty throat and moved my empty stomach. The smell and taste of my imagined food seemed to be present in my mouth and nose. Restlessly, I speeded up a little faster.

The dark overcast hid my view of the road and the area around faded away into darkness so I had to turn on the headlights. My face was now tired of being fixed in the same direction, down the long, dirty highway. My eyelids were so weak that they closed by themselves. I should have slept longer last night. Again, I rolled down the window. The cold air poured in, caressing me with its moistened chill. It awoke me completely.

I would have brought my brother, Teddy, along to accompany me, but he was fast asleep so I didn't bother. I reckoned he'd rather work in the field than to sit all day long. Somehow I was glad he hadn't come because I wouldn't want him to fear this killer storm. If anything should happen, I'd be the only one to die. Sadly, I kept on counting the dips, rocky hills, and the zigzagging curves as I drove on.

The sudden forceful blow jolted the car and waved it like a rolling wagon. The screaming wind began to knock at my windows. I clung hard on the steering wheel to fight the rushing wind. I slowed almost to a stop and peered out through the blowing dust at the hood, trying to keep on the road. Flying soil and tumble weeds crashed against the car. I could not tell what ran beside the highway—a canyon or maybe a wash. The angry wind roared and blew so strong that the car slanted. I didn't know how to escape the Wind Monster. I sat motionless, feeling death inside my soul.

And then the car was rocked by falling raindrops as if it were a tincan being battered by flying stones. The downpour came too quickly for me to see the first drops on the wind-shield. The whole rocky land shook when a loud cracking lightning shot into the nearby ground.

"Oh no! The devil is coming." I frightened myself, but I had enough courage to pick up my speed a little, thinking that I might escape his aim. I strained my eyes to see through the glare on the windshield. The pouring raindrops were too heavy for the wipers. It was like trying to look under water. Another swift stripe of lightning exploded into the ground. This time, it was closer. I kept myself from panicking. I drove faster, hoping the devil wouldn't see me.

The storm calmed and turned into a genial shower. Then I could see where I was. In sight, through the crystal rain, a green-and-white-lettered sign showed up in the headlights: LITTLEWATER 12 miles; SHIPROCK 32 miles. At last, I felt relieved. I would be home in less than an hour. Never in my life did I ever long for home so much until this day. The windshield cleared and the rain had passed.

Again it was quiet except this time I heard a splashing sound at the tires. My ears missed the hard rhythms of smashing rain. I felt as if I had been closely missed by a rifle shot.

Even though I didn't see any of the monsters, still I looked out, but shamefully, for the two rainbows. They weren't there. I scolded myself for looking. It was ridiculous to fear something that didn't exist, like fairies. Yes, I'd heard thunder, seen lightning, and felt the terrifying wind, but I'd come out alive. Only for a moment was I trapped and my minutes numbered. I'd probably confronted the stormhead.

"Standing ghost," I scoffed and laughed to myself.

"It's too bad I can't see anything except the light-struck black pavement," I thought. I always rejoiced to see and smell the land where the rain had spread its tasteful water. It's refreshing to watch the plants drink from the puddles around them.

I hoped the rain had traveled across the farmlands near

Shiprock. I was supposed to irrigate the corn tomorrow, but luckily the rain would take good care of it. I might do something else instead. Maybe I'd go to the store or to the cafe and eat three or four hamburgers. I liked to see that cute waitress there.

With the scary storm passing, and my being penetrated by the superstition over, I felt as if I'd awakened from a nightmare. My hunger, too, had surrendered, but the crampy stiffness still tightened my body. I didn't bother to stop for a rest. I rushed straight home. I hoped my supper would be waiting. The clouds slid away and it wasn't as late as I'd thought.

By now, some twinkling stars appeared over the northern horizon. The found moon cast its light on the soggy ground as the silky white clouds slid after the rain. The water reflected the light so that the standing water shone like the moon itself. I could see the whole area as if in daylight. I ran the tires through the shallow puddles on the pavement to feel it splash. I imagined myself running and playing along the San Juan River shore. I constantly hastened on, looking for the lights at Littlewater over on the other side of the next hill.

Littlewater is a small store standing alongside the highway. Besides the two trailer houses in the back of the store, there are several hogans and log cabins standing in view of the flat valley, but tonight, I can see them only as dark objects at a distance. During warm wintry days, the local people gather together on the sunny side of the trading post walls to chat or watch the travelers stop for gas or supplies. But at this time in the summer, they all move to the cool mountains.

A few electric lights appeared within range of my headlights. Three dull guide lights shone at the store. One larger light showed up the whole front porch. As usual, there wasn't anybody around at this late hour of the night. I slowed to glance at the porch as I passed by. At the same time as I turned back to the road I saw a standing object about fifty yards ahead.

I had always feared dark objects at night. My soul tensed with a frightening chill as I trembled. I drove closer, telling myself it would be a horse or a calf.

The lights reached the dark image as I approached. Surprisingly, it was a hitchhiker. I didn't think anything about the person. All that came to my mind was to offer someone my help. Then I saw it was a girl.

I stopped a little way past her.

She slowly and shyly walked to the car window. She was all wet and trembling from the cold air. "Can you give me a lift to Shiprock?" she politely asked in her soft, quivering voice.

"Sure. That's where I'm going, too." I quickly offered the warm empty seat.

She smiled and opened the door. Water dripped to the floor from her wet clothes. She sat motionless and kept looking away from me.

I thought she was just scared or shy. I, too, was shy to look, and we didn't talk for a long time. It wasn't until a few miles from Shiprock that I finally started a conversation.

"I guess the people around this area are happy to get such a big rain," I finally dared to utter. "I was supposed to water our farm field tomorrow, but I guess the good Lord did it for me," I joked, hoping she would laugh or say something. "What part of Shiprock are you from?" I questioned her.

"Not in Shiprock. About one mile from there," she carefully murmured, using the best of her English.

She looked uneducated by the style of the clothes she wore. She was dressed in a newly made green velvet blouse and a long, silky white skirt. She wore many silver and turquoise necklaces and rings. A red and orange sash-belt tightly fitted around her narrow waist. She was so dressed up that she looked ready for going to town or a squaw dance.

Her long black hair hung loosely to her small, round shoulders and beside her light-complexioned face. In the glow from the instrument panel I could tell she was very pretty. She didn't look like some other Navajo girls. Her skin was much lighter than their tannish-brown skin color.

Finally, I gathered enough guts to offer her my school sweater. "Here. You better put this on before you catch cold. I hear pneumonia is very dangerous," I said, as I struggled about to take off the sweater.

She kindly took it and threw it around herself. "Thank you." She smiled and her words came out warmly.

I looked at her and she looked at the same time, too. I almost went off the road when I saw her beautiful smile of greeting. She was the prettiest girl I have ever seen. I jerked the steering wheel and the car jolted back onto the highway. We both laughed. From that moment on, we talked and felt as if we'd known each other before. I fell in love and I guess she did, too.

"Where have you been in this kind of bad weather?" I began to ask questions so we could get better acquainted with each other.

"I visited some of my old relatives around Littlewater." She calmly broke her shyness. "The ground was too wet to walk on so I decided to get a ride."

"I've been to Window Rock to get a scholarship to an art school. I started this morning and it isn't until now I'm coming back. I'm late for my supper because of the storm."

I knew she was interested in me, too, as she asked me, "Where do you live?"

"I live on one of the farms down toward west from Shiprock. I live with my family next to Thomas Yazzie's place." I directed her to the place, too.

"I used to know Thomas and his family when I was very small," she almost cried. "It's always sad to lose friends."

I felt sorry for her losing her friends. Right then I knew she was lonely.

"Where do you live?" I asked, as I looked straight down the lighted road.

She hesitated to answer, as if she weren't sure of it. Then she said, "I live about four miles from Shiprock." Then she lowered her head as if she was worried about something I'd said.

I didn't talk any more after that. Again it was quiet. I kept my mind on the road, trying to forget my warm feelings for her beauty.

The night settled itself across the desert land, making stars and the moon more bright. The night sky and the dampness made me sleepy. I felt in a dreamy, romantic mood. The rain still covered the road. It was too quiet for comfort.

"Let's listen to some music," I interrupted the silence as I turned on the radio. I tuned to some rock 'n' roll music. So now, with the cool night, beating music, and our silence we drove until she asked me to stop. It was just about a mile over two hills to Shiprock. I stopped where a dirt road joined the highway.

"Is this the path to your place?" I quickly asked before she departed.

"Yes. I live about three miles on this road." She pointed her lips for direction as she placed her hand on the door handle.

"I wish I could take you home, but the road is too wet. I might never get home tonight. Well, I hope I'll see you in Shiprock sometime. By the way, what's your name?" I tried to keep her there a while longer by talking to her.

She took a long time to say her name. "Susan Billy," she said finally. Then she added, "Maybe I can visit you some of these nights." She smiled as she opened the door and stepped out of the car.

"All right, goodbye." I tried not to show how I felt as I said those last words.

I looked back in the mirror as I dropped over the hill. She stood waving her hand. I felt proud to find someone like her who wanted so much to see me again. I already missed her. Or was she just joking about her visit? Why would she want to visit me at night? I smiled, hoping she'd come very soon.

Before I knew I was home, I stopped at our garage. The lights in the house were out and the rain had wet the red brick building to a deeper red. I couldn't wait to get into the bed where I could freely think about Susan. I didn't bother to eat or wake my folks. I just covered myself with the warm blankets.

Another sunny morning turned into a cloudy and windy afternoon. Rain clouds brought another chilly breeze as they had two evenings ago when I went to Window Rock. I had not forgotten Susan and, deep in my heart, I kept expecting her visit which she had spoke of. Today, though, we must go to the field to plant new seeds. The cold called for a warm jacket. I glanced around the room where I usually placed my sweater, a maroon-and-gold-colored school sweater. I walked through the house, but I didn't find it. I used my old jacket instead, hoping my sweater was in the car at the hospital where my brother-in-law, Martin, was working.

The movements of my arms and legs, my digging and sowing seeds were in my usual routine for the last few weeks. I could let my mind wander to Susan while my body went on with its work. Suddenly I remembered offering her my sweater on that trip.

"Are you tired already? What are you thinking about? Supper?" my brother asked when he saw me standing with a smile on my face.

"I remembered where I left my sweater. What time is it?" I asked him, wishing the time for Martin to come home with the pickup were near, but I remembered that our noon lunch wasn't even thought of yet.

"Don't know. I know it's not lunch time yet," he joked and kept on hoeing the small weeds along the corn rows.

It wasn't until late that evening, about six-thirty, that I was on my way to see Susan. My whole life filled with joy. The dirt road leading off the highway where Susan had stood seemed dried enough for the tires to roll on.

Slowly and very nervously I approached the end of the three miles to her place. I rode over the last hill and stopped at a hogan. The people were still outside, eating their supper under a shadehouse. A familiar man sat facing me from the circle around the dishes on the ground. I was sure I'd seen him someplace, but I couldn't recall where. His wife sat beside him, keeping busy frying some round, thin dough. Three small children accompanied them, two older girls and a child—I couldn't tell whether it was a girl or a boy. I politely asked the man where the Billys lived. He pointed his finger to the west from his crosslegged sitting position. It was at the next hogan where I could find Susan.

"Their hogans are near, over beyond that rocky hill," he directed me in his unmannered way. His words came from his filled mouth.

"They moved to the mountain several days ago," his wife interrupted, "but I saw a light at the place last night. The husband might have ridden down for their supplies."

Hopefully I started again. Sure enough, there were the mud hogans, standing on a lonely plateau. As I approached, a man paused from his busy packing and stood watching me.

He set down a box of groceries and came to the car door. I reached out the window and shook his hand for greeting.

"Hello. Do you know where Susan Billy lives?" I asked, pretending I didn't know where to go to find her.

"Susan Billy?" He looked down, puzzled, and pronounced the name as if he'd never heard it before. After a while of silence, he remarked, "I don't know if you are mistaking for our Susan, or there might be another girl by that name."

My hope almost left as I explained further. "Two nights

ago I gave her a ride from Littlewater to the road over there. She told me she lived at this place."

His smile disappeared and a puzzled, odd look took its place.

"See that old hogan over in the distance beyond the three sagebrushes?" He pointed to an old caved-in hogan. "Susan Billy is there," he sadly informed me.

"Good. I'll wait here until she comes back." I sank into the car seat happily, but why was he looking so shocked or worried?

"You don't understand," he went on, explaining, "she died ten years ago and she is buried in that hogan."

At first, I thought it was a joke. I knew how some parents would try to keep their daughters or sons from seeing any strangers. His black hair and light complexion, not so smooth or whitish as Susan's, somehow resembled hers.

Then I knew he was lying. "I loaned her my sweater and I forgot to get it back." I tried to convince him to tell the truth.

He seemed so shocked as he looked more carefully at the old hogan again. "See that red object on one of the logs?" He pointed out that it hadn't been there until recently.

I saw the maroon object. I could instantly recognize my sweater at a distance. My heart almost stopped with the horrible shock. I struggled to catch my breath back. I didn't believe in ghosts until then, but I had to believe my sweater. I had to believe the beautiful girl who had ridden with me, who had promised to visit me. Still, why hadn't she killed me like the rest of her victims? Was it because of my sweater or because of the love we shared?

From that day, I had proven to myself the truth of the Navajo superstitions. I know I shall never get my sweater back, but, on one of these windy nights, I will see Susan again as she promised. What will I do then?

SIMON J. ORTIZ

Woman Singing (1969)

Reflecting Ortiz's lifelong commitment to activism and Native rights, "Woman Singing" is graced with a profound lyricism balanced by a tightly controlled, almost reportorial style. Fusing the position of a woman to that occupied by Indian people of both genders, as so many of his predecessors did, Ortiz contributes a powerful Pueblo voice to the emerging written aspect of the Native Narrative tradition.

Far from home, subject to a variety of brutalizations that they have sometimes incorporated into themselves, sometimes reacted to with self-destructive acts, the People endure, and from their imposed situation of near-hopeless deprivation, and loneliness, something remains. Held through the ages, it persists in dignity. There is a Navajo prayer that contains the refrain, "May it be beautiful all around me; In beauty is it finished," that forms the subtext of "Woman Singing." Out of centuries of silence, out of deep despair and degradation, Turtle's voice reminds us who we are and what life's journey is for.

"Yessir, pretty good stuff," Willie said. He handed the bottle of Thunderbird wine to Clyde.

Clyde took a drink and then another before he said anything. He looked out the window of their wooden shack. Gray and brown land outside. Snow soon, but hope not, Clyde thought.

"Yes," Clyde said. But he didn't like it. He didn't drink wine very much, maybe some sometimes, but none very much.

Willie reached for the bottle, and Clyde thought that Willie didn't mind drinking anything. Any wine was just another drink. But he knew, too, that Willie liked whiskey, and he liked beer, too. It didn't make any difference to Willie. Clyde wished he had some beer.

They had come from the potato fields a few minutes before. It was cold outside and Willie threw some wood into the kitchen stove as soon as they came in. He poured in kerosene from a mason jar and threw in a match. After a moment, the kerosene caught the small fire and exploded with a muffled sound. Willie jumped back and laughed. Clyde hung up his coat and then put it back on when he saw there were only a few pieces of wood in the woodbox. He looked over at Willie, but Willie was taking his coat off and so Clyde went on out to get the wood. Willie didn't do anything he didn't have to.

There was singing from the shack across from theirs. Singing, The People singing, Clyde said to himself in his Native Indian tongue. It was a woman. Sad kind of, but not lonely, just something which bothered him, made him think of Arizona, his homeland. Brown and red land. Piñon, yucca, and his father's sheep, the dogs too around the door of the hogan at evening. Smoke and smell of stew and bread, and the older smell of the juniper mingled with the sheep. His heart and thoughts were lonely. Woman singing, The People singing, here and now, Clyde thought to himself. He stood for a while and listened and then looked over at the shack. The door was tightly shut, but the walls were thin, just scrap lumber and roofing paper, and the woman's voice was almost clear. Clyde was tempted to approach the shack and listen closer, his loneliness now pressed him, but he would not because it was broad daylight and it was not the way to do things. The woman was Joe Shorty's wife, and she was the mother of two children. Clyde picked up an armful of wood and returned to his own shack.

"Have some more, son," Willie said. Willie was only a few years older than Clyde, but he called him son sometimes. Just for fun, and Clyde would call him father in return. Willie was married and the father of two children. They lived in New Mexico while he worked in the Idaho potato fields.

"I think I'll fix us something to eat," Clyde said after he had taken a drink. He began to peel some potatoes. Willie's going to get drunk again, he thought. Yessir. They had gotten paid, and Willie had been fidgety since morning when they had received their money from Wheeler, their boss. He had told the Indians who worked for him, "Now I know that some of you are leaving as soon as you get paid, well, that's okay with me because they ain't much to do around here until next year. But some of you are staying for a while longer, and I'm telling those guys who are staying that they better stay sober. Besides, it's getting colder out, and we don't want no froze Indians around." Wheeler laughed, and Willie laughed with him. Clyde didn't like the boss, and he didn't look at him or say anything when he received his pay. He was going to stay for at least another month, but he didn't want to. But he figured he had to since he wasn't sure whether he could get a job around home right off or even at all. Willie was staying, too, because he didn't feel like going home just yet, besides the fact that his family needed money.

"I think I'm gonna go to town tonight," Willie said. He was casual in saying it, but he was excited and he had been planning for it since morning. "Joe Shorty and his wife are coming along. You want to come?"

"I'm not sure," Clyde said. He didn't know Joe Shorty too well, and he had only said Hello to his wife and children.

"Come on," Willie insisted. "We'll go to a show and then to the Elkhorn Bar. Dancing there. And all the drunks have left, so it'll be okay now. Come with us."

"Yeah, I might," Clyde said. He listened for the woman's singing while they ate, but the fire crackling in the stove was loud and Willie kept talking about going to town. "Isn't Joe Shorty and his family going back home?" Clyde asked.

"I don't know," Willie answered. He pushed back his chair and carried the dishes to the sink. Clyde began to wash the dishes but Willie stopped him. "Come on, let's go."

When they knocked on Joe Shorty's door, a boy answered. He looked at the two men and then ran back inside. Joe came to the door.

"Okay, just a little while," Joe said.

Willie and Clyde sat down on the front step. They could hear movement and mumbled talk inside. Clyde thought about the singing woman again. He felt uncomfortable because he was thinking of another man's woman. It was a healing song, strong mountains in it, strong and sharp and clear, and far up. Women always make songs strong, he thought. He almost told Willie about the song.

Joe and his wife and children, two boys, came out and they all began to walk on the road towards town. It was five miles away, and usually someone was driving into town and would give them a ride. If not, they would walk all the way. The children ran and walked ahead. They talked quietly with each other, but the grownups didn't say anything.

When they had walked a mile, a pickup truck stopped for them. It was Wheeler. "Hey, Willie. Joe. Everybody going to town, huh? Come," Wheeler called.

Willie and Clyde got in front with Wheeler, and Joe and his family got in the back.

"Well, gonna go have a good time, huh? Drink and raise hell," Wheeler said loudly and laughed. He punched Willie in the side playfully. He drove pretty fast along the gravel road.

Willie smiled. The wine he had finished off was warm in him. He wished he had another bottle. Out of the corners of his eyes, he searched the cab, and wondered if Wheeler might have a drink to offer.

"You Indians are the best damn workers," Wheeler said. "And I don't mind giving you a ride in my truck. Place down the road's got a bunch of Mexicans, had them up at my place several years back, but they ain't no good. Lazier than any Indian anytime, them Mexicans are. Couldn't nothing move them once they sit down. But you people—and for this reason I don't mind giving you a lift to town—Willie and your friend there do your work when I tell you, and that means you're okay for my farm."

Clyde felt the wine move in his belly. It made him swallow and he turned his head a little and saw that the woman's scarf had fallen away from her head. She was trying to put it back on.

"That Joe's got a pretty woman," Wheeler said to Willie. He looked at Clyde for comment, but Clyde would not look at him. Willie smiled and nodded.

"Yeah, don't get to see too many pretty Indian women around the camps, but she's a pretty one. You think so, Willie?" Wheeler nudged Willie with his elbow.

"Yes," Willie said and he shrunk down in his seat. He wished that Wheeler would offer him a drink if he had any. But he knew that he probably wouldn't.

"Hey, Clyde, you married? A woman at home?" Wheeler asked, but he didn't look at Clyde. They were approaching the town and Clyde stared straight ahead at it but he decided to answer.

"No," Clyde said. "Not yet, maybe when I get enough money." He smiled faintly to show that he was making a minor joke.

"Someday you'll get a woman, maybe a pretty one like Joe's, with or without money," Wheeler said. And he laughed loudly. He pulled the pickup truck over to a curb in the center of the small town. "Well, take it easy. Don't over do it. Or else you'll land in jail or freeze out in the cold or something," Wheeler said with no special concern.

"We're going to the show," Willie said, and he smiled at Wheeler.

"Okay," Wheeler said, gave a quick laugh, and turned to watch Joe's wife climb out of the truck. He wanted to catch her eye, maybe to wink at her, but she didn't look at him. He watched the Indians walk up the street towards the town theater. The woman and her children followed behind the men. Wheeler thought about all the drunk Indians he'd seen in his life. He shrugged his shoulders and turned down the street in the opposite direction.

The movie was about a singer. Hank Williams was the singer's name. Clyde knew who he was, used to be on the Grand Ole Opry on radio, he remembered, sang songs he remembered, too. Clyde thought about the singers back home. The singers of the land, the people, the rain, and the good things of his home. His uncle on his mother's side was a medicine man, and he used to listen to him sing. In the quiet and cold winter evenings, lying on his sheepskin beside the fire, he would listen and sing under his breath with his uncle. Sing with me, his uncle would say, and Clyde would sing. But he had a long ways to go in truly learning the songs; he could not sing many of them and could only remember the feeling of them.

Willie laughed at the funny incidents in the movie, and he laughed about the drunk Hank Williams. That made him wish he had a drink again, and he tried to persuade Joe to go with him, but Joe didn't want to leave. Joe's wife and children watched the movie and the people around them, and they watched Willie fidget around in his seat. They figured he wanted to go drink.

At the end of the movie, they walked to a small cafe. On the way Willie ran into a liquor store and bought a pint of whisky.

"Come on, son," he said to Clyde. "Help your father drink this medicine." Joe followed along into an alley where they quickly gulped some of the liquor.

"Call your woman and ask if she wants some," Willie said to Joe. He was in good spirit now. The whisky ran through him quickly and lightly.

"Emma, come here," Joe called to his wife. She hesitated, looked up the street, and stepped into the alley. Her husband handed her the bottle and she drank quickly. She coughed and gasped for a moment, and Willie and Joe laughed.

Clyde saw the two children watching them. They stood in the weak overhead glare of a streetlight. Traffic barely moved, and a few people from the movies were walking on the streets. The children waited patiently for their parents.

They ate a quick dinner of hamburgers and Cokes. And when they finished, they paid up and walked to the Elkhorn Bar a couple of blocks away.

"Do se doe," Willie said when he heard the music coming from the bar. Saturday night was always a busy night, but most of the Indian potato pickers were gone now. There were only a few cars and trucks; some men and women stood by the door. A small fire blazed several yards from the bar, and around it were a few Indians quietly talking.

Willie walked over to the fire, and Clyde followed him because he didn't want to be left alone. Joe and his family stood beside the door of the bar and peered in.

"Here comes a drunk," someone in the circle of Indians said as Willie and Clyde walked up. They laughed, but it was not meant in harm. For a moment, as he did upon entering a crowd away from his home, Clyde felt a small tension, but he relaxed quickly and he talked with an acquaintance. Willie passed him a bottle, and he made a small joke, and Clyde laughed. He felt better and took a long drink. Whisky went down into the belly harder than wine but it made him feel warmer. And when he thought that it didn't make any difference to Willie what he drank he laughed to himself. The men talked.

The talk was mostly about their home and about The People at home. Clyde again felt the thought travel into his heart. It made him long for his home. He didn't belong here even though he had friends here, and he had money in his pocket and a job. He was from another place, where his people came from and belonged. Yet here some of them were around this fire, outside the Elkhorn Bar, and they worked in the Idaho potato fields cultivating, irrigating, and picking potatoes. Someone began a song. It was the season for sings back in The People's land. The song was about a moving people.

When no one passed a bottle for a while, Clyde decided to go get a drink at the bar. The liquor in him made him sleepy, but he was getting cold too. There was no wind, but it was getting colder. He remembered Wheeler's words, thought about them for a moment, but he knew it would not freeze tonight. The bar was crowded. Someone was on the floor near the doorway, and others stepped over him without taking much notice.

Clyde met Joe Shorty and his wife, and they drank some beer together. Joe was getting drunk and his wife was drinking quietly. It was too noisy for Clyde to remember the song anymore. The children were standing by the jukebox, watching the revolving discs. Clyde wondered when they were going back to the camp by the potato fields, and he went to look for Willie.

"So there you are, son," Willie said when Clyde found him. He was with the men around the fire. "Come join us." He was drunk, and he handed Clyde another bottle.

The Indians, who were very few now, were singing in the high voice of The People. Like the wind blowing through clefts in the mountains. Clyde wondered if it was only that he was getting drunk with the liquor that he could make out the wind and the mountains in the song. But it was the men getting drunk, too, which didn't make it sound like the wind, he thought. He drank some more, but he was getting tired and colder, and he told Willie he wanted to go.

"No, stay," Willie said. "It is still a long night. These nights are long, and at home the sings last all night long."

This Idaho was not where The People's home was, Clyde thought. And he wanted to tell Willie that. He wanted to tell the others that, but they wouldn't pay attention to him, he knew.

The women would sit or stand quietly by the singing men at home. The fire would be big, and when it got smaller someone would bring an armload of wood and throw it in. Children would hurry through the crowd of The People until they were tired and sleepy. Here there were no children except by the jukebox, watching it play records. In the morning, there would be newly built fires before camps of families. In the mountains of The People. And the light beginning in the East would show that maybe it will snow sometime soon, but here by the Elkhorn Bar there would be no fires and no one to see the light in the East. Maybe, like Wheeler talked, there'd be some frozen Indian left lying around.

Clyde walked away. The town was quiet. A police cruiser went in the direction of the bar and the officer looked at Clyde. When he got to the edge of town, he lengthened his stride.

When he had walked for a while, he saw that someone was walking in front of him. He slowed down, and he saw that it was a woman and two children. Joe Shorty's family. Joe must have stayed, drunk I guess, Clyde thought, and his family had left without him. Clyde didn't want to talk with them because

they were another man's wife and children. They heard him
and one of the boys said loudly, "It's Clyde. Clyde, come walk
with us."

The woman was slightly drunk. Clyde could see her smile.
She staggered some. "It's cold," she said. "We left Joe Shorty.
He's going to come home in the morning."

Joe Shorty's wife and sons and Clyde walked quietly and
steadily. The children stepped carefully in the dark. Once, Clyde
looked back, and he could barely make out a pale light over the
town. He thought about Willie and thought he would be all
right. It was cold and Clyde let his hand out of his pocket to test
the cold. Willie would be all right. Joe Shorty and Willie would
probably come back to the camp together in the morning.

The lights of a truck lit them up and Clyde said, "We better get on this side of the road." The younger boy stumbled and
grabbed for Clyde's hand. The boy's hand was cold, and Clyde
felt funny with Joe Shorty's son's hand in his.

The truck was Wheeler's. It passed them and then slowed
to a stop fifty yards ahead. Wheeler honked his horn. Clyde and
Joe Shorty's family walked toward the truck as it backed towards them.

"It's Wheeler, the potato boss," Clyde said to the woman.
She did not look at him or say anything. The younger boy
clung to his mother's skirt.

The pickup truck drew back alongside of them and
stopped. Wheeler rolled down his window and studied them for
a moment. He looked at Clyde and winked. Clyde felt a small
panic begin in him. He realized that he still held the child's
hand in his. What did this mean to the potato boss, Clyde asked
himself.

"Well come on," Wheeler said. "Get in, but just a minute,"
and he got out. He stood by the side of the truck and urinated.
The woman and her children and then Clyde climbed into the
back of the truck.

When Wheeler saw that they had climbed in the back, he said gruffly, "Come on, get in front." And then with a softer tone, "There's enough room and it's colder than hell out," and he reached out a hand to one of the boys. But the boy hung back. Wheeler grabbed the other and swung him over the side. The woman and the other boy had no choice but to follow.

Clyde felt his feelings empty for a while and then he slowly felt himself burning. He watched the woman climb out of the back into the front. It was not cold as before and it was the liquor, he thought. When he jumped down from the back and got into the front he felt light and springy. He smiled at Wheeler.

Joe Shorty's wife did not say anything. She was looking at the dashboard and her children huddled against her.

"Well, Joe Shorty must be having a good time," Wheeler said. He laughed and steered wildly to keep the truck on the road.

The woman did not say anything. She held one of her children, and the other huddled against her tightly. Clyde was on the side against the door. He could feel her movement and her warmth. But he looked straight ahead until Wheeler spoke to him.

"Weren't you having a good time, Clyde? Maybe there's good times other places, huh?"

Clyde felt a hot liquid move in him. It was warm in the truck. The heater was blowing on his ankles. It's the whisky, he thought. What does this man think of this, he thought. And then he thought of what all the white men in the world thought about all the Indians in the world. I'm drunk, he thought, and he wanted to sing that in his own language, The People's language, but there didn't seem to be any words for it. When he thought about it in English and in song, it was silly, and he felt uncomfortable. Clyde smiled at Wheeler, but Wheeler wasn't paying attention to him now.

Wheeler drove with one hand and with the other he patted Joe Shorty's older son on the head and smiled at Joe Shorty's wife.

"Nice, nice kid," Wheeler said. The woman fidgeted, and
she held her other son tightly to her.

Clyde felt her move against him and he tensed. He tried to
think of the son then. The People singing, he thought, the
woman singing. The mountains, the living, the women strong,
the men strong. But he was tense in his mind, and there was no
clear path between his mind and heart. Finally, he said to himself, Okay, potato boss, okay.

They drove into the camp and stopped in front of Clyde's
and Willie's shack. Clyde thought, Okay, Potato boss, okay. He
opened the door and began to climb out. The woman and her
children began to follow him.

"Wait," Wheeler said. "I'll drive you home. I'm going your
way." His voice was almost angry.

Wheeler grabbed her arm, but she wrenched away. Clyde
stopped and looked at Wheeler.

"She lives over there," Clyde said, pointing to Joe Shorty's
shack, but he knew that Wheeler knew that.

Wheeler scowled at him and then he searched for a bottle
under the seat. The woman did not move away anymore. She
watched Wheeler and then said something to the children.
Clyde looked at her. The song, he thought, and he tried very
hard to think of the woman singing. The children ran to the
shack, and Joe Shorty's woman and Wheeler followed.

For a long time, Clyde stood behind the door of his and
Willie's shack. Listening and thinking quiet angry thoughts. He
thought of Willie, Joe Shorty, the Elkhorn Bar, Hank Williams,
potatoes, the woman and her sons. And he thought of Wheeler
and himself, and he asked himself what he was listening for. He
knew that he was not listening for the song, because he had decided that the woman singing was something a long time ago

and would not happen anymore. If it did, he would not believe it. He would not listen. Finally, he moved away from the door and began to search through Willie's things for a bottle. But there was no bottle of anything except the kerosene and for a moment he thought of drinking kerosene. It was a silly thought, and so he laughed.

When the bus pulled out of the town in the morning, Clyde thought of Willie again. Willie had come in when the sun was coming up. He was red-eyed and sick.

"We had a time, son," Willie said. He sat at the table woodenly. He did not notice that Clyde was putting clothes into a grip bag.

"That Wheeler, he sure gets up early. Joe Shorty and I met him outside his house. 'The early bird gets the worms,' he said. Sure funny guy. And he gave us some drinks," Willie mumbled. He was about to fall asleep with his head on the table.

"I'm going home," Clyde said. He had finished putting his clothes in the bag.

"You never have a good time," Willie said. Clyde thought about that and asked in his mind whether that was true or not.

When Clyde thought about the woman's singing he knew that it had been real. Later on he would hear it someplace again and he would believe it. There was a larger hurt in his throat and he began to make a song, like those of The People, in his mind.

About the Authors

Estelle Armstrong (Colorado River, Arizona; tribe unknown) Dates unknown: There are several tribal communities along the Colorado River in southwest Arizona from which Estelle Armstrong might have come: Yuma, Chemahuevi, perhaps Pima (the tribe of Congressional Medal recipient Ira Hayes). She wrote her stories in the late 1920s while she attended Carlisle Indian School in Pennsylvania, and they were about boys from the Colorado River region of Arizona.

Black Elk (Lakota) 1863–1950: Black Elk was a medicine man, chosen by the Spirits in childhood. He gave accounts of his life (*Black Elk Speaks*) and of Lakota spiritual teachings, which appeared in *The Sacred Pipe: Black Elk's Account of the Seven Rites of Oglala Sioux*, recorded and edited by Joseph Epes Brown. He toured Europe with Buffalo Bill's Wild West Show, where he performed for Queen Victoria and other royalty. He seemed as impressed with the queen as with the Iron Horse, the railroad upon which he traveled to New York City, where the company boarded a ship to Europe.

Grey Cohoe (Navajo) Dates unknown: Cohoe was born at Shiprock, New Mexico. He attended the Institute for American Indian Arts in the 1960s and was an instructor there in the 1970s. His stories and poetry have been anthologized, and his paintings have been exhibited in Oklahoma City, New York City, Washington, D. C., and countries in South America and Africa. Cohoe, homeless, died of exposure in Santa Fe in January 1993. A memorial was held for him there at the Institute for American Indian Arts.

Charles A. Eastman [Ohiyesa] (Wahpeton Sioux) 1858–1938: Eastman was born near Redwood Falls, Minnesota, and was raised by his grandmother and uncle in the Manitoba borderlands area. When he was fifteen his father brought Ohiyesa to live with him at Flandreau, where Ohiyesa was given the Christian name Charles. He was educated at Dartmouth College and Boston University School of Medicine, receiving his M. D. in 1890. He held a number of significant positions as spokesman and leader of Native people during his long life, and achieved considerable recognition for his literary work, produced with effective editorial aid from his wife. His major works include *From the Deep Woods to Civilization: Chapters in the Autobiography of an Indian, Indian Boyhood, Red Hunters and the Animal People*, and *Old Indian Days*; collections of short stories: *The Soul of the Indian, The Indian To-day: Past and Future of the First American*, and *Indian Heroes and Great Chieftains*, all having to do with Native life and thought; and, in collaboration with Eliza Eastman, *Wigwam Evenings*, a collection of traditional narratives.

E. Pauline Johnson (Mohawk) 1861–1913: Johnson was born on the Ontario side of the Mohawk Nation of an activist father, George Martin, and an English-descended mother who was a cousin of William Dean Howells, the renowned American writer and critic. Her fiction was first published in popular magazines, supplementing her small income. Her poetry and fiction were concerned with Native and western themes, and many revealed her activist and feminist sympathies. Three volumes of her work—*Flint and Feather*, collected poems; *The Moccasin Maker*, short stories; and *Legends of Vancouver*, a collection of Kutenai stories—are available in recent editions.

Frank Bird Linderman (Anglo-American) 1869–1938: Linderman was born in Ohio but in 1885 moved to Montana, where he spent most of his time among Native people. He worked as a trapper, farmer, and cowboy, eventually turning to ethnography. His studies—*Plenty-coups, Chief of the Crows* and *Prettyshield, Medicine Woman of the Crows* (originally published as *Red Mother*)—established him as one of the early leaders in the field of "as told to" autobiographies.

John Joseph Mathews (Osage) 1894–1979: Mathews was born at the Osage Agency at Pawhuska in Indian Territory. He attended the University of Oklahoma but dropped out to enlist in the cavalry during World War I. He switched to the Signal Corps, serving as a pilot in France. After the war he returned to the University of Oklahoma, took another degree at Oxford University, then attended the University of Geneva's School for International Relations. Eventually he returned to Pawhuska, where he devoted himself to Osage tribal affairs and his writing. His words include *Wah'Kon Tah: The Osage and the White Man's Road*, a historical narrative based on the diaries of Indian agent Laban J. Miles; *Sundown*, his somewhat autobiographical novel; *Talking to the Moon*, reflections on man and nature; *Life and Death of an Oilman: The Career of E. W. Marland*, a biography of his friend the Oklahoma governor Ernest Marland; and *The Osages: Children of the Middle Waters*, an eight-hundred-page historical work based on Osage oral history. His two-volume autobiography, "Twenty Thousand Mornings," remains unpublished.

D'Arcy McNickle (Creek; adopted by the Confederated Salish and Kootenai Tribes) 1904–77: McNickle was born in St. Ignatius, Montana, on the Flathead Reservation, and educated at mission schools, public schools, the University of Montana, Oxford University, and the University of Grenoble. He was active in Indian affairs and co-founded the National Congress of American Indians. He taught as a professor of anthropology at the University of Saskatchewan and is thought by many to be the most important Native American fiction writer until N. Scott Momaday. He wrote three novels: *The Surrounded, Runner in the Sun* (young adult fiction), and *Wind from an Enemy Sky* (published shortly after his death). In addition to his novels, he wrote a number of short stories; these, along with several that remained unpublished during his lifetime, were recently collected in *The Hawk Is Hungry.* He has also written *They Came Here First: The Epic of the American Indian, Indians and Other Americans* (with Harold E. Fey), and *Native American Tribalism*, all historical-ethnographic studies; and *Indian Man*, a biography of the anthropologist and novelist Oliver La Farge.

N. Scott Momaday (Kiowa-Cherokee) 1932– : Momaday was born in Lawton, Oklahoma, and raised in New Mexico, where his parents, writer Natachee Scott Momaday and painter and Peyote Road man Al Momaday, ran the Day School at Jemez Pueblo. Momaday attended the University of New Mexico and Stanford University, where he received his Ph.D. He has taught at a number of major institutions, including the University of California–Berkeley, Stanford, and the University of Arizona–Tucson. He received a Pulitzer Prize in 1969 for his novel *House Made of Dawn*, and the Native American Prize for Literature in 1989. His paintings of Kiowa shields have shown in a number of galleries. He is a member of the Kiowa Gourd Dance Society. His works include *An Angle of Geese and Other Poems* and

The Gourd Dancer, poetry; *The Journey of Tai-me* and *The Way to Rainy Mountain*, mixed genre tribal history and biomythography; *The Names*, a family history; *The Ancient Child*, a novel; and *In The Presence of the Sun: A Gathering of Shields*, a collection of stories, poems, and shield sketches. He has also published several essays on Kiowa tradition and ecology.

Mourning Dove [Humishuma; Cristal or Christine Quintasket Joseph McLeod Galler] (Okanogan) 1885–1936: Mourning Dove was born near Bonner's Ferry, Idaho, married twice, and died in an asylum in Washington, where the Coleville Reservation on which she lived is located. She made up her pen name, Morning Dove, a character in the Salishan narrative tradition; later she changed the spelling to the ornithologically correct Mourning Dove. She received a sporadic white education during about eleven years of childhood and adulthood. Active in Indian affairs, she was the first woman elected to the Coleville Tribal Council, shortly before her death. Working as a migrant farmworker or housekeeper, often typing far into the night after a ten-hour day in the field, she collected and wrote two volumes of "folklores" as she called them, *Coyote Stories* and *The Tales of the Okanogans*, finished the first draft of her novel, *Cogewea: The Half-Blood*, in 1912; completed its revised version in 1916; and saw it published in 1927. *Mourning Dove: A Salishan Autobiography* was published in 1990.

John G. Neihardt (Anglo-American) 1881–1973: Neihardt was born in Illinois. He was primarily a writer of fiction and poetry, though he worked at farming and teaching. He published several epic poems. His works include *The Song of Hugh Glass, The Song of Three Friends, The Song of the Indian Wars, The Song of the Messiah,* and *The Song of Jed Smith*, all gathered as *A Cycle* *of the West; Collected Poems* includes lyric poems published earlier. Other books include *The River and I, The Lonesome Trail, Indian Tales*, and *Others*, short stories; *Life's Lure*, a novel; *The Splendid Wayfaring*, a biography of Jedediah Smith; *Two Mothers*, drama; *Poetic Values*, essays; *When the Three Flowered* and *Eagle Voice*, fictional accounts of Sioux life; and *All Is but a Beginning* and *Patterns of Coincidences*, memoirs.

Simon J. Ortiz (Acoma Pueblo) 1941– : Ortiz was born at Acoma Pueblo. He attended the day school there and then St. Catherine's boarding school in Santa Fe, New Mexico. He has served as lieutenant governor at the pueblo and has been involved in traditional life there. Ortiz is a multigenre writer, and has published several volumes of poetry including *Going for the Rain, From Sand Creek*, and *A Good Journey; For the Sake of the People, For the Sake of the Land*, and *Woven Stone*, mixed-genre collections; *Welcome Howbah Indians* and *Fightin'*, short stories; and *The People Shall Continue*, a children's book.

John M. Oskison (Cherokee) 1874–1947: Oskison was born in Vinita in Indian Territory, attended Willie Halsell College, Stanford University, and Harvard, where he did some graduate work in literature. He served on the staffs of the *New York Evening Post* and *Collier's Weekly* as journalist and editor, and contributed articles on Native subjects to the *Quarterly Journal of the Society of American Indians*. He served as a lieutenant in the army in World War I, then became a correspondent. He published extensively as a journalist, short story writer, and novelist. Oskinson died in Tulsa, Oklahoma. His published works include *Wild Harvest, Black Jack Davy*, and *Brothers Three*, novels; *A Texas Titan: The Story of Sam Houston*, a biographical novel; *Tecumseh and His Times*, a historical study; and a vast number of short stories and articles, as yet uncollected.

Arthur C. Parker [Ga-wa-so-we-neh] (Seneca) 1881–1955: Parker was born on the Cattagaurus Reservation in New York State, near Cattagaurus Creek, where it is said the Little People are wont to reside. His grandparents were of the Sachem lineage, and they were related to the Seneca prophet Handsome Lake. Parker was educated at Indian district school and public school in White Plains, New York, often returning home for traditional dances and ceremonies. Under the mentorship of Professor F. W. Putnam of Harvard, Parker became professionally involved in archaeology, ethnography, folklore, and museumology. In addition to *Seneca Myths & Folk Tales*, Parker authored a historical account about his grandfather in *The Life of General Ely S. Parker; Skunny Wundy and Other Indian Tales*, a collection for children; and edited and annotated *Myths and Legends of the New York State Iroquois*, collected and recorded by his friend Harriet Maxwell Converse.

Pretty-shield (Crow) 1858–?: " 'I was born across the Big [Missouri] river from the mouth of Plum creek in the moon when the ice goes out of rivers [March] of the snow that Yellow-calf, and his war-party, was wiped out by the Lacota . . .' " Her biographer, Frank B. Linderman, wrote that "Pretty-shield is a 'Wise-one,' a medicine woman, of the Crow tribe [whose lands are in Montana]. She not only belongs to a great Crow clan, the 'Sore-lips' that has given her people many leaders and chiefs, but to a prominent Crow family." *Pretty-shield, Medicine Woman of the Crows* was originally published as *Red Mother*.

Ronald Rogers (Cherokee) 1948– : A poet and fiction writer, Rogers was born in Claremont, Oklahoma, and was a student at San Francisco State University in the late 1960s, when his story was included in John M. Milton's groundbreaking collection *The American Indian Speaks*. Rogers' work was anthologized in several collections in the 1970s.

Luther Standing Bear [Ota K'te] (Lakota) 1868–19?: Chief Luther Standing Bear was born to the Lakota people just as the great Sioux Reservation was formed. Changing circumstances led his father to send him to Carlisle Indian School in Pennsylvania. Standing Bear's books were reviewed in the *New York Times* and other major newspapers. In 1933 he wrote a letter to President Franklin D. Roosevelt proposing a bill to require public schools to teach a course on Indian history, religion, philosophy, art, and culture. His proposal has remained unanswered by the United States for over sixty years. Standing Bear wrote three books about Lakota life: *Land of the Spotted Eagle, My Indian Boyhood, by Chief Luther Standing Bear, Who Was the Boy Ota K'te (Plenty Kill),* and *My People, the Sioux.*

Don C. Talayesva (Hopi) 1890–19?: Born at Old Oraibi in Hopiland (Arizona), Don Talayesva spent some ten years at a white school, where he learned the skills that made writing *Sun Chief* possible. He submitted his eight-thousand-page manuscript to Dr. Leo Simmons, a professor at Yale University, who prepared it for publication. *Sun Chief* is a landmark volume. As Robert V. Hine remarked in his 1963 foreword to the volume, "*Sun Chief* puts us inside Don, like his Spirit Guide, beside him throughout his life. Within its literary framework, we are convinced, removed from our pretensions, momentarily certain that . . . Spider Woman and the Two Heart(s) exist."

Zitkala-Ša [Gertrude Simmons Bonnin] (Sioux) 1876–1938: Zitkala-Ša was born at the Yankton Sioux Agency in South Dakota. Her mother was a full-blood Sioux, while her father seems to have been an Anglo-American. She attended a Quaker mission school for native children in Wabash, Indiana, then completed her studies at Earlham College in Richmond, Indiana. Bonnin was active in Indian rights, at both local and national levels, forming the National Council of American Indians, a major Indian rights organization that kept Native people from diverse regions abreast of legislative concerns and provided them with a centralized focus for a variety of local issues. She published sketches and short stories in several popular magazines and two book-length collections—*Old Indian Legends* and *American Indian Stories*, a collection of her fiction and sketches. Bonnin collaborated with William E. Hanson on an Indian opera, *Sun Dance*, that was selected as the 1937 Opera of the Year by the New York Light Opera Guild.

Bibliography

Brandon, William. *The Last Americans, The Indian in American Culture.* New York: McGraw-Hill, 1974.

Black Elk and John G. Neihardt. *Black Elk Speaks: Being the Life Story of a Holy Man of the Oglala Sioux.* Introduction by Vine Deloria, Jr. Lincoln: University of Nebraska Press, 1988.

Eastman, Charles A. (Ohiyesa). *Old Indian Days.* Introduction by A. LaVonne Brown Ruoff. Lincoln: University of Nebraska Press, 1991.

Johnson, E. Pauline *The Moccasin Maker.* Introduction, annotation, and bibliography by A. LaVonne Brown Ruoff. Tucson: University of Arizona Press, 1987.

Linderman, Frank B. *Pretty-shield, Medicine Woman of the Crows.* Lincoln: University of Nebraska Press, 1972.

Mathews, John Joseph. *Sundown.* Norman: University of Oklahoma Press, 1988.

McNickle, D'Arcy. *The Hawk Is Hungry & Other Stories.* Edited by Birgit Hans. Tucson: University of Arizona Press, 1992.

Milton, John M. *The American Indian Speaks.* South Dakota Review, Special Issue. Vermillion: University of South Dakota, 1969.

Momaday, N. Scott. *House Made of Dawn.* New York: Harper, 1968.

Mourning Dove (Humishuma; Christine Quintasket). *Coyote Stories.* Notes by Lucullus Virgil McWhorter. Foreword by Chief Standing Bear. Edited by Heister Dean Guie. New York: AMS, 1977.

————. *Cogewea, the Half-Blood: A Depiction of the Great Montana Cattle Range.* Notes and biographical sketch by Lucullus Virgil McWhorter. Introduction by Dexter Fisher. Lincoln: University of Nebraska Press, 1981.

Parker, Arthur C. *Seneca Myths & Folk Tales.* Introduction by William N. Fenton. Lincoln: University of Nebraska Press, 1989.

Peyer, Bernd, ed. *The Singing Spirit: Early Short Stories by North American Indians.* Tucson: University of Arizona Press, 1989.

Standing Bear, Luther. *My People, the Sioux.* Edited by E. A. Brininstool. Introduction by Richard N. Ellis. Lincoln: University of Nebraska Press, 1975.

Talayesva, Don C., and Leo W. Simmons. *Sun Chief: The Autobiography of a Hopi Indian.* New Haven: Yale University Press, 1974.

Zitkala-Ša (Gertrude Simmons Bonnin). *American Indian Stories.* Introduction by Dexter Fisher. Lincoln: University of Nebraska Press, 1986.

A major Native American poet, fiction writer, lecturer, and scholar, PAULA GUNN ALLEN was born in 1939. Her mother was of Laguna Pueblo, Sioux, and Scottish descent, while her father is Lebanese-American. She was raised in a New Mexico village bounded by a Laguna Pueblo reservation on one side and an Acoma reservation on the other. Spanish, German, Laguna, English, and Arabic were all spoken at home. She spent the ages between six and seventeen at a convent school, yet was strongly influenced by her mother's stories of Native American goddesses and traditions. It was after earning a B.A. in English literature and an M.F.A. in creative writing that Allen seized the opportunity, as she puts it, "to return to [her] mother's side, to the sacred hoop of [her] grandmother's ways."

Now one of the most visible spokespeople for Native American literature, Allen is currently a professor of English at the University of California at Los Angeles. Her poetry and prose appear widely in anthologies, journals, and scholarly publications. A recipient of numerous awards, including the 1990 Native American Prize for Literature, she is the author of seven volumes of poetry (most recently *Skins and Bones*, 1988); a novel, *The Woman Who Owned the Shadows* (1983); and a collection of essays, *The Sacred Hoop: Recovering the Feminine in American Indian Traditions* (1986). She edited the anthologies *Studies in American Indian Literature* (1982) and the highly acclaimed *Spider Woman's Granddaughters: Traditional Tales and Contemporary Writing by Native American Women* (1989). Her most recent book is *Grandmothers of the Light: A Medicine Woman's Sourcebook* (1991).